THE H
THE A
AN[
KHORENATS'I

ՀԱՅՈՑ
ՊԱՏՄՈՒԹԻՒՆԸ
ԵՒ ՄՈՎՍԷՍ
ԽՈՐԵՆԱՑԻ

THE HISTORY OF
THE ARMENIANS
AND MOSĒS
KHORENATS'I

GABRIEL SOULTANIAN

BENNETT & BLOOM

First published
in 2011 by

BENNETT & BLOOM

www.bennettandbloom.com

PO Box 2131
London WIA 5SU
England

© Gabriel Soultanian 2012

Typeset and designed by Desert♥Hearts

Printed and bound by
Marksprint

British Library Cataloguing in Publication Data
A catalogue record for this book is available from the British Library

ISBN 978-1-898948-13-1 (paperback)
ISBN 978-1-898948-89-6 (hardback)

Dedicated to the memory of
Mar Abas Katina
and his unknown Editor

Contents

Sulumal (Gełama) assisted by his son slays the dragon Illuyanka (see page 193). Perhaps this is the source of the Vishaps (dragons) of the Geł Mountains in later Armina, where the progeny of Sulumal had settled.

Treasures from the Phrygian tumulus burials at Gordion (see pages 201-202) — Top: A bronze situla in the shape of a lion's head. Identical vessels appear in Assyrian reliefs from the eighth century BC. Below: A colourless glass bowl with moulded ornaments, an extremely rare material in the eighth century BC.

Preface

The case of Khorenats'i is rather difficult to deal with since he is among the most problematic writers to understand and explain. His History has been used as a textbook for centuries and it thus contains interpolations, abstractions and a multitude of mistakes due to careless copying scribes and editors who had tried to update its contents, acts which are at times impossible to pinpoint. His language and sentences, though appropriate, are mostly written in a few well-chosen words which makes the sense for us potentially obscure and their misunderstandings innumerable.

Khorenats'i is not a historian but a philosopher and a rhetorician, though he has a natural ability to grasp what is of historical value and what is trivial. Many times he preserves ancient sayings, demotic tales and subjects of which he has no proper understanding. His attitude is that of a philosopher, which always reflects a healthy position and yet many times he writes about events so concisely, and expects the reader to understand him since he himself knows the answer.

I have devoted many years to the understanding of the History of Mosēs, and still there remain dark parts which cannot yet be explained. However, I have reached a more fortunate position than any other scholar who has had the courage to explain the obscure areas of the History with no thorough knowledge, since I had translated and published the hieroglyphic inscriptions which the Proto-Armenians had left behind for posterity while they were living in the country of Aram (southeastern Turkey) between 1200 to 600 BC. The information contained in these inscriptions I have always considered a gift from the past and, combined with the Assyro-Babylonian sources, they also confirm the majority of the names and a number of events that Mosēs records in Book 1.12, 14, 19 & 22 and throw light on many frustrating or ill-understood problems.

In this work I criticize many scholars for their poor knowledge and understanding of the History, and yet a dozen years ago I was one of their number. At the present I cannot but admire Mosēs even despite its failings, as I know only too well: when one considers that this man created from seemingly nothing a complete history, employed an honest attitude at all times and never sought to mislead the reader, I cannot but admire his genius, and it is my hope the reader of this book will appreciate my sincere words and see Mosēs's History as a remarkable product of fifth-century thought and methods.

In this study there will be found a number of unavoidable repetitions, particularly in Part ɪᴠ, due to the fact that related subjects are examined in more than one section in order to provide a thorough explanation of an event or article discussing certain of the more obscure parts of the History. These repetitions are intended to make it easier for the reader to grasp the various misunderstood parts but if there are some who may find it tiresome, I appeal to their indulgence and understanding that a history, which has been subjected to such fault finding over a century and a half, is not easy to immediately rationalize and vindicate.

I express my gratitude to my editor and publisher Nicholas Awde for his efforts to present this study in a good and orderly manner. Other scholars who have been of help while I was finalizing this study have been acknowledged in the appropriate places within this book.

Gabriel Soultanian
Yerevan
Armenia
2009

Introduction

In the second half of the fifth century, acceding to the request of Prince Sahak Bagratuni, a cleric by the name of Mosēs Khorenats'i wrote the History of the Armenians, starting from their beginning and ending with the death of Ss Sahak and Mesrop (AD 439/440). This History has been the mainstay of the Armenian people from the time it was discovered, a hundred years or so after it was written, up to the first half of the nineteenth century. The first Book of the History in particular is a unique document with much truth to captivate one's attention as well as to provoke diverse opinions since its chronology is practically non-existent—there is some telescoping—and it contains much that scholarship has misunderstood or even not understood at all.

However, when one realizes that Khorenats'i has created a history of the Hay people (later the Armenians) from nothing, from the non-existent, for the first time, and that he approaches his subject matter with sympathy and is willing to work hard by carefully examining all the evidence and thoroughly analyzing the alleged impediments, one will be amazed at the validity of the greater part of what is written as well as appreciate the enormity of the task undertaken by this great man. Needless to say, the History has been acknowledged as a great work by most commentators and has justly earned for him such epithets as the 'Father of Armenian History', the 'Father of Writers' and 'Philosopher Mosēs'.

The interest of Western scholarship in this History begins in the eighteenth century when, in 1730, M. V. de la Croze wrote a letter to G. Whiston expressing his opinion that Khorenats'i was a historian of the ninth to tenth centuries,[1] living at the time of the princes of the house of the Bagratunis, which view due to lack of supporting evidence was

---

1.   Fr V. V. Hats'uni, *Movsēs Khorenats'i Returns to the Fifth Century*, Mkhitarian Press, St Lazar, Venice, 1935 [in Armenian].

ignored. The main thrust of scholarly interest in Khorenats'i and his History starts in the second half of the nineteenth century when A. von Gutschmid wrote an article in the *Encyclopaedia Britannica* in the 1880s and gave the date of 634-642 for Khorenats'i.[2] Following Gutschmid, the list of interested parties grew dramatically, being divided into three groups in accordance with the dates they ascribe to Khorenats'i and his History.

The first group, claiming a date for the seventh century, comprises G. Ter Mkrtichian, V. Ter Movsesian and A. von Gutschmid; the second group, claiming the eighth century, includes A. Carrière, H. Gelzer, P. Vetter, C. Toumanoff, R. W. Thomson and J. P. Mahé; and the third group, claiming the ninth century, includes M. V. de la Croze, G. Khalat'yants', N. Adontz, J. Marquard, H. Manandyan, A. Madikian and N. Akinian. Of these scholars I shall briefly discuss the opinions of Carrière, Khalat'yants', Adontz, Manandyan, Madikian and Akinian; and at length the works of Toumanoff, Thomson and Mahé, who being more recent represent the prevailing accumulated views of scholarship.

The majority of these scholars selected certain events, idiomatic phrases and excerpts, analyzed and compared certain passages of the History with the works of other ancient writers, and in the process their conclusions differed from each other. Each was trying to prove his expertise and excel over their fellow experts and even contradict them. Due to a misunderstanding of parts of Khorenats'i's unique History or due to their limited knowledge of events, their efforts had little to offer in the way of true criticism, particularly when aspects of ancient history and certain basic truths, including source materials invalidating their opinions, were ignored. To this we may add the contradictions inherent in their own works and the non-availability of important source materials at the time.

In general, most of those who have studied the History, be they Western or Armenian, belong to this category. The conclusion that the History was not written in the fifth century, but in the seventh, eighth or ninth centuries was and still is based on misguided assumptions, to which we must add the fact that at the time these scholars were writing, they claimed that they knew of no other medieval writer who acknowledged the History until the tenth century, which was not true. Scholarship knew of at least three sources but instead of directing their

---

2. S. Malkhazyants', *History of the Armenians* by Mosēs Khorenats'i, translation into Modern Armenian with commentary, Yerevan University, Yerevan, 1981. On p62 of his commentary Malkhazyants' discusses von Gutschmid and his article.

efforts towards a true understanding of them, they tried to destroy the true order of chronology pertaining to one, and created imaginary or unnamed derivations or authors for the other two. Furthermore, they justified their claim, quite prematurely, that the History was replete with second-hand borrowings, similes and historical extracts belonging to writers from after the fifth century or foreign works that had been translated into Armenian after this period. Now I am well aware of the gravity of what I say here, a fact that compels me to highlight in this study the various contradictory statements that exist in the works of such scholars.

Malkhazyants', for example, declares that the entire History has been subjected to editing around the seventh or eighth centuries AD,[3] and that it contains interpolations and mistakes committed and perpetuated by various scribes who have copied it. And yet he overlooks, or does not comment on, two of the most basic reasons that would have demonstrated the unreasonableness, or even the futility of some of the arguments of himself and his peers. Here I shall explain these two basic reasons, which most of the scholars interested in the History know but fail to consider.

Firstly, what were the conditions at the time of publishing the History? These conditions directly affect the availability and the acknowledgement of the work. Scholars claim, wrongly in my opinion, that it is only in the tenth century that such acknowledgement of the History and of the author starts. Logically one must first ask how many copies had Mosēs Khorenats'i produced of his History? Of course, the answer is one—it was sent chapter by chapter to his patron, the young Sahak Bagratuni, who had commissioned it. The History was completed in 474, which was before Mosēs became bishop to the Bagratunis. Sahak was appointed Marzpan by the Armenians in 482, but unfortunately he died in the same year in the battle of Charmanay and, I am certain, with his death his papers, including the History, were locked up and none could have known of the existence of such a document. Also, one must consider that it takes another writer to acknowledge a work, and it is a matter of chance whether such acknowledgement survives to our own times. Besides, how many writers of the sixth century do we know beside Łazar P'arpets'i, the subject of Part II of this study, and At'anas Tarawnts'i who acknowledges the History? At'anas was the first to acknowledge the History in the second half of the sixth century and, it

---

3. Ibid., pp 18 & 67.

appears, he used it in the preparation of his own chronology.[4] The implication of this discovery by At'anas is that for the first time, after the discovery, copies of the History started to appear, a conjecture that is supported by two clerics, Bishop Sebēos[5] and Kałankatuats'i,[6] both of whom acknowledge that they benefited from Mosēs Khorenats'i soon after the middle of the seventh century.

Secondly, since its acknowledgement by At'anas, Mosēs's History became for at least 1,250 years the history textbook in learning centres (i.e. monasteries) in Armenia and Cilicia. It has been replicated over and over again (at the present there are more than 48 extant manuscripts,[7] the bulk of which are to be found in the Matenadaran in Armenia). It is to be expected that such a textbook would be updated from time to time: not necessarily interpolating the actual text but marking in the margins (this method of marking is seen on most extant manuscripts). Each new scribe copying the History would take note of these additions and in accordance with his knowledge and opinions he would either insert them into the text or keep the notes as he found them in the margins. This unavoidable procedure accounts for many interpolations and feigned corrections by various scribes.

It would be logical to state that preconceptions do not have a place in critical analysis. Yet one finds the opposite in the criticisms of those who have studied Mosēs. Besides tampering with his History they have also sought to create an imaginary order of chronology for other ancient Armenian works in order to support their claims such as removing chapter 3 from Sebēos' History and marking it as an 'Anonymous History' of the eleventh to twelfth centuries, because the heading of this chapter mentions the name and the History of Khorenats'i.[8] My copy of Kałankatuats'i's History comprises 267 pages: of these, 222 pages belong to him and the remaining 45 pages are written by Mosēs Daskhurants'i. In other words, Kałankatuats'i of the seventh century had written more than eighty per cent of the book and Daskhurants'i of the tenth century had completed the remaining part of the present History. Having this in

4. A. S. Matevosyan, 'Movses Khorenats'i and At'anas Tarawnts'i's Chronology', *Patma-banasirakan Handes*, pp 220-234, Academy of Armenia, 1989 [in Armenian].
5. Sebēos, *The History of Bishop Sebēos*, critical edition by S. Malkhazyants', Armfan, Yerevan, 1939; see the heading of chapter 3.
6. Mosēs Kałankatuats'i, *The History of the Albanians*, translated into Modern Armenian by Varag Aṛak'elyan, Hayastan, Yerevan, 1969; see chapter 8 where the author acknowledges Khorenats'i and in chapter 15 borrows the list of the ancient names.
7. See note 2 above, p83 of the Commentary.
8. G. Soultanian, *The History of Bishop Sebēos*, Bennett & Bloom, London, 2007; a critical analysis of the first five chapters, and see pp 85-103.

mind one may ask whose name should appear on this book as the author? Of course, the sceptics entitle the book 'The History of Daskhurants'i', because in the part written by Kałankatuats'i (Book 1, chapter 8, pp 8-9) Khorenats'i is cited, which impels, at least one of the scholars whom I shall discuss to ascribe the book to Daskhurants'i with the following note in parenthesis: 'Called (has the sense of alleged) Kałankatuats'i.'[9] This is not an isolated case,[10] as we shall see in the course of this study.

As a last word, I would reiterate, once again, that my examination of scholarly opinions shall concentrate on Toumanoff, Thomson and Mahé. This should not be taken as a move to isolate these scholars as foremost sceptics (for in such case I would have concentrated on the works of G. Khalat'yants', Y. Daghbashyan and N. Akinian)—in fact I consider their works otherwise as serious and worthy of the effort, particularly since they encapsulate all previous scholarly opinions. Besides, it is now nearly fifty years since Toumanoff's *Study*, thirty years since Thomson's and more than fifteen years since Mahé's translations, which means it is time for these works to be re-evaluated in the light of new interpretations and discoveries.

*

9. N. V. Akinian, *Movsēs Daskhurants'i (called Kałankatuats'i) and his History of the Albanians*, Mkhit'arian Press, Vienna, 1970.
10. C. J. F. Dowsett, *The History of the Caucasian Albanians by Movsēs Daskhurants'i*, Oxford University, London, 1961 (translation into English).

Part I
Criticisms
and
Commentaries

In 1892-93, A. Carrière, a learned professor of oriental languages in Paris, embarked on a series of articles about the 'History of Khorenats'i and his sources' in the *Handes Amsorya* journal of the Mkhit'arians of Vienna, which later in 1893 was published in a booklet.[1] A second series of articles on the same subject was written in 1893-94, also published later in 1894 in another booklet.[2] These articles created a great stir in the learned circles and soon Carrière had his allies and opponents.

Carrière had noticed that chapter 11.83 of Khorenats'i's History had similarities with the Greek version of the *Life of Silvester*, according to him translated from Latin (the *Vita Silvestri*) into Greek in the sixth century. Therefore he concluded that Khorenats'i had taken his information from this work, which meant that Khorenats'i could not have been a writer of the second half of the fifth century. As Carrière himself admits (note 1, p5, 1893) his article was not well researched. Soon after writing his first article, he learned from the critics of his ideas that there was a translation into Armenian of the *Life of Silvester* attached to the *Ecclesiastical History* of Socrates.

The translations of both works were produced in the last quarter of the seventh century, which made Carrière change his stance and conclude that Khorenats'i had taken his material from the Armenian

1. A. Carrière, *Nouvelles Sources de Moïse de Khoren*, translated into Armenian by Fr Y. V. Tashian, Mkhit'arian Press, Vienna, 1893.
2. A. Carrière, *Nouvelles Sources de Moïse de Khoren, Supplement*, translated into Armenian by Fr Y. V. Tashian, Mkhit'arian Press, Vienna, 1894.

translation of the Life of Silvester, and therefore he was a writer of the eighth century. He did not accept Khorenats'i's citation of Agat'angełos as the source of his narrative. Critics of Carrière's views, such as N. Buzandats'i, S. Paronian, F. C. Conybeare, B. Sargisian and S. Malkhazyants', pointed out that there is much in the Armenian translation of the *Life of Silvester* that are similar to what Khorenats'i writes and which is to be found in neither the Latin nor Greek versions. Therefore it is clear that the translators of *Silvester* and Socrates had borrowed from Khorenats'i and not the other way round. Paronian went further to claim that the Latin work was based on older sources, but he failed to substantiate this claim.

However, what Paronian had not done, Buzandats'i completed. This philologist produced practically all the excerpts the translators of the *Life of Silvester* and Socrates had borrowed from Khorenats'i's history in his 1898-99 articles in *Mshak*,[3] a daily paper published in Tbilisi. In an impressive feat of memory, he pointed out the excerpts that occur in neither the Latin nor in the Greek versions, and identified all the compound words, mainly invented or composed by Khorenats'i, which were part of his vocabulary. He also made many corrections to the text, which the producers of the 1913 critical edition of the History[4] consulted.

Buzandats'i also indicated various events, persons and writings that supported his insistence that Khorenats'i was a writer of the second half of the fifth century and therefore Carrière and his allies were sensationalist sceptics to be ignored. Unfortunately, the more recent commentators ignore Buzandats'i, and instead they rely on a few historical events that appear in the History. Due to their unwillingness to penetrate and understand these, they move Khorenats'i to later times, insisting that Carrière and others of his opinion were correct. We shall see these historical objections in Part II.

Problematic sources

In 1893 Fr B. Sargisian published a well-researched study on the *Life of Silvester* and Khorenats'i's sources (this work is not referred to in most later commentaries).[5] He indicated that Zosimos, a pagan historian, in

---

3. N. N. Biwzandats'i & M. Minasian, *Collection: Mose Khorenats'i's History of the Armenians*, M. Minasian, Geneva, 1991.
4. M. Abełian & S. Yarutiwnian, *Movsēs Khorenats'i's The History of the Armenians*, Critical Text and Commentary, Academy of Armenia, Yerevan, 1991.
5. B. V. Sargisian, *Observations on the Story of Silvester and the Sources of M. Khorenats'i*, Mkhit'arian Press, St Lazar, Venice, 1893.

the period 410 to 431, had written six books: in Book 11.7 he wrote about Constantine I (306-337), the bastard son of Constantius (293-306), and in 11.29 confirmed that Constantine was born to Helen, his going to Rome, the Ariolian priests and their advice on a cure for his illness, and his acceptance of Christianity, and so on. Sargisian adds that Zosimos' writings derive from an older biography of Constantine, which was known to James of Sarug (also known as Srchets'i, 452-521), bishop of Batnan (518-521) and Khorenats'i.

In other words the story had originated in Anatolia, and then gone to the west, where it was rewritten in Latin, translated into Greek and returned to Anatolia. But such was also the opinion of the Abbé Duchesne, author of the *Liber Pontificalis* of 1886.[6] Sargisian on pages 32-34 of his commentary says that three centuries prior to the Armenian translations of the *Life of Silvester* and *Socrates' Ecclesiastical History* there was a Greek version of the *Life of Constantine and his Mother Helen, the First Christians* written by an unknown sophist named Eusignius of Cappadocia from which both Khorenats'i and James of Sarug had benefited. He quotes the Mkhit'arians of Venice manuscript 1441, which apparently was also known to Aṛagel Patmich' of Ispahan. In addition to this manuscript he also quotes an old Greek version found in the Vatican in fol.356 of manuscript 866 and says 'this manuscript was known to Lambigius'. Sargisian's explanation of the name Eusignius is interesting: he says it is composed of Greek *eu* + Latin *signum* and means a 'good sign' or 'good mark'. This is very close to the meaning of the name of the Armenian Agat'angełos, which means 'good messenger' (at this point this much should suffice concerning the name).

In his booklet of 1894, Carrière advanced the view that Khorenats'i had used the works of Malala, a Syriac writer of the sixth century, for the description of Abgar of Edessa and his acceptance of Christianity; however the books of Malala were not translated into Armenian. He also compares an extract from Procopius (War of the Vandals, 11.ii—an incorrect reference, it should be History of Wars, Book iv.x., ed. Loeb, vol. 11, p289). The reference from Procopius is compared with the footnote in Khorenats'i's chapter 1.19 for the name of Sur, in connection with Joshua and the flight of the Canaanites to Tigisis. However, at the end of his article he quotes the Phoenician History by Mauverse (col. 11.2, p428, written in 1850), and tells us that like Mauverse, he too came

6.   Ibid. See his introduction, page IV.

to the conclusion that this part of the History of Mosēs is an interpolation of later years.

The reader may be interested to know that in reality Sur was a contemporary of Jehu and not of Joshua. In Armenian Joshua is written as 'Hesu' and Jehu as 'Heu', which demonstrates how the interpolation of a simple 's' alters sense and chronology. It also means that the anecdote of the Phoenicians is no interpolation, aside from the addition of the 's'.

Carrière also wrote a booklet in 1899, published by the Mkhit'arians of Vienna, about the 'Eight Temples of Pagan Armenia'.[7] This is a substandard study which gives the impression that Carrière, encouraged by his converts, was now looking for further anomalies in the History of Khorenats'i—it would not be incorrect to say that this study is a nit-picking exercise. A couple of examples to support my view are where, on pages 28-29, he states that 'King Trdat went (from Vałarshapat) to Artashat but on his way he came across the temple of Tir' (Agat'angełos §778)'. He then compares this sentence with what Khorenats'i had written: 'Artashēs II removed the idols (from Armavir) to his new capital city, but the idol of Tir he placed outside of the city, on the way (to Artashat).' Carrière concludes that 'what Khorenats'i had written is absolutely wrong since there were many roads to Artashat' and yet his statement is devoid of reasoning. Artashat was no more the capital city or a trade centre by Trdat's time, while in Artashēs' time it was a new city which could not yet have many roads leading to it. Another objection in this respect is that in order to go down to Artashat from Armavir, the old capital city, one had to follow the same route as the one from Vałarshapat, which Trdat had followed.

Another of Carrière's poorly conceived assertions occurs on page 37: 'At the time Khorenats'i lived, one could only have an elementary idea about the ancient Armenian religion as traditions were lost. The books circulating in those days had little to say about the ancient religion, except for a few, which struggled against Mazdaeanism.' But the Mazdaean religion together with the Sassanian kingdom of Iran had come to an end in AD 651 with Islam established by the Arabs long before Khorenats'i's time, if one accepts the dates of the eighth or ninth centuries. So what is the precise connection here with Mazdaeanism? Does Carrière place Khorenats'i back in the fifth century?

---

7. A. Carrière, *Les Huit Sanctuaires de l'Armenie, d'après Agathange et Moïse de Khoren*, étude critique, Paris, 1899, translated by Y. V. Tashian, Mkhit'arian Press, Vienna, 1899.

Conflicting dates

F. C. Conybeare in a 1901 article on dating Mosēs of 'Khoren' had rather uncomplimentary words for von Gutschmid:[8] 'It will surprise no one to learn that he [Gutschmid] is rather a compiler than an original historian, a compiler moreover devoid of critical sense and ability to distinguish between legend and sober fact.' As for Carrière's hypothesis that Khorenats'i borrowed from the *Life of Silvester* and *Socrates*, Conybeare writes: 'For a long time I accepted Carrière's view, but I had always an uneasy feeling . . . for a time his "pièces justificatives" appeared to me to bear it out. I am glad to have been able to liberate myself from the yoke of a hypothesis which appeared inevitable and yet involved such difficulties.'

G. Khalat'yants' became a staunch ally of Carrière's and, confirming the same opinions, he wrote about the subject of new sources[9] claiming that Khorenats'i had borrowed from *The Life of Silvester and Socrates* and many other authors whose works or translations into Armenian belong to periods later than the fifth to sixth centuries. And yet, in his previous study of the History of Łazar P'arpets'i, dated to *c.*500, he had claimed in 1883 that Łazar had used Khorenats'i and Ełishē.[10] He was clearly a meticulous and hardworking scholar but, unfortunately for him, his assertions went beyond the acceptable—in fact his unending parallels between Khorenats'i's History and the works of Eusebius, Diodorus Siculus, Fl. Josephus, the Bible and so on proves tiresome. Khalat'yants' went on to write *The Armenian Arsacids According to Mosēs Khorenats'i*,[11] a work in which he unwittingly negated both Carrière's and his own claims.

On page 3 Khalat'yants' enumerates all the sources, naming the creator of the Armenian alphabet as Mashtots'. In this list he includes 'Mosēs Kałankatuats'i (the seventh-century edition)', which is correct and yet it nullifies previous arguments that Khorenats'i was a historian of the eighth or ninth century because Kałankatuats'i and his 'seventh century edition' belong to the early second half of the seventh century. In Kałankatuats'i's Book 1, chapter 8, we read 'In this part K'ert'ołahayr

---

8.   F. C. Conybeare, 'The Date of Moses of Khoren', in *Byzantiniche Zeitschrift*, 10, 1901. pp 489-504.
9.   G. Khalat'yants', *Movsēs Khorenats'i and His Newly Found Sources*, Mkhit'arian Press, Vienna, 1898.
10.   Ibid., *Łazar P'arpets'i and His Works: A Historical and Philological Study*, Moscow, 1883, pp 51, 59 & 60.
11.   Translated from the Russian into Armenian by Deacon A. Simonyants', Mkhit'arian Press, Vienna, 1906.

Mosēs will help us', and in chapter 15 of the same book are mentioned all the ancient names of Hay kings that appear in Khorenats'i's Book 1, chapters 12, 19 & 22, as well as borrowing many other descriptions of events. I do not know of any other recent scholar who has remarked on this contradictory reference: Khorenats'i is clearly cited by Kałankatuats'i, therefore he could not belong to the periods indicated by some scholars nor could he have borrowed from the works mentioned, which were written or translated after the last quarter of the fifth century and onwards.

Khalat'yants' also published two books on the subject of Khorenats'i's History, on which, being as they are in Russian, I am unable to comment except in quoting the remarks of Adontz, one of the class of scholars who believe that Khorenats'i's work belongs to the ninth century. Nevertheless he appears to have been the harshest critic of Khalat'yants', pointing out Khalat'yants' extreme theories and his sense of animosity directed towards Khorenats'i and his History.[12]

Most of Adontz's articles are speculative. In his article reviewing Akinian's discourse of 'Łevond and Khorenats'i', he admits that the only real objection to Khorenats'i being a personality of the fifth century is the fifteen-line verbatim extract which appears in the longer recension of the translation of the *Life of Silvester* of 678,[13] a subject dealt with above while discussing Carrière's position. In his criticism of the article ('Łevond and Khorenats'i'), writing about the 'Lament', the last chapter of the History, Adontz is adamant that it belongs to Khorenats'i and that Akinian's ideas are ineffectual and misguided.[14] In this case I agree with what Adontz writes but at the same time I see an inconsistency in his theories. Adontz believes that Khorenats'i and his History belong to the ninth century, the time when the Bagratid Ashot became 'Prince of Princes' (862) and in 884-5 achieved kingship. How could Khorenats'i, so enamoured of the Bagratids according to Adontz, write a 'Lament' about the termination of the Arsacid kingdom of Armenia (AD 428) and the deaths of his teachers Sahak and Mesrop (AD 439-40) in the second half of the ninth century?

J. Marquard was of the opinion that Khorenats'i was an author of the second half of the ninth century. In *The Origins of the Bagratunis*

12. N. Adontz, *Collection*, University of Yerevan, 2006.Critical article in vol. 11, pp 294-312, re. G. Khalat'yants', *The Armenian Arsacids in the History of Movsēs Khorenats'i*, Moscow 1903.
13. Ibid. See p309.
14. N. Adontz, 'Łevond and Khorenats'i: A Review of Fr N. Akinian's Article', in *Collection*, vol. 11, University of Yerevan, 2006, pp 323-51; see pp 332-41.

(Mkhitarian Press, Vienna, 1915) he declared that '[the Georgian] chronology up to the second half of the ninth century, from a historical point of view, is completely worthless, since for the older periods it is based on Pseudo-Mosēs Khorenats'i's work.'[15] An amazing claim! Does this mean that the Georgians have no history for a period of more than 400 years since we know Mosēs' History ends on AD 440? Is it not remarkable that a document written in the second half of the ninth century, if we believe Marquard, became the basis for the older periods of the Georgian history written in the second half of the ninth century? Had the Georgians no traditions of their own and had to wait for Mosēs to write his History of the Armenians? And by what means do the Georgians receive this History which, according to Marquard and others, is not known until the tenth century? Or has the timing of Mosēs' *floruit* deliberately been distorted to fit certain scholarly opinions?

According to Marquard and many other critics of the History, Khorenats'i glorified and extolled the Bagratunis at the cost of the Mamikoneans, and yet after 440—the date he finishes his history, when the true elevation to power of the house of the Bagratunis starts—he has nothing to say, even about one of the most famous of their sons, Smbat Khosrov Shum, or the initial years of their aspirations to create the kingdom of the Bagratunis. Furthermore, after writing his 'Lament' adverse conditions were created by the Arabs and their invasions of Armenia, starting with 640, but on this Mosēs is silent! As for Mosēs being the enamoured of the Bagratunis, this is explained below (see Part III), in view of which it is surprising that Marquard had not examined the matter thoroughly prior to making such a claim.

Some contradictory opinions

In 1934 H. Manandyan published his study *The Solution of the Enigma of Khorenats'i*,[16] which was not a well-argued work. It contains much material from Khorenats'i's History and ascribes him also the authorship of *Geography*, which is nowadays accepted as the work of Anania Shirakats'i. On page 50 Manandyan quotes Hübschmann, who had stated: 'Mosēs knows the district of Great Tsop'k' as just Tsop'k'' (Sophene), but this district in 591 had passed to Byzantium and was

---

15. J. Marquard, *The Origins of the Bagratunis*, in two parts, trans. M. Hapozian, Mkhit'arian Press, Vienna, 1915.

16. H. Manandyan, *The Solution of the Enigma of Khorenats'i*, State Press, Yerevan, 1934; see p50.

joined with Ałdznik' and thereby was renamed Np'rkert District. Mosēs knows none of these.'

Another of Manandyan's arguments asserts that 'Anania could not know the name Tork' Angeł, since this "house" and the district had assimilated and vanished by his time'. Anania is a writer of the middle seventh century and Khorenats'i, according to Manandyan, is a writer of the ninth. Again, is it not remarkable that Khorenats'i of the ninth century does not know of Np'rkert district yet knows Tork' Angeł and much that is connected with both the person and the dukedom. In fact, he is our only source, and yet Anania of the seventh century knows the first but knows nothing of the latter. All the same, it is interesting to see how Manandyan resolves these contradictory expositions. According to him, Hubschmann's opinion is due to misunderstanding and Mosēs while writing his History had consulted older sources. It is well known that Mosēs is our only source for Tork' Angeł, so what then are these 'older sources' that Manandyan knows of yet does not disclose? On page 151 of his study, Manandyan says: 'It is not difficult to guess why Khorenats'i in line with his city names of Artashat and Eruandashat also names the place Erazgavork-Shirakavan as Shirakashat-awan and Mavrikopolis.' Manandyan is extremely happy with his discovery since none commented on the subject prior to him. Unfortunately, Khorenats'i's History does not have such place names and this discovery is useless because these quotations are from Anania Shirakats'i's Geography.[17]

H. Adjaryan on page 430 of his *Dictionary of Armenian Personal Names*, under the name of Mosēs says that 'Mosēs knows the concealed Greek inscriptions from Garṇi, which in recent excavations Manandyan discovered and translated. But, if Mosēs is moved to the ninth century, he could not have known this'—since the place was destroyed during the Arab invasions, which started in 640.

Fr A. Matikian has a great deal to say about Khorenats'i in his two books *Ara Gełets'ik (Ara the Fair)* and *Ananuna kam Kełts-Sebēos (The Anonymous or Pseudo-Sebēos)*.[18] His views in connection with Ara the Fair are imaginary and unrealistic, moreover they do not consider the times when such indigenous myths were created by the local minstrels (see 'Ara the Fair' in Part IV). He pushes Mosēs and his History to the ninth century, and yet I see no worthwhile argument for doing so. In the book

---

17. Anania Shirakats'i, *Geography*, Soviet Writer, Erevan, 1979, p296.
18. Fr A. V. Matikian, *Ara the Fair*, 1930; *The Anonymous or Pseudo-Sebēos*, 1913 (both published by the Mkhit'arian Press, Vienna).

on Ara, Matikian says on page 7: 'Here Khorenats'i has slavishly followed Ananun [Anonymous History] and therefore he does not any more have the old significance or merit.' As the case has been with others offering such opinions, Matikian on page 70 of his commentary on Sebēos' History makes a contradictory statement: 'It is no more possible to rely on the genealogy of the noble houses of Khorenats'i, since he has not seen [the Anonymous History of] Ananun, nor was it possible to find these true legends in the ninth century.'

Matikian, intentionally or otherwise, tries hard to diminish the importance of Khorenats'i—but that is not all. He also tries to destroy the History of Bishop Sebēos because he has come up with the idea that P'awstos is the author of the first four chapters labelled as the 'Anonymous Histories' by previous scholarship (see *Ananunə kam kełts Sebēos*, pp 9-28). P'awstos Biwzandats'i's History that has reached us starts with Book iii. This enumeration belongs to later times and it is, most probably, the marking of a copying scribe, since there have never been first and second books (see below). But Matikian thinks otherwise, and borrows from other authors such as events that are found in Sebēos History, and tells us that these belong to the lost first two books of P'awstos.

In the first chapter of Book iii, P'awstos has an ambiguous phrase: 'There are places wherein our history is the first and there are places wherein it is the last and what is in between had already been written by others.' In my opinion Madikian explains this reasonably well on pages 12-16 and yet he fails to realize that P'awstos's sentence is a declaration of his intention and an explanation of what the history will involve—something that one expects to find at the beginning of any book. Although this 'declaration' comes at the start of what has been designated Book iii, it is obvious that there were no previous books here by P'awstos—a fact confirmed by Łazar P'arpets'i's lack of awareness of such books[19] when, at the end of the fifth century, he became the first to write about P'awstos and his History. According to the opinion of most scholars P'awstos is also of the fifth century, and therefore practically a contemporary of Łazar's, whom one expects to know better than a twentieth-century commentator.

In 1935 Fr V. Hats'uni delivered a lecture in Venice at the Mkhit'arian Congregation, which later on that same year was published as a

---

19. Łazar P'arpets'i, *History of the Armenians & Letter to Vahan Mamikonian*, critical edition by G. Ter Mkrtch'ian & S. Malkhazyants', Mnats'akan Mardirosian, Tbilisi, 1904; see the first three pages of the Introduction.

booklet.[20] Hats'uni directs some of his remarks to prevailing scholarship, saying: 'But when in the name of criticism we hear utterances from scholars, and these utterances are intended to demonstrate something different from others that contradicts each other rather than Khorenats'i, this means criticism is not the primary intention of these scholars.' He is adamant that Khorenats'i and his History belong to the second half of the fifth century and as supporting evidence he cites the Histories of Sebēos and Kałankatuats'i, both from early second half of the seventh century. Note that at the time of his lecture nothing was known of At'anas Tarawnts'i.

Fr Nersēs Akinian, in his 1970 study of the History of Kałankatuats'i (whom he calls Mosēs Daskhurants'i but adds in parenthesis 'the alleged Kałankatuats'i'), refers to Hats'uni's booklet and exposes his own preconceptions by asserting that 'Hats'uni tried to exploit the truth in order to prove that Khorenats'i was a fifth-century historian . . . He would not have made this mistake if he was aware of the verdict of the critics that prior to 850 no History of Khorenats'i existed.'[21] But in the third volume of his *Bibliographical Studies* (1930) in connection with Łevond's History and Khorenats'i, Akinian claims that 'following the artificial Classical Armenian of the Hellenistic school ... it was Khorenats'i who made it prominent'. Though correct, this statement contradicts Akinian's other claim, his main thesis, that there was no History of Khorenats'i prior to 850,[22] because it is well known that the post-golden age Armenian language of the Hellenistic School lasted from the sixth to eighth centuries.[23] In addition to these assertions, Akinian tells us that chapters 8 and 15 of the first book of Kałankatuats'i's History, where Khorenats'i is cited, belong to the tenth-century Daskhurants'i.[24] No doubt he has forgotten to mention Bishop Sebēos' History.

Akinian advocates that the last chapter (III.68), the Lament of the History of Khorenats'i does not belong to it—in later years someone had placed it there by removing it from Łevond's History, since in his opinion it belongs to Łevond. He presents the reader with incredible events as

20. Hats'uni; see 'Introduction' above, note 1, p78.

21. N. V. Akinian, *Movsēs Daskhurants'i (Called Kałankatuats'i) and his History of the Albanians*, Mkhit'arian Press, Vienna, 1970, p52.

22. N. V. Akinian, *Bibliographical Studies*, vol. III, Mkhit'arian Press, Vienna, 1930, p122.

23. H. Adjaryan, *The History of the Armenian Language*, vol. II, Haypedhrat, Yerevan, 1951, pp 142-68; H. Manandyan, *The Hellenistic School: The Periods of Its Progress*, Mkhit'arian Press, Vienna, 1928, see 'Introduction'.

24. Akinian, *Movsēs Daskhurants'i*, 'Introduction', pp 53-58.

contributing factors to the Lament, such as the earthquake in Khorasan (eastern Persia) in 764-5 and 768-9; the flooding and destruction of Mosul in 762-3; the famine in Syria, Assyria and Mesopotamia of 772-3, which was also prevalent in the countries to the east and south (what about the north, Armenia, for which the lament was written?); swarms of locusts and the death of 20,000 in Basra in 768-9; and the pillages of Mesopotamia, Antioch and Palestine in 772 by the Arabs.

It is interesting to note his interpretation of a section of the Lament (Book III.68), which starts halfway down paragraph five (I quote Thomson's translation): 'And while they hoped for our return to glory in my most erudite wisdom and perfect aptitude, while we swiftly making for Byzantium hoped to dance at marriages, being bold and nimble of foot, and to sing wedding songs—now instead of festivities I lament over a tomb and piteously sigh.' It appears that everybody has understood this excerpt except Akinian. He argues that the plural pronouns such as 'our' and 'we' of the extract are wrong and that these should be in the singular; thus he decides the whole extract is written in inferior language and therefore is an interpolation!

Toumanoff's quandary

Of the more recent scholars, Cyril Toumanoff is of the opinion that the History of Mosēs Khorenats'i is a 'great work' and was written by an 'erudite, clever and a deliberate mystifier in the eighth century'.[25] It follows that this person, whom he labels 'Pseudo-Mosēs', suffered from pangs of altruism and decided to present his great work in the name of Mosēs of Chorene (this is how he puts Khorenats'i) of the fifth century.

Toumanoff's naming Khorenats'i 'Pseudo-Mosēs' is amusing but wanting in reason. People want to perpetuate their own name: to this end they may steal the works of others and pass it as their own. A great work that does not carry the writer's name does nothing for the ego of the writer (the case of corruption or interpolation falls into a different category). Nevertheless, Toumanoff admits that there were two Mosēses, i.e. the real one known as Mosēs of Chorene and a second writer from the eighth century whom he calls Pseudo-Mosēs. Therefore, in the course of this study it is incumbent on me to prove which of these alleged Mosēses, if there was any truth in such a claim, is the actual writer of the History and in which period he operated.

25. C. Toumanoff, 'On the Date of Pseudo Moses of Chorene', *Handes Amsorea*, 75, 1961, p467; see also his *Studies in Christian Caucasian History*, Georgetown University, 1963, p108.

Incidentally, there are other authors of the early twentieth century and some modern writers who follow Toumanoff in using the same label of Pseudo-Mosēs. However, their articles will not be discussed here since they are far-fetched, speculative or else tell us nothing new.

Tumanoff's baseless inferences

Thomson does not use the label Pseudo-Mosēs. He is of the opinion that Mosēs of Chorene was the actual person who wrote the History of the Armenians during the first decade of Abbasid rule (starts AD 750), in the second half of the eighth century.[26] Mahé does not directly commit himself to any date, but says that Mosēs had benefited from both Łazar P'arpets'i and Anania Shirakats'i.[27] The latter author, Shirakats'i, wrote his studies early in the second half of the seventh century, and so it is obvious that in Mahé's opinion the History of Mosēs was written in the eighth century, which also finds confirmation in his citing and acceptance of Carrière's theories.

Toumanoff in his article 'On the Date of Pseudo-Mosēs of Chorene' (1961), accepts that scholarly opinion varies in the case of the true date of Mosēs' activity. He believes it was the eighth century and tries to disprove other theories that lay claim to the fifth, seventh or ninth centuries. He avoids any involvement in arguments as to which author used Mosēs or vice versa. His position is clear: he has identified eight anomalies in the History which preclude it from being a work of the fifth, seventh or the ninth centuries. He outlines these objections in his article, the influence of which unfortunately may also be seen in his major work *Studies in Christian Caucasian History* of 1963, which has much to recommend itself but remains seriously flawed. Toumanoff's intention is to give us a complete history of the Armenians, i.e. from the very beginning. In doing so he resorts to some fantastic conjectures which affect his later conclusions. The other main shortcoming of the work is his reliance on the so-called *Primary History of Armenia*, which on many occasions leads him down the wrong path. In my study of the History of Bishop Sebēos,[28] I have conclusively proven that no such *Primary History* ever existed and that the whole thing is a scholarly invention. It is remarkable that scholarship, in order to disprove the validity of a written

26. R. W. Thomson, *The History of the Armenians*, by Moses Khorenats'i, translation with commentary, Harvard University, Cambridge, Mass., 1978.
27. Annie & Jean-Pierre Mahé, *Histoire de l'Arménie*, par Moïse de Khorène, translation with commentary, Gallimard, Paris, 1993.
28. G. Soultanian, *The History of Bishop Sebēos*, Bennett & Bloom, London, 2007.

document, feels it has to invent and then pass judgement relying on their invention.

Toumanoff states: 'The *History of Armenia* of Pseudo-Mosēs and that of the *Primary History of Armenia* present two different versions of genealogy of the early, mostly mythical, kings of Armenia. The genealogy represents a blend of theogonies of the pagan past—divinities became heroes in the Christian monuments—with a pellmell of reminiscences about the Vannic, Scythian, Proto-Armenian, and early Armenian rulers' (*Studies*, 1963, p108). When he mentions the *Primary History* in this paragraph, Toumanoff refers to the first chapter of the History of Bishop Sebēos. Sebēos replicates Mosēs in the chapter, but if one moves Mosēs from the fifth century to the eighth then one is hard-pressed to find an explanation for the genealogy provided by the seventh-century Sebēos and his mention of the name of Mosēs Khorenats'i in it—except, as is the case here, one invents a second non-existent *Primary History* belonging to the twelfth century![29] Furthermore, I do not understand Toumanoff's motive when he mentions 'two different versions of genealogy of the early mythical kings' since this statement is untrue. In chapter 5 of Book 1, Mosēs demonstrates the concordance of the generations of Noah's sons with others; in the case of the Hays he quotes the longest line taken from the list of names of chapter 12 (see the 'Family Tree of Hayk', page 255), which gives: Hayk, Aramaneak, Aramayis, Amasia, Gełam, Harma, Aram and Ara the Fair. This same list of names is repeated by Sebēos in paragraph 7 (page 3) of his chapter 1. For what precise purpose has Toumanoff created two different versions of genealogy I am unable to say.

In the case of the following sentence—'Mostly mythical kings of Armenia'—we must concede that at the time Toumanoff was writing his study no one had carried out any thorough research into these kings, and what he says appears to be the prevailing view of his time. However, in Volume I of *Pre-History of the Armenians*,[30] I have proved that there was nothing mythical about these kings, while in Volume II I have produced their inscriptions and translated them into English. These kings, every one of them, existed in the countries of Aram, Tabal and Cilicia, but not Armenia (see this king list in 'The Proto-Armenian Kingdoms' in Part IV, pages 247-252). In their epoch there was no territory known as Armenia, whose origin in reality starts with the movement into Urartu

29. G. V. Abgaryan, *History of Sebēos*, Academy of Armenia, Yerevan, 1979.
30. G. Soultanian, *The Pre-History of the Armenians, Volume I*, Bennett & Bloom, London, 2003.

of the descendants of these kings, who called themselves the Hay people. 'Armenian' means 'People of Aram', i.e. belonging to the *land* of Aram and not the progeny of a person known as Aram. Mosēs, unable to find the names of individuals whose deeds he describes, had used—and believed to be correct—the country name of Aram as a person responsible for the various battles and the migration of the Hays into Urartu. It is unfortunate that after saying 'Tigran extended the borders of our country up to the edges of our ancient habitation places' (1.24), Mosēs did not make the connection between the land of Aram and the ancient habitation places of the Hays, even though he knew that Tigran had conquered Cilicia, Aram (which he mentions as Cappadocia although he knew the location of the land of Aram)[31] and Syria.

Toumanoff's sentence continues: 'The genealogy represents a blend of theogonies of the pagan past—divinities became heroes in the Christian monuments.' This is another scholarly invention. Toumanoff, in the first place, says the genealogy is 'mostly mythical kings of Armenia', and yet it seems this speculation was not convincing enough for him since he knows nothing about the subject of the said kings, therefore he intensifies his conjecture by adding 'theogonies of the pagan past—divinities became heroes in the Christian monuments'. How indeed can such a conclusion possibly be reached? When one reads my *Pre-History Volume I*, one realizes that all these kings were down-to-earth people and that there is nothing remotely divine about them. In *Pre-History Volume II*, there are a number of inscriptions that describe the death and burial of a king. On reading these inscriptions, one realizes that even kings were treated as ordinary people—of course, exortations and wishes were always added, such as 'he is now with the Sun' or 'he is entrusted to the care of god Tark'. The people of Armenia knew none of the names Mosēs gives us in his chapters 1.12, 19 and 22 until the end of the sixth century, the time of the discovery of the manuscript of the History by At'anas Tarawnts'i, when copies started to be produced. This claim is supported by the Histories of Sebēos and Kałankatuats'i. But even after such copies of the manuscript were made, the people of Armenia would not know who these named kings were nor where had they reigned, since Mosēs himself and the entire world of scholarship did not know until the publication of *Pre-History Volume I* in 2003. How could, in such circumstances, anybody know of 'mythical kings' and make them

31. Koryun, *Life of Mashtots'*, translation into Modern Armenian with commentary by M. Abełyan, Haypethrad, Yerevan, 1962; see chapter 7, where it is stated that Mashtots' arrived in the country of Aram.

into 'divinities become heroes, etc'? Was it not also such scholarly presumptions that had ascribed to Ara the Fair and Tork' Angeł divinity, which Mosēs with his honest and healthy attitude had rejected?

There are a few interesting demotic tales which professional minstrels or *gusans*, making the rounds of the country, composed and recited in public gatherings in order to make a living. Using imaginative and parabolic language they had to captivate their listeners and were wide-ranging in their subject matter: it could equally have been Hayk and Bēl, Ara the Fair and Semiramis, Tork' Angeł, Vahagn or Artashēs. But even then we do not know except what Mosēs writes as to how these *gusans* presented their heroes. The extent of our knowledge derives from Mosēs' History where he preserved a few of these poems, of which the oldest relates to Vahagn (Heracles) at the end of the fifth century BC. Most of these poems relate to subjects from the second century BC onwards, perpetuated by oral tradition. It was because of such poems and songs that Mosēs had written to his patron 'not to believe that the princes, as the poets say, were of the kin and seed of the gods' (III.65). Toumanoff quotes this (1963, pp 108-9) without realizing how out of time and place such a remark would have been in the eighth century. It is modern scholarship that transforms the ancient kings to divinities, which demonstrates that Mosēs, 1,500 years ago, had a far healthier attitude towards the miraculous.

At the time of the translation of the Armenian Bible (404-430?—we do not know exactly when the translation was completed since it was improved for a long time, but by 339/40, prior to the deaths of Ss Sahak and Mesrop it would have been in the state it has reached us), the Orion constellation was named Hayk, but that was to honour the memory of Hayk, who had slain Bēl; he was the only person that had prevailed against the Assyrian might. But did the translators of the Bible associate Hayk with divinity? Or does Mosēs give us any hint of such a divinity concerning the most ancient hero and primogenitor of the Hays? Scholarship usually identifies Ara the Fair with Er, son of Armenius of Pamphylia,[32] mentioned in the Republic of Plato.[33] What therefore has Ara of the Hays (Armenians) to do with the Pamphylian Er? The case of Tork' Angeł is worse still. A disgraced person known in the ancient times as Tarkhunazi (Thunder Devoid of Fire), whose name was recomposed in Classical Armenian as Tork' Angeł (Tork' the Ignoble), suddenly acquires divinity in the accounts of certain scholars—one of them is

---

32. A. V. Matikian, *Ara the Fair*, Mkhit'arian Press, Vienna, 1930, pp 254, 272.
33. Plato, *The Republic*, J. M. Dent, London, 1950; see Book X, §314.

Toumanoff. Why all these inventions and distortions? What benefit is to be derived from such imaginative but absurd innovations? In the History of Mosēs (or in any History written in the fifth-sixth centuries) there is only one person, Vahagn (borrowed from the Iranians) with a temple at Ashtishat, who has acquired divinity and is equated with Heracles of the Greeks (Hercules of the Romans).

In the last phrase of his excerpt Toumanoff employs the description 'a pell-mell of reminiscences about the Vannic, Scythian, Proto-Armenian and early Armenian rulers'. By 'Vannic' Toumanoff is referring to the kingdom of Urartu. Well, the whole known world, including the Armenians who were living in the same highlands, knew nothing relating to Urartu (an anomaly explained in *Pre-History, Volume 1*). Mosēs writes nothing about the subject since he knows nothing (writing about the building of Van by Semiramis, which happens to be a surreal concoction, does not count as knowledge of the Urartians). Other Armenian clerics who wrote histories similarly knew nothing about Urartu. It would take more than 1,400 years from the time of Mosēs for the world to show an interest in the inscriptions of Eastern Anatolia, the study of which, combined with Assyrian inscriptions, would throw light on the subject of the Vannic kingdom. As for the Scythians, the only one mentioned by Mosēs was Niwk'ar Mades with whom the Proto-Armenians battled and prevailed (1.23). But Khorenats'i did not know that Niwk'ar was a Scythian, nor did the other historians. Where do these reminiscences of Scythians come from? Is Toumanoff in his imagination equating Aramu of Urartu with the country of Aram, and Bartatua of Herodotus with the non-existent Paroyr of Mosēs and thus making baseless inferences? Mosēs certainly does not know Aramu or Bartatua.

Toumanoff's nescience of the Hay migrations

Toumanoff writes that 'one of the errors that both Pseudo-Mosēs and the Primary History [Sebēos] must have derived from an older tradition the idea that the Artaxiads have been a branch of the Iranian Arsacids; the rise of the latter in Parthia being contemporaneous with the rise of the former in Armenia' (*Studies*, p111). Toumanoff's scepticism, his reliance on the alleged Primary History and ignorance of the fact that the Paeonians, the inhabitants of Gordyene and Mygdonia in Eastern Anatolia, were Hays (Proto-Armenians), leads him astray.[34] Mosēs too is

34. H. Manandyan in his *Critical Survey of The Armenian History* (Haypethrad, Yerevan, 1957), on page 45 tells us that Harran in the second century AD was a city of Macedonians and, in his work *Tigran II and Rome* (Armfan, Yerevan, 1940) on page 207, he

under a misapprehension: he writes correctly 'the world of Armenians' (*'Hayots' Ashkharb'*) but considers this to be Armenia, whereas 'the world of Armenians' means the place where Armenians have settled, which does not necessarily imply Armenia.

It is a historical event that the king of the Parthians, Phraates II, subdued Mesopotamia and appointed his younger brother, Vałarshak, viceroy of Atropatene with his capital city at Nisibis. There is nothing unusual in this since in every district conquered, large or small, Phraates had to appoint a viceroy or a satrap. The population of Atropatene consisted in the main of Hays (Armenians), because the old Kadmeans of the district of Kadmukhi, with Nisibis as its centre, had multiplied with the arrival of the Paeonian population of Gordyina on the Axius river in the Balkans (this migration was soon after the passage of Xenophon and his army through these lands). This took place during the fourth century BC and their new settlement area was named Gordyene—by themselves or by others—after the name of their previous habitation place. The second century, after the year 182 BC, saw the arrival of a large population of Mygdonian, Laioi and Doberes Paeonians, who settled in and around Nisibis—and the land was named Mygdonia after them. A little earlier, the northern Paeonians, the Agrianes, had settled to the west of Sebastia; after 217 BC the population of Bylazora (present-day Titov Veles in Macedonia) settled to the north of Gordyene and founded the city of Bayazet,[35] to the south of the Ararat mountains (later this place was better known as the Dariwnk' fortifications of the Arsacids, and still later of the Bagratids); and the population of Astibus (present Shtip in Yugoslavia) settled to the northwest of Lake Van, naming the district Tarawn after the name of their royal family of Derrones (the name of their god of healing was also Darron) and founding the city of Ashtishat in remembrance of the holy city of Astibus they had left behind in their Balkan homeland.[36]

After the middle of the second century BC, Atropatene had the largest number of settled Hays (Armenians). Therefore the new viceroy Vałarshak was bound to be interested as to who these people, the Hays, were.

writes that in 65-64 BC Afranius, the Roman general, returning from Mesopotamia, encountered hardships and the Carrhaean Macedonians (Harran population) received and helped him on his way (the same event is repeated by Dio Cassius, book xxxvii, §5.5, Loeb Edition, vol. III, pp 107-9). After 150 BC the population of Harran comprised wholly of Mygdonian Hays, but since in the Balkans Mygdonia had become part of Macedonia, the migrant Hays settled in Harran, too, have been made Macedonians!

35. John Wylkes, *The Illyrians*, Blackwells, Oxford, 1992, pp 149-154. See also: Polybius, *The Histories*, Loeb Classical Library, Harvard University Press, Cambridge, Mass., 2003/6; see vol. III, p233 (Book v.96-97) and vol v, p417 (Book xxiii, 10).

36. N. G. L. Hammond, *Macedonia*, Sidgwick & Jackson, London, 1991, pp 22, 183.

Khorenats'i writes that Vałarshak sent a learned wiseman, named Mar Abas Katina, to Nineveh (Nineveh has the sense of Assyro-Babylonia) to consult the archives and find out what kind of people the Hays were. Mar Abas accomplished his mission and presented Vałarshak with a document giving all the names of the Hay kings of Aram (and not Armenia as Mosēs has it) as well as some complementary information, which all proves to be correct as shown in *Pre-History Volume I*. Scholars did not know the existence of the Mar Abas Katina's document and so could not explain how Mosēs had managed to find out all the names of the kings; instead they have claimed that these were fictitious; these names could only derive from the Assyro-Babylonian inscriptions.

Toumanoff too proffers his disbelief and calls the viceroy Vałarshak a mythological figure, hence his inability to discover why Mosēs had ascribed Iranian origin to the Artaxiads. If for the time being we ignore the names of Vałarshak and Mar Abas, we must at least agree that a person had to be the viceroy of the large country of Atropatene and govern it on behalf of the Parthian king Phraates II and another person, Mar Abas, had to research and find the truth about the Hay kings of Aram country in order to account for the Assyrian versions of the ancient Hay names. But, why should Mosēs give us fictitious names of Vałarshak and Mar Abas, two non-Armenians, when everything else he writes about them are factual and verifiable,[37] for which we should be thankful to Khorenats'i instead of doubting every word he has written, and trying to find parallel expressions within historical works of his time in order to prove a point. And so this brings us to the crux of the matter, namely why does Mosēs ascribe to the Artaxiads an Iranian, specifically Parthian, origin?

Mosēs' conundrum of the Artaxiads

Mosēs had in his possession the book of Mar Abas Katina (I have dealt with the subject of Mar Abas in a separate article on pages 169-212, here I simply mention the name as found in Mosēs' History without going into details) which is supported by the names of the ancient Hay kings of Aram country. Mosēs refers to Mar Abas's book in Book 1.8, but he does not tell us how he came across it. It is also true that Mosēs was writing in the fifth century, as no such written record in those days and conditions in practice could have lasted up to the eighth century. The lifetime of a manuscript was limited for many reasons such as wear and tear, humidity, storing method and place, and atmospheric conditions.

---

37. G. Soultanian, *Pre-History Volume I*; see Part II.

This point may be particularly appeciated when we consider the manuscripts or copies thereof that have reached us, mostly written between the fourteenth and eighteenth centuries.

Following Mar Abas's document it was easy for Mosēs to write his First Book. He had all the names and various events, albeit in a mixed-up state as we see, in addition to the local lore. However, being of the opinion that the Armenian highlands were the place where all these kings and the Parthian Vałarshak reigned, Mosēs was placed in an impossible position. He had to write about the Artaxiad dynasty of Armenia, which as we now know was older than the rule of Vałarshak of Atropatene, but he had no sources or written account to confirm this fact or the existence of dynasty, which he admits by telling us that the account of Mar Abas ends with the death of Arshak, Vałarshak's son (II.9). To complicate things further, Mosēs has collected part of his material from unreliable sources and has sifted inexact local stories. It is not surprising therefore that Mosēs is confused: he does not have answers to many questions and what he has found in his sources are misleading. Therefore the only way he could solve his problem was to present the few names of the Artaxiad kings that he had found as a continuation of the dynasty starting with Vałarshak and his son Arshak. This was a reasonable solution for such a conundrum, since the Artaxiad dynasty of Armenia proper, in Mosēs' way of thinking, was sandwiched between the Parthian Vałarshak of Nisibis and Trdat the first of the Arsacids (AD 66). This created a single line of the Arsacid dynasty for Armenia, and it accounted for the gap of more than 150 years that is from Vałarshak's son Arshak of Nisibis (Mtsbin, *c.* 100 BC) to the time of the first Arsacid king Trdat I of AD 66. Unfortunately, this was also responsible for ascribing the deeds of Tigran the Great (90-55 BC) to a previous Tigran (Sakawakeats') of *c.* 560 BC.

On the same page 111 of his study, Toumanoff writes: 'Adontz begins by equating the princely class with feudalism; he thus fails to discern the dynastic-allodial order from, and parallel to, the feudal-administrative one. For him the Armenian social process consisted in passing from the primitive tribal to the more advanced feudal phase; this feudalization was the origin of the princes.' If Toumanoff has in mind just Armenia, the last stage in the life of the Hays, than he and Adontz are both wrong because the original system within Armenia cannot be compared with feudalism of Medieval Europe, nor with 'primitive tribal'. This is an important point, on which both scholars have prematurely expressed opinions, and I feel obliged to deal with it in a concise manner by presenting what is known of the past Hay people's endeavours and organizations which may give a better idea of the state Armenia was in during the period c. 580 BC to c. AD 150.

When one discusses the social order of Armenia, one must take note of the more ancient times these people existed as Hays in the countries of Paeonia (in the Balkans) and in Aram (in southeastern Anatolia), which was not available to Adontz and Toumanoff. The political divisions of Hays in Armenia, within themselves and from the other different cultures, the various ethnic units within the highlands and the various stages in the life of all these peoples have to be considered, since each stage and period has its influence on the next one.

Our knowledge of the ancient Paeonians amounts to very little, as all the information available derives from Greek literature, which neglects the social and similar other aspect of these people. However, Homer tells us that the Paeonians sent two corps in aid of Priam, the king of Troy. The first was under the leadership of Pyraechmes (Zarmayr) when the Trojan War started (*Iliad*, book 2, 848-50) and the second under Asteropaeus eleven days prior to the end of the war (book 21, 140-180). A nation in such a primitive tribal state clearly could not send two corps to Troy—the dispatch of such a force presupposes an organised nation.

Another stage parallel to that of Paeonia in the life of the Hay people starts after the Trojan War (c. 1200 BC) in south-eastern Anatolia in the land known as Aram. We know very little about the social order of the Hays of Aram, and what we do know derives from a few inscriptions, in hieroglyphic or Assyrian cuneiform, and are insufficient for an in-depth study. Nevertheless we understand that each city-state had its own satellites of minor kings or chiefs, who as vassals paid homage to a superior in addition to being the advisers of the monarch. It is not known whether the monarch had appointed these minor chiefs or they had worked their way up and achieved higher positions (in the Sultanhan inscription there is the case of an unnamed person working his way up to become adviser to Harma/Wasusaramimasa—see *Pre-History, Volume II*, pp 167-172).

The Hays of Aram beginning with the tenth century BC succeeded in creating the kingdoms of Carchemish and Marash. In time, with the arrival of additional migrants from Paeonia, the number of the kingdoms increased, spreading over Malatya, Tabal, Cilicia and its north-western regions. With the establishing of the Hay kingdoms, the kings of the various districts adopted the hieroglyphic script for their various inscriptions, the earliest of which starts in the first decade of the tenth century BC. Near the end of the eighth century BC Sargon II of Assyria put an end to all the Hay kingdoms (718-708 BC), but the former royal houses survived, becoming responsible for the welfare of the people.

A third stage parallel to both Paeonia and the land of Aram starts in 588 BC in Armenia proper, when the Urartian kingdom had fallen with the country under attack by the Medes and in flames. To save the people and halt the complete destruction of the country the Urartian surviving nobility came to an understanding with the ex-royal houses of the Hays of Aram. In 588 BC when the Hays entered Urartu, and thereby were named Armenians, they spread to the periphery of the country, each ex-royal house of the Hays settling in previously agreed regions, which were named after the dynastic names of the ex-royal houses (see Part IV, 'The Enigma of Mar Abas Katina'). The Hays never fought with the Urartians and the proof of this agreement between the two nations to share the land can be seen in the original dispersion of the Hays and in the future settlement areas of the newcomers from the Balkans, such as the people of Odomantis in the fifth century BC, Gordyene in the fourth century, Bylazoreans at the end of the third century, the Mygdonians, Astibuseans, Derrones, Edesseans and so on in the early second century (the dates for Amid, Harran and Europus are not known). The Hays in compliance with their agreement never impinged on the Urartian lands.

The dispersion of the Hays in the periphery of the new country was their weakness and they soon became prey to the Medes, who conquered the whole of the territory and placed their satrap, one Eruand Sakawakeats', the father of Tigran, as mentioned by Xenophon in his *Cyropaedia* (the main theme is in Book III).

The Hays, therefore, were already organised in the Balkans before the twelfth century BC before moving on to having kingdoms and adopting the hieroglyphic script (a legacy from the Hittites) after the tenth century BC in Aram. Such a people must be called civilized, which renders the conjectures of both Toumanoff and Adontz questionable. But what type of label do we assign the Hays after their entry into Urartu when they were called Armenians (people of Aram)? Does the label dynastic-allodial fit such a unique people? The Armenians themselves call the ancient system patriarchal houses, but that label was created at a time when they had no idea about the past of the nation. What is of further interest is that this system of patriarchal houses continued through the years until the time of Vałarsh I (AD 117-140/4) when a system near enough to feudalism was imposed on all the houses.

The case of princes—Toumanoff discusses whether their origin was in feudalism or not—is a very involved subject that would require a whole section to elucidate and involves a great deal of questions and aspects of the Armenian language which do not form an essential part of this study. Therefore this part of the generalisations made by Toumanoff and Adontz I shall leave for the time being and, hopefully, some time in the future I shall be able to revert to this subject.

The misunderstood Ostan

Toumanoff on page 125 of his *Studies* writes: 'Pseudo-Mosēs is responsible for a certain amount of confusion among modern historians regarding the subject of Ostan. He offers two statements about this: in I.30 he mentions the "nobility called Ostan" while in II.7 he is more explicit—here he speaks of the guard called Ostan, regiments founded by the first Arsacids and manned by descendants of the ancient Haykid kings.'

I have thoroughly discussed the subject of Ostan in *Pre-History Volume I*, but here I shall examine Toumanoff's assertation, which is based on misunderstanding and mistranslation of the excerpt from Mosēs. I find further fault in his argument, such as on page 114 where he claims '*Ostan* literally means "threshold", i.e. "*court*", and, on page 124, note 215, that '*Ostanik* signified "men of Ostan" i.e. "*court*", in other words "*courtiers*".' If his claims about *Ostan* and *Ostanik* were correct, which they are not, how can we square them up with his translation of 'the guard called *Ostan*, regiments manned by the descendants of ancient Hay kings, founded by the first Arsacids'? His definitions of *Ostan* and *Ostanik* are not acceptable. Scholarship claims that *Ostan* is borrowed from Iranian, which does not have such a root (Adjaryan). In fact *Ostan* is an indigenous word and means 'branches'—the various Hay or Proto-Armenian kingdoms of the land of Aram are referred to as the branches of the Proto-Armenians. *Ostan* is composed from *ost* ('branch') + *an* (collective suffix), along the lines of *hawr* > *hawr-an* ('cattle'), *ma* > *ma-r-an* ('storerooms'), *esh* > *esh-an* ('donkeys'), *dzi* > *dzi-an* ('horses'), *chori* > *chori-an* ('mules'), *movpēt* > *movpētan* ('chief magi'), *avag* > *avagan-i* ('nobility'); this is similar to the English *-en* suffix in *ox* > *ox-en*; *child* > *child-r-en*, *brother* > *brethr-en*. Hence *Ostanik* (*ost* + *an* + *ik* [diminutive suffix]) means 'Little Ostan'.

Thomson's translation (p138) of the same part of II.7 highlighted above by Toumanoff, is as follows: 'He established four companies of palace guards, each one with ten thousand armed men from the same ancient race of kings descended from our ancestor Hayk, who were called the original Ostan.' We note that according to Mosēs (II.7) it was the progeny of Hayk, 'the ancient race of kings who were called the original Ostan' and not the 'guards or regiments'.

The four descendants from the ancient race of kings mentioned were the Sisakeans in the east, the Kadmeans in the south (this house was later taken over by Arzanene), the Angełats' Tun in the southwest, and the Shahunis in the west (the Gusharids were not members of the original Ostan since they were a later branch of this house in the north). In other words these guards or regimental companies were to guard the four corners of Armenia. The remaining four members of the original Ostan were the Gełark'unik' (at the time of Artashēs I this branch had ceased to exist) in the northeast, the Manawazeans (they would expire in the fourth century) centrally situated and known as the 'Fathers' (Hark'), the Bznunik' (they would have their end at nearly the same time as the Manawazeans) to the northwest of Lake Van, and lastly the Khorkhorunik' (they would be given the title of Malkhaz, and survive up to the seventh century BC) to the north of Lake Van.

Toumanoff says: 'Pseudo-Mosēs is responsible for the confusion among modern historians' (p125, see also p108). To make such an accusation one must have access to the facts of the subject, which he does not. While he describes the principalities of Angeł Tun and Andzit as being ruled by one dynasty, and further two separate dynasties ruling the Greater and Lesser Tsop'k', he claims that these houses were of Orontid origin (p131)—in reality all three were Haykids. It does not occur to Toumanoff that modern historians, himself included, are responsible for the confusion since it was by their doing that Mosēs was removed to the seventh to ninth century. Moreover, besides not believing Mosēs they also failed to undertake any meaningful research. Other historians, such as P'awstos, Ełishē and P'arpets'i mention Ostan and Ostanik, but within the context of the history they are writing, which involves the time when the Arsacids (Khosrov Kotak and after) had usurped the title. Their definitions are therefore those prevailing in the fourth and fifth centuries AD, whereas the Ostan mentioned by Mosēs belongs to the period covered between the sixth century BC to the second century AD.

The misunderstood Tork' Angeł and Sebēos

On page 168, note 109, Toumanoff writes: 'Tork'-Angł represents a syncretistic figure, at one Tarkhu, the Anatolian divinity of fertility and vegetation, and the Hayasa-Armenian god of the netherworld, an equivalent of the Sumero-Akkadian Nergal, the solar deity of war and the dead (in the Armenian Bible, 'Angł').'

What is written here cannot be considered even conjecture. The only part that one may consider valid is the claim in parenthesis that in the

Armenian Bible Nergal appears as Angł (*Studies*, p299) note that it is not Angł, but Angeł. This substitution only happens, as far as I know, in the Zohrapian (1805) and Bałtatlian (1895) editions, which may be a legacy of Bishop Sebēos who in his chapter one had written the nonsensical phrase: 'Because of this he was called Bagarat and Angeł, whom the barbarians of his time called god.' The Armenians never had a god named Angeł. As for Khayasha, we know the names of its gods, which did not include Angeł, but Baltaik, Shillili, Tarumush, Terittitunish, Zakkan, Unagashtash and two more whose names are partially obliterated. Besides, Khayasha of the fourteenth century BC had no connection with the Hays, who entered Urartu only at the start of the sixth century BC. It is remarkable that the nonsense written in the seventh century by Sebēos has become the byword of present-day scholars. The Proto-Armenians in the country of Aram worshipped god Tark (Tork') as the head of their pantheon. He was the god of thunder, but a single rock relief at Irviz presents him holding grapes and corn, which one might interpret as 'harvest'. How is it possible to equate such a god with Nergal, the god of the underworld and death?

As I have stated before, my study of the History of Bishop Sebēos clears up these misunderstandings and corrects many existing theories. At this point I feel obliged to reprise some of the points in support of my assertions, based on what Sebēos actually says and not on invented theories such as the *Primary History*.

Sebēos starts his first chapter with the following words: 'It was not due to the personal desire of a learned researcher [that I heedfully undertook to write this History, but because I was asked to], I shall obediently go back in time and record a few legends in connection with the ancient heroes.' Misunderstanding of this and much more that follows has led various scholars to incorrect explanations which in turn have been used for interpretations that corrupt the text.

The second to fourth paragraphs continue: 'There, I shall look into the scroll of Maraba, the philosopher of Mtsurn, the contents of which were found inscribed on a stele at Mtsbin city, at the palace of King Sanatruk, opposite the gate of the royal court, covered by the ruins of the royal abode. *Paragraph 3*: since the court of the Persian king had requested the pillars of the palace, the ruins were opened, when an inscription was found, incised in <u>Greek letters</u> on stone, with the years and days of the five [this should be old – *hing > hin*] kings of <u>Armenia and Parthia</u>, and which I found [copy of the inscription] with his [Marapa's] disciples in Mesopotamia; this I wanted to relate to you, since it had the following title. *Paragraph 4:* I Agat'angełos the scribe wrote on this stele with my own hand the years of the first <u>Armenian kings</u> taking them from the royal archive at the command of the valiant Trdat.'

On page 307 of his *Studies* Toumanoff comments: 'The Primary History forms the opening part of the History of Heraclius written by Bishop Sebēos in the seventh century. It purports to be the (original) Greek work [*ardzanagir*—this word was composed and first used by Khorenats'i] by Agat'angełos, and to have been found in the Book of one Maraba, the Philosopher of Mtsurn. Pseudo-Mosēs claims that the text of his History corresponds to an extract made by one Mar Abas Katina from Greek translation. The two texts are thus associated.'

The phrase 'Greek work' is misleading. Sebēos has 'stele incised with Greek letters' (underlined above) and explains what was written, which were the names of the Parthian and ancient Armenian Arsacid kings (underlined). As he explains, the ruins of the palace were excavated and only then was the stele discovered, the inscription on the said stele was then copied by Maraba, the Philosopher of Mtsurn. Of this list of names, those of the Parthians and the ancient Armenian Arsacid kings, Sebēos says that he will let us see it a little later at its appropriate place, and at the end of chapter 2 he lists both the Parthian and the Armenian kings.

Sebēos says that the pillars of the palace, for which the ruins were excavated, were requested by the Persian king. I have demonstated in my study of the History of Bishop Sebēos (2007, pp 70-71) that this ruler was Khusru II Parviz, (AD 590-628), and thus the ruins of the palace could not have been excavated prior to his accession. Furthermore, Maraba, who copied the names incised on the stele, belongs to the same time as Khusru. At this period there could not have been a city of Mtsurn, since it was ruined either by an earthquake or by the forces of Shapur II (309-379) before the middle of the fourth century, which means that 250 years after its destruction and abandonment there could not be a philosopher named Maraba of Mtsurn. However, if there is any truth in the matter, there could be one of Mtsbin (Nisibis). It is also notable that the Armenians having had their new script for 250 years earlier than Sebēos, were not short of scribes for the job of copying the inscription and there was no need for a Syriac-speaker.

It is clear that Sebēos is emulating Mosēs in creating a Maraba of his own, besides replicating Mosēs' History in a sub-standard manner. Indeed in the heading of his chapter 3 he admits that he is following Mosēs. Since Mosēs wrote his History in the second half of the fifth century (the date he finished writing is 474) and Sebēos finished his own in the second half of the seventh century (the History finishes in AD 661), it is hard to see where this alleged *Primary History* fits in.

Toumanoff's Orontids

Parts II and III of Toumanoff's study (1963) are devoted to the Orontids, Angeł Tun and the Bagratids. Again, the basis of the argument is undermined by drawing selectively what is termed as Sebēos' *Primary History*. Bagarat P'arazian is mentioned as a 'great feudatory' and a descendant of Aramaneak, but (unknown to Sebēos) the name Aramaneak in fact means the 'circuit of Aram', i.e. a land and not a person. Mosēs was unable to find information as to where the ancient kings ruled and who were responsible for the various Proto-Armenian battles, and so he created the two distinct persons of Aramaneak and Aram. Toumanoff adds that P'arnavaz 'was none other than the eponym of the Iberian royal house of the Pharnabazids (P'arnavaziani)', and repeats the absurd claim by Sebēos that this same P'arnavaz paid homage to Nabuchadnesser. The latter's dates are 605-562 BC, which means that P'arnavaz belongs to a period before the country was called Armenia, unless his obedience falls in the last years of the monarch, i.e. between 588 and 562 BC! It should not also be overlooked that P'arnavaz's son Bagarat pays obedience to Vałarshak of Nisibis in Atropatene of 132 BC (a full 430 years later) according to Sebēos.

Mosēs insists that the Bagratids were of Jewish origin while Toumanoff says that they were Orontids. Although there is no way of verifying either claim, the former is by 1,500 years the older which, to my way of thinking, is more likely to hold truth. Toumanoff also claims that Orontes was 'as Iranian as the dynasty itself', which one cannot dispute since they were originally Iranian satraps. But we part company with Toumanoff when he also claims that the Bagratids and princes of Angeł Tun were Orontids. He quotes Drastamat of P'awstos (5.7) (Drastamat was a Mardian and his title *mardpet* means 'head of the Mardians'), saying that 'Drastamat was governing (*ishkhum ēr*) Angeł district and all the royal castles, including Bnabeł, where the royal cemeteries and treasures were found.' This does not imply that Drastamat was the prince of Angeł Tun nor of the other castles that were under his charge, rather he was a servant of the king and part of his duties was to look after the crown possessions stored in various castles for safekeeping.[38]

---

38. P'awstos Busant, *Armenian History*, University of Yerevan, 1987. The Classical Armenian text is that of K'. Patkanyan and the translation into Modern Armenian that of S. Malkhazyants'; see book V, chapter 7, second paragraph.

Toumanoff also claims that the Gnunis and Artsrunis belonged to a branch of the Orontids, citing Manandyan—that Tigran the Great removed people from the northwest of Armenia and settled them in the south. But there is no proof that these resettled people were the Artsrunis. As much as I can make out, the Artsrunis, Gnunis and Rshtunis were of Urartian origin. This is inferred from the division of the highlands between the Hays and the Urartians at the time the Hays entered Urartu (588 BC), in addition to the fact that these houses first received recognition as dukedoms only during the time of Vałarsh. But according to the history of T'ovma Artsruni (pp 72-73), the Artsrunis were of Assyrian origin.[39] The Hays never impinged on the Urartian lands, which we see even in the case of the last Paeonian arrivals, in the course of the second century BC, of the Agrianes, Mygdonians, Laioi, Doberes, Astibuseans and Bylazoreans, which is four centuries after the Proto-Armenian entry into Urartu. The Agrianes settled to the west of Sebastia, the Mygdonians, Laioi and Doberes settled south of the Urartian lands around Nisibis, the Astibuseans created the name Ashtishat and Tarawn for their settlement places, and the Bylazoreans founded Bayazet to the east of the Urartians.

The commentary of Thomson

Now we must look to the translation and commentary on the History of Moses by R. W. Thomson, published in 1978 by Harvard University Press. Here the translation is a work of different order to that of Toumanoff's 1963 *Studies*. Whereas Toumanoff is more interested in the history of the Armenians and only cites quotations from Moses in support of his opinions or criticism, Thomson in his commentary to his translation devotes some 61 pages examining the written History itself, passing judgement in accordance with his own opinions and asserting that Moses wrote this work after the middle of the eighth century. His criticism is rather severe and, in places, derisory for such a serious academic study. Nevertheless, on reading his commentary one has to agree that Thomson is a clever and erudite sceptic who has mastered the Armenian language well.

However, the commentary and footnotes he places in the study reflect personal opinions that in some cases have not been subjected to serious analysis and are flawed, since he refers to the opinions of previous scholarship on the alleged *Primary History* and on the preconception that

---

39. T'ovma Artsruni, *History of the House of Artsrunis*, University of Yerevan, 1985.

the History was written in the eighth century. Therefore, if one successfully invalidates his six major historical objections, which appear on pages 58-59 of his commentary, and is able to demonstrate that the true period when the History was written was the second half of the fifth century, then his arguments and the commentary as a decisive document become worthless save for the wealth of information contained therein. I must also state that at the time Thomson wrote his commentary, At'anas Tarawnts'i and his manuscript were still undiscovered.

In general, Thomson's case is sometimes exaggerated and on occasion he quotes parts of the sentences in support of his views, at least a couple of times mistranslates the text, which may be due to misunderstanding, and there are quite a few instances in his criticism where he does not understand the text (in this he is not alone), as we shall see below and in Part III in the course of this study.

Thomson: a harsh critic

On page 3 of his commentary, Thomson asserts that 'a historian Mosēs is unknown before the tenth century', and that 'John Catholicos (850-c.931) has only one specific reference to the History of Mosēs'. This claim is not valid, as we shall see in Part II.

The History was not a publication in the modern sense when multiple copies are distributed—Mosēs did not write his history in duplicate or triplicate, rather it was a period when a single text would be handwritten and sent to the patron who had requested such a book. In this case the patron was Sahak Bagratuni, who died in 482, and it is only reasonable to assume that the History was available only to Sahak and would have remained in the house of the Bagratunis for a long while after the death of Mosēs' patron. The implication is that there could not be many who saw the manuscript except for those who were in the service or confidence of Sahak. However, even in such a case it would take another writer who was aware of the History of Mosēs and whose manuscript has survived to our own times to acknowledge the History.

It appears that the few to have seen the manuscript were not writers. Smbat Bagratuni, one of the more famous sons of the Bagratunis, also known as Khosrov Shum of the late sixth to early seventh centuries, knew this History, since he took a literary idiom from it as we shall see in Part II. No one can say with any certainty how long it took for the manuscript to be known more widely or how many copies were made of it, but we do have the first acknowledgement of the History in the person of At'anas Tarawnts'i, who had also made extracts of it. At'anas' *floruit* is accepted as the second half of the sixth century, since in 582-4 he was requested to work, together with some learned clerics, on the Armenian calendar,[40] which may be the reason he made an effort to find the manuscript in the first place. But the evidence for Mosēs and his History does not stop with At'anas, as we shall see in Part II.

The case of the brother of Mosēs, called Mambrē, is not discussed in this study but considering what Thomson (p4) says—'The only reference to Mambrē is in the preface to "Elegy on the Cross", ascribed to David of the seventh century, which makes the evidence useless'—I can confirm that Thomson is partially right since the cited elegy is accepted as belonging to David. And yet, what of the sermons ascribed to Mamprē, such as the 'Sermon on the Resurrection of Lazar' and the 'Sermon on the Advent of Christ to Jerusalem' (Adjaryan)?

Thomson discusses Eusebius of Caesarea and tells us how Mosēs plagiarised his Chronicle and the Church History, 'giving only a passing reference (II.10), and then in an obscure and deliberate false manner'. Here I must insist that Mosēs, being a devout cleric, could not resort to falsities nor intentionally corrupt his quotations. As for the 'passing reference', my answer is twofold. Firstly, there is a lack of desire amongst scholars to reason and understand precisely what it is that Mosēs is saying, creating preconceptions, which reflects badly on their own capabilities as truth-seeking academics—in Part III of this study, in chapters II.10 (page 153) & II.75 (page 160), I explain what Mosēs actually intends and how to reason and understand him. Secondly, Thomson's remarks are questionable considering that he himself writes on page xIvii (section VI, 'Literary Characteristics') of his translation of Sebēos' History: 'Although Armenian historians often mention their predecessors, they rarely name their sources for the specific events described.'[41] However, one concedes that this is also one of the shortcomings apparent in Mosēs' writings; others include his uncertain referrals to sources with such formulas as 'he says', 'he also writes' or just 'he', where one has to work hard in order to identify the person referred to. At other times, Mosēs, after saying that his information derives from, say, Mar Abas Katina, also mentions the name of Mar Abas' source, e.g. Book 1.9 starts with Mar Abas' History—but Mosēs also mentions the names of Berossus and Abydenus who were the true sources of Mar Abas

---

40. A. S. Matevosyan; see Introduction, note 4 above.
41. R. W. Thomson, translation with commentary of *The Armenian History Attributed to Sebēos*, in two volumes, with a historical commentary by James Howard-Johnston. Liverpool University Press, 1999, p xlvii.

Katina. But these are the characteristics of a writer, which are not intended to misguide or deceive or seek praise. I, at least, am one who is grateful for information deemed by sceptics as 'fraudulent, false, imaginary, faked', facts that helped me to untangle the whole pre-history of the Armenians while they were in the Balkans and later inhabited the country of Aram (southeast of Anatolia) for 600 years prior to their move into Urartu. Without Mosēs there is no pre-history of the Armenians since he alone provides us with the key.

The archives of Nineveh and Mar Abas

On page 12 of his commentary Thomson observes that: 'Mosēs makes Nineveh the site of the archives. Nineveh, however, contained not the Parthian but the Assyrian records.' It is unclear why Parthian is mentioned since Mar Abas was sent to Mesopotamia in order to extract information from the archives of Nineveh concerning the Hay people, and the archives contained Assyro-Babylonian records. The Parthians having only just dominated the land could not have had archives of their own. Thomson adds: 'According to Mosēs archives had been translated from Chaldaean (cuneiform) to Greek at the command of Alexander the Great. And these, claims Mosēs, were his source for the legendary history of Armenia.' Thomson possibly does not appreciates the veracity of the 'claim' since everything Mosēs writes about the ancient (and not legendary) Hay kings is correct (see *Pre-History Volume I*). And, on page 14, writing on the same subject, Thomson adds: 'Mosēs claims that the Chaldaean books used by Mar Abas Katina are more reliable. These books were kept in the archives at Nineveh, and from them Alexander the Great had a Greek translation made. Making extracts from this Greek text, Mar Abas Katina brought them, with a Syriac translation to Nisibis.' For a further explanation of this matter of archives, see chapter 11.10 in Part 111.

There are a few points that require elucidation here. To start with, when Mosēs writes Nineveh or Babylon, these must be understood as Assyro-Babylonia or Mesopotamia and not necessarily the city of Nineveh or Babylon, because the Greek translation of the records referred to by Mosēs contained both Assyrian and Babylonian histories (chapters 1.3 & 9), as we see in the names he has set down for posterity in Book 1, chapters 12, 19 & 22.

When one carefully studies what Mosēs is saying in Chapter 1.9 concerning these Greek translations one realises that the information derives from Mar Abas' book (they were also, four hundred years later, a source for Eusebius), and were not the inventions of Mosēs, even though he uses the same theme of 'historical records' to reproach his ancestors in chapter 1.3. It is true that the Assyro-Babylonian archives contained the records of their own two nations, but it is also true that the Hay (Proto-Armenian) kingdoms of Aram were irretrievably intertwined in their history starting with the tenth century BC, for which Mosēs gives his explanation in 1.21: 'Our ancestors were their satraps, vassals and prefects.' Mosēs is correct on all counts.

In Part II of *Pre-History Volume I*, I set out all the branches of the Hay (Proto-Armenian) city kingdoms of Aram, starting with the tenth century BC. The names, recomposed in Classical Armenian, of the dynasties and individual kings are given with explanations. Also included are the names of the kings recorded by Mosēs, except for two important names and a few minor ones that he omits; there is also a single name, Zrvan, in Mosēs' list that I have not managed to locate. While there is no need to mention all the names here I shall demonstrate why they derive from Mar Abas Katina's book, the first history written about the Hay people (Proto-Armenians). I shall also prove that these names could only derive from the Assyro-Babylonian records and never from the memory of the people themselves.

Mosēs himself did not know even a single example of the Proto-Armenian names of these ancient kings of Aram; in fact, in his confusion, he makes them all kings of Armenia. What he records are the translations and recompositions of the names in Classical Armenian belonging to the end of the second century AD. We know no other person than Mar Abas Katina, who was sent to Mesopotamia to extract these names from the records, therefore, one has to accept that all the names derive from his book, but the (recompositions of the) same names in Classical Armenian are the work of an editor. Some scholars, such as Carrière and Khalat'yants', have expressed doubt as to the existence of Mar Abas Katina, and have claimed that Mosēs and Mar Abas are the same person, and have ascribed the ancient names of Chapters 1.12, 19 & 22 to the imagination of Mosēs. Thomson on pages 54-55 of his Commentary expounds on the subject of Mar Abas and related various aspects of it, which I find extemely interesting, at the very least for the clear logic of what he writes. But when such a well reasoned exposition is based on false premises to what benefit does it serve except try to degrade the standing of Mosēs and his History? The other point related to the subject discussed is when in this section Thomson expresses the opinion that Mosēs is establishing a 'historical tradition' for the Armenians. The natural question that comes to mind in this connection is why should such a writer, i.e. Mosēs, credit a non-Armenian, a Syriac, with so great a discovery unless it was true?

The names listed by Mosēs as mentioned above cannot be challenged, but the name of Mar Abas Katina lacks solid proof: what Sebēos writes in the first chapter of his history is worthless, since we know that Mtsurn or Mtsurk as a city ceased to exist in the course of the fourth century AD (see P'awstos, Book iv.14), therefore it could not have a Mar Abas of the city of Mtsurn at the end of the sixth century, which implies that Sebēos is replicating Mosēs and there is no such a work as the Primary History. Thomson advances the opposite opinion, which creates yet another false premise as basis for his arguments. Once more scholarship in general has failed to consider the most basic details, just as they have failed to understand the meaning of each name (ancient or recomposed) in the Assyrian inscriptions or Mosēs' lists in the light of the fact that it is now more than a hundred years since the Assyrian texts were translated and more than 1,500 years since the completion of Mosēs' History.

In the Assyro-Babylonian inscriptions we find a few of the names not spelled or pronounced identical to those inscribed in the Proto-Armenian hieroglyphic inscriptions of Aram, since the Assyrians record only the demotic names of their vassal kings, e.g. Larazamasa in the Assyrian inscriptions is Palalam (P'arokh), Wasusaramimasa as Uassurme (Harma), Warpalawa as Urballa (Arbak). Also there are a number of names which Mar Abas has not understood and has shortened as a result. For example, the name of the Proto-Armenian king of Tuwana (Tyana in Roman times) was Warpalawa (meaning 'One Who Conducts Good Conversation'), which may be seen on his stele, the inscription from Bor. Warpalawa was a vassal of the great king Wasusaramimasa of Tabal. The Assyrians called the former Urballa and the latter Uassurme, which means Mar Abas Katina could not have known the ancient Proto-Armenian names of these two kings, and had only the Assyrian versions through the works of Abydenus, the Babylonian scholar and priest who translated the archives into Greek. Mar Abas therefore can only translate the names as he has found them (here in Part iv under 'The Enigma of Mar Abas Katina' we shall see that the translations of the names belong to Mar Abas' editor), such as Urballa as Arbak, where both *urb* and *arb* have the meaning of 'satellite', 'orphan' or 'vassal'—the *al* means salt, the ancient diminutive suffix equivalent of the present-day Armenian *-ak*. The final form has no relationship with the Iranian name and the resemblance is incidental. I suspect that Mar Abas does not understand the complete name of Uassurme, except for the *surma* part which he translates as *harma* (both Surma and Harma [*s* → *h*] are names of the god Saruma, whom the Proto-Armenians worshipped in Tabal). We can only wonder what would have been Mar Abas's understanding if he had been given the full Proto-Armenian name of this king, Wasusaramimasa, which means 'Kingdom (*wasu*) of the God (*masa*) Sarami' (for further details see *Pre-History Volume 1*).

Here I must also explain the name of Hrant (a word that cannot be explained in the Armenian language), who was a king of Gurgum (Marash, where there were three kings with this name) although Toumanoff has made him an Orontid in his *Studies*. The ruler's Proto-Armenian name was Khalparutiya, and Mar Abas has used the same method as in the case of Wasusaramimasa in renaming this king Hrant, which represents only the *rutiya* part of the old name—Rutiya was the Anatolian god Runzas, worshipped by the Proto-Armenians of Tabal and Cilicia. Since in the Armenian language there are no indigenous words that start with an initial *r*, Mar Abas has armenicised the name by adding initial *h*, which is a normal procedure (cf. Rufus → Hṛup'os, Ruth → Hṛut').

Shirakats'i and Olympiodorus

We learn from Thomson that 'Mosēs used other texts to give the impression that he had received a good classical education' (page 21)— but it is unclear what is meant by 'other texts'. The following page contains the confident assertion that 'none of Mosēs' references to Classical authors is based on a personal reading of the original texts. His reference to Ptolemy and the geographers (1.30) is based on the first section of the *Ashkharhats'oyts'*.

The *Ashkharhats'oyts'* or *Geography* is one of the works of Anania Shirakats'i of the seventh century that has reached us. In this work Anania tells us (p260) that he is following Pappus the Alexandrian (third century AD), who in his turn had benefitted from the works of Ptolemy (Claudius Ptolemaeus, AD 90-168). Anania has also compiled a chronology known as the Anonymous Chronology of the seventh century. The work does not carry his name as author but, according to Ashot Abrahamyan (1940) who has analysed it in minute detail, there is no doubt that the chronology was compiled by Anania. Remarkably, the same claim was made some 36 years earlier by Fr B. Sarkissian of the Mkhit'arian Congregation of Venice. The chronology comprises, in the main, of four lengthy extracts from Mosēs Khorenats'i, Andreas,

Eusebius and Epiphanius, of which the extract from Mosēs occupies the first three pages and are from his first book of the History, chapter 4 (third paragraph to the end). In addition to the *Ashkharhats'oyts'* another study from Anania that has reached us called *Zinch' ē Amisn* ('What is a Month', so far unpublished), wherein there is an extract from Mosēs relating to Patriarch Hayk.[42] One may challenge the authorship of both of these works, since the manuscripts do not bear the name of Anania, but the fact that these manuscripts belong to the second half of the seventh century is beyond any doubt, and the extract relevant here of the Chronology is entitled 'From Mosēs Khorenatsi', bearing as with the other three the name of the original writer. Therefore, Thomson's claim that Mosēs' reference to Ptolemy in actual fact is based on the *Ashkharhats'oyts'* is baseless. Thomson says, on page 40: 'It is clear that Mosēs was a writer of considerable erudition. Although, most of his demonstrable sources were available in Armenia, he had read widely in history, theology, rhetoric and philosophy.' What of Mosēs' own translations which Łazar confirms?[43] The way Thomson presents Mosēs as erudite, widely read etc. etc. sounds rather derisory, since this learned cleric, according to Thomson's commentary and his translation of the History, had no higher education, was not well versed in the Greek language and produced nothing except a load of fiction and fraudulently pretended to be a personality of the fifth century.

Another of Thomson's statements, which I can only describe as academic nitpicking with the aim of degrading both Mosēs and his History, appears on page 14 of his Commentary: 'Mosēs gives a long account of the origin of certain Armenian place names, which he ascribes to a Greek, Olympiodorus [the name is mentioned in 1.6 & 11.74]. There were various Greek writers of that name but none is likely to have had that interest in implausible etymologies for Armenian names that was so dear to Mosēs, and Thomson places in parenthesis chapters 1.6 & 12 and 11.7 & 8 to support his claim. How does Thomson know of other people's interest and what purpose does this statement serve? How does it help us to understand the history or the person of Mosēs? Surely judging a document of over 1,500 years old at the end of the twentieth century and, at that, presenting it in a misleading fashion appears to have been designed to support his arguments. I use the word misleading for the simple reason that the etymologies of only four place names appear

42. H. Adjaryan, *Dictionary of Armenian Personal Names*, Sevan, Beirut, 1972.
43. Łazar P'arpets'i, *History of the Armenians and Letter to Vahan Mamikonean*, translated into Modern Armenian by B. Ulubabyan, University of Yerevan, 1982, pp 483-85.

in chapter 1.6, which are ascribed to Olympiodorus. The other chapter numbers, 1.12, 11.7 & 8, have nothing to do with this Greek writer; their presence in the same parenthesis is at the very least an unfair manner of presentation. Because, Thomson says, 'in the same chapter he gives a long account of the origin of certain Armenian place names, which he ascribes to a Greek Olympiodorus'. Therefore, chapters 1.12, 11.7 & 8, as mentioned above, have no place in the same parenthesis.

We do not know exactly who this Olympiodorus was. Malkhazyants' thinks on chronological grounds that it is the fifth-century writer from Thebes, Egypt. Moses' writing gives the impression that it was the one from Athens the teacher of David,[44] his nephew, since he quotes the name of David as the storyteller. For me the name of Olympiodorus after fifteen hundred-odd years is not important, particularly when Moses has not given a concrete reference. What is important is the story that Moses has heard and he is repeating it for us with a proviso at the end of the chapter: 'whether these stories are true or not is not important for us, I am mentioning them so that you are informed.'

All the same, of the four etymologies contained in chapter 1.6 and ascribed to Olympiodorus only three are in Armenia; the fourth one refers to Bactra (see Part III, chapter 6), which is not found in Thomson. The discussion attributed to Olympiodorus is not about Armenian place names, but about Xisitra (Biblical Noah) sailing to Armenia. The three place names are the mountains Sim, the districts of Tarawn and Ts'rawnk'. Of these names Sim and Tarawn were already known and recorded by Strabo. So, why should the Greeks not be interested in creating their own entertaining stories and speculate on various aspects of divine and human origins? If one carefully reads what is written in the History, one will realize that the whole thing is the idle talk or pastime of a few learned individuals while they were together. Olympiodorus and his company know that Xisitra landed in Armenia. They are also Christians and know Noah and his three sons and the rest of the tale from the Bible. And exceptionally, Olympiodorus also knows that Bactra and its districts were also known as Zariaspa, which translates into Armenian as Zaruand (Thomson identifies Zaruand with the district of similar name in the south of Armenia!). While old men are having fun and discussions, why should Olympiodorus, too, not take part in it? Moses does not say that such a story was written by him. And, in 11.74 Moses refers to him in a

44. Davit' Anhalt', *Collection*, Armenian Academy, Yerevan, 1983; see Thomson's article 'Notes on the Armenian Version of Davit' the Invincible's Definitions of Philosophy', pp 390-401, & note 2 on p397.

manner to confirm that such stories were told from father to son and onwards 'like those of Olympiodorus about Tarawn'.

Subject not understood, yet criticism continues

In view of the fact that Thomson placed chapters 1.12, 11.7 & 8 in the same parenthesis as 1.6, I feel obliged to explain what these additional chapters are all about, particularly 1.12, which is the masterpiece of Book One.

Chapter 1.12 is all about the generations that sprang from Hayk down to Aram (see Hayk's Family Tree, page 255), while 1.15 starts with 'Ara, a few years before the death of Ninos, acquired the government of his ancestral lands... like his father Aram', which makes it clear that Ara was the son of Aram. In chapter 1.19 the list of the Proto-Armenian kings (29 names) starts with Ara, the son of Ara, and continues down to Skayordi. Therefore, Aram being of the generation of Hayk, his son Ara and grandson Ara and all the other remaining 29 names are all from the same line, i.e. all the names found in chapters 1.12 & 19 represent the generation of Hayk, or Hayk's descendants. So why is it that this long line of Hayk's descendants has been divided into two groups (chapters 12 & 19)? Do we see Thomson, Mahé and the other sceptics ask themselves such a question? Mosēs has no hand in these lists, indeed, like all scholars for the next 1,500 years, he does not even understand the reason for this division. It is remarkable that no one has questioned this arbitrary looking division of names, and none has expressed a meaningful view except to ascribe the names to the imagination of Mosēs and consider them fictitious.

Whenever I think of these names and the division of them into two groups, I cannot but admire the man Mar Abas Katina, or the Editor of his work, and his intellect for devising such a simple but effective scheme in order to allow future generations to know their pre-history. The names in the first group of chapter 12, are all remembered in later Armenia either as a place name or as 'patriarchal houses' (later dukedoms). None of the names in the second group of chapter 1.19 are to be found, in any capacity, in later Armenia. The exception is the name Anushavan, in chapter 20, which in my opinion is due to interpolation—the sentence says: 'he had been dedicated to the cult at the plane trees of Aramaneak in Armavir' (1.19). The final phrase 'in Armavir' has been added by someone who had not understood what is being said, since the real meaning of the sentence is: 'he had been dedicated to the cult at the plane trees of "the circuit of Aram".' In other words Aramaneak means 'circuit of Aram' (*Aram + maneak*), which cannot be transported to Armavir; this fact makes it clear that he is not remembered in later Armenia and that Armavir is an interpolation.

So, if we sort the names of the patriarchal houses from those of place names in the first list (Hayk's progeny, chapter 12), we end up with the following: Khor (Khorkhorunik'), Manawaz (Manawazeans), Baz (Bznunik'), Kadmos (Kadmeans), Shara (Shahunis), Gełam (Gełark'unik'), Sisak (Sisakeans) and Tork' Angeł (Angełats' Tun). Looking at an ancient map of Armenia we notice that these are the names of the houses that have encircled the Highlands, save for the Manawazeans, Khorkhorunis and Bznunik', who have settled centrally north of Lake Van and who border each other. Of these latter three, the Manawazeans come from Marash and it was their land in Armenia that was named Hark'. This is the picture of the Ostan organization, meaning the 'Branches', i.e. branches of the Proto-Armenian ex-royal houses of Aram entering and settling in the lands of Urartu. In other words, the various kingdoms that were established in the country of Aram, in unity entered Urartu and by previous agreement took up their settlement areas in the periphery of the Highlands (the full explanation of these settlement places may be seen in 'The Enigma of Mar Abas Katina' in Part iv). And is it not remarkable that the Armenian capital cities have always been on the periphery, to the northeast—except for Tigranakert, which was designed to administer to an empire?

Since Moses does not understand any of these, even though he says that the Armenians take their name from Aram, and due to his inability to penetrate Mar Abas' divided name list, he makes Aram a person instead of the country. And yet he knows that everything is not as it should be, since Aram as a person is not named in the records of the Assyro-Babylonians, a fact that he admits in chapter 1.14 with the words: 'these things were not recorded in the books of kings nor in temple histories.' Can a person be more truthful?

The case of chapters ii.7 & 8 is different. This applies to the period of the middle second century AD (Moses telescopes these and presents them as in the time of the Nisibis kingdom of Vałarshak of the second century BC), when a feudalistic type of rule was being established. Again Moses has no hand in the etymologies of any of the new dukedoms nor the explanations of their names. Like a good reporter he is simply writing down whatever he has managed to glean from a variety of sources. This is obvious, since in the case of the Artsrunis, Gnunis and

Dziwnakans he expresses his disapproval and tells us that in his opinion it is more likely that the explanation should be such and such.

The misunderstood ambiguous chapter II.75

Chapter 11.75 is ambiguous due to its compact style and doubtless it could have been better written. The translations and the opinions of scholars, however, are completely off the mark, including even the great Malkhazyants'. For his part, Thomson expresses the opinion that Moses' 'historical work is a complete fake, replete with extraordinary anachronism' while Mahé (p.45) discovers that: 'Nous savons par example que Firmilien de Césarée mourut peu après 268. Il semble donc impossible que, dans l'Histoire des persecutions qui lui est attribuée (11.75), il ait mentionné le martyre de Pierre d'Alexandrie, qui eut lieu en 311.' I feel dispirited when I read such accounts about a subject that could have been thoroughly understood if only these scholars had had the will to approach it without preconceptions and devote a little of their time to research, analysis and reasoning instead of following each other like lambs. Please see Part III, chapter 75 of this volume for the correct explanation.

On page 16 of his Commentary, Thomson writes: 'He (Moses) claims to be basing chapters 22-65 of his second book on the temple history of Olympius, priest of Ani Kamakh. But in fact it is primarily to Josephus, Eusebius, Labubna and Agat'angełos that Moses is indebted here.' Unfortunately, anyone reading this who knows little about Moses or his Armenian history will not be in a position to question such a statement. The name of Olympius is supposed to be the transcription of the name Ułiwp in the History; this is how my copy records it, which Malkhazyants' in his translation into Modern Armenian writes as Ułyump. This priest of the temple of Ani Kamakh is mentioned only once in the entire History of Moses, in chapter 11.48 (as mentioned before, throughout this study I quote the English translations of Thomson):

This is accurately told us by Olympius, priest of Ani and composer of temple histories, as are also many other deeds that we have to relate and to which the books of the Persians and the epic songs of the Armenians bear witness.

The quotation, the only one in the entire History concerning Olympius the priest, is indeterminate and there is no additional information to make one think that chapters 11.22-65 derive from this Olympius the priest of the Temple of Ani. From the translation of Thomson it can be seen that the statement 'this is accurately told' refers only to the previous sentence, that 'Artashēs satisfied them [the Romans] with supplications and by paying double tribute'.[45] The second part of Thomson's translation of the sentence says: 'as are also many other deeds that we have to relate...', which implies that after the present chapter 11.48 there may be some subjects derived from the Olympius the priest's Temple Histories. It is impossible to pinpoint any event that occurs in the History after chapter 11.48 that one can with certainty ascribe to Olympius the priest as a source. But reading chapters 11.49, 50 & 61 of the History one notes that these chapters are the allegorical stories of the minstrels, which Mosēs, as he confirms in these chapters, tries to interpret and elucidate their concealed messages. As for those previous chapters 11.22 up to the present 48, where does Mosēs imply that the source is Olympius? After writing 26 chapters (11.22 to 48) has he suddenly realized that he is using the Temple Stories of the priest? Or, is it not Thomson who, rather than adhere to what is written, conjectures instead a line of discussion conducive to degrading the History and Mosēs by adding 'but these facts derive from Josephus, Eusebius, Labubna and Agat'angełos'?

The Edessa archives and the Sibylline Oracle

Khorenats'i's History in 111.68 says (again, Thomson's translation): 'who will express the delight of a father in part exceeded by his son?' But in his commentary (page 2) Thomson writes: 'The claim to possess erudition and rhetorical aptitude far superior to those of his teachers.' I am unable to make out Thomson's motive for this exaggeration.

In the case of the archives at Edessa, Mosēs in 11.10 claims that Eusebius in his Church History bears witness to it. Mosēs correctly quotes the book and chapter number. Apparently Thomson does not agree with what Mosēs says, and expresses the view that 'Mosēs' patently false claim in 11.10 that Eusebius in his Church History (1.13) bears witness to the existence in Edessa of Archives dealing with Armenia'. Since Thomson's assertion highlights only part of what is written, I

45. Note that Thomson's translation of 'double tribute' is misleading, since it may give the idea that the Romans were paid double the usual tribute. The translation should have said 'for the second time', since the first amount of tribute was sent to Persia, ignoring the Romans. But when the Roman army arrived, Artashēs had no alternative but pay them the usual tribute.

quote what Mosēs writes (11.10): 'Africanus ... transcribed everything from the ... archives of Edessa ... which concerned the history of our kings. These books had been transported there from Nisibis and from the temple histories of Sinope in Pontus. Let no one doubt this, for we have seen that archive with our own eyes. And as a closer witness the Ecclesiatical History of the translation of Eusebius of Caesarea is a guarantee...'

The Loeb edition (volume 1, section 1.13, p87) of Eusebius' Ecclesiastical History says: 'There is also documentary evidence of these things from the archives of Edessa, which was at that time a capital city. At least, in the public documents there, which contain the things done in antiquity and at the time of Abgar...' There is a pertinent remark on page xxxix of the translator's introduction, that 'these appear to have consisted of two divisions. There was an ancient royal archive and a later ecclesiastical one which was probably not instituted until the beginning of the fourth century. ... It is not certain whether Eusebius had himself seen these archives or made use of it only at second-hand through the writings of Africanus.' Mahé too refers to Mosēs' claim (p35 and note 12 of 11.10) that the Edessan archives contained the acts of ancient Armenian kings. He says: 'The reference to Eusebius' Church History is correct but the citation is inexact, since these archives contained all the acts of the ancestors up to Abgar (tous les actes accomplis depuis des ancêtres jusqu'à Abgar).'

Mahé and Thomson both fail to mention that Mosēs considers King Abgar and his father Arsham (this is how he understands the names) to be Armenian (11.26), therefore the acts of the ancients recorded in the archives must also be those of our kings (albeit not necessarily of Armenia). To this explanation one may also add that Edessa up to the middle of the second century AD was an Armenian city, and so my quotations from Thomson and Mahé in respect of Edessa and its archive may be of interest to the reader to compare how these two recent scholars approach the matter.

Mosēs in 1.6 writes 'i Biwroseann Sibylleay', which means 'Sibylla by Berossus'. Malkhazyants' translates it as 'Berosyan Sibylla', and in his note 21 relates that 'the Sibylla mentioned by Mosēs was a Babylonian Sibyl with a name of Sabbe or Sambeta, the daughter of Berossus'. As Pausanias in his 'Description of Greece' in Book x.xii.8 (Loeb edition, vol. 4, p437) relates: 'There grew up among the Hebrews above Palestine a woman who gave oracles and was named Sabbe. They say that the father of Sabbe was Berossus, and her mother Erymanthe. But some call her a Babylonian Sibyl, others an Egyptian.' Mahé translates this correctly as *'la Sibylle, fille de Berose'*, and in his note 2 mentions 'Sambéthé, la Sibylle babylonienne' and cites Nikiprowetzky, 1970, page 15.

Thomson's version is *'Sibyl, Berossus'*, and in his footnote 4 (p78) he observes that 'the passage attributed to Berossus is based on the Sibylline oracles', while in his commentary, page 14, he adds that 'in 1.6 Mosēs ascribes a quotation from "Oracula Sibyllina" to Berossus'. I am unable to understand the reasoning behind Thomson's mistranslation since he clearly knows the exact meaning of *i Biwroseann*. In his translation of Sebēos' History, Book 1, chapter 44 (page 104), he renders the Armenian phrase *'i Mavrinea'* correctly as the '(Son of Heraclius) by Martinē',[46] and the beginning of the heading of chapter 21 of Book 1 (page 108) of Mosēs, where it is said *'i Skayordvoyn Baroyr'* he has the correct 'Paroyr, son of Skayordi'.

In the History of Mosēs the large district named Atērpatakan (southeast of Armenia) occurs eight times. Atērpatakan is the same as the Greek Atropatene and one expects that that is how it should be translated. Not with Thomson. He translates all the Atērpatakans as 'Azerbaijan', a country that did not exist for many centuries after the History was written.

Thomson and Mahé claim that Mosēs has made use of the *Bible*, *Book of Maccabees*, *Josephus*, *Book of Pidoyits* (both mention this book as *Book of Chries*), Agat'angełos, Theon's *Progymnasmata*, Nonnus' *Scholia*, Julius Africanus, Eusebius' *Church History* and *Chronicle*, Pseudo-Callisthenes' *Alexander Romance*, Gregory Nazianzenus, Labubna, Philo and Socrates. This is an involved subject and cannot be discussed in this study. Suffice to say that, any work by the authors mentioned available in Armenia later than AD 474 could not have been used by Mosēs, who finished his History in that year.

The commentary of Mahé

Mosēs in 1.30 quotes the three lines of an ancient poem that has reached us: *'Tench'ay Sat'enik tikin tench'ans zartakhur khawart ew ztits' khawartsi i bardzits'n Argawanay'*, which Thomson translates as 'Queen Sat'enik had great desire for the vegetable *artakhur* and the shoot *tits'* from the table of Argavan'. Mahé makes no such attempt, quoting instead a translation by Dowsett which he finds agreeable: 'La reine Sat'enik

---

46. Thomson, see note 41 above.

convoite avec ardeur la tiare de verdure et le bandeau de fleurs du cousin brodé d'Argavan.' Both of these translations are nonsensical. If all Queen Sat'enik wanted was 'vegetable *artakhur*' and the 'shoot *tits*' ' or green bands and embroidered cushions, she could have had the choicest in the palace of Artashēs, the king and her husband. Neither Malkhazyants' nor Adjaryan have attempted to translate these three lines, furthermore no one so far has solved their meaning except to say that it has erotic undertones (see explanation in Part III, pages 146-150).

Now let us look to the French translation and commentary by Annie and Jean-Pierre Mahé. After providing biographical details and mentioning a few of the works ascribed to Mosēs, Mahé comments that these are all later attributions and therefore suspect. He then mentions what Łazar had written in his Letter to Vahan Mamikonean, which I discuss in Part II, and makes up his mind that it is not evident from what Łazar writes that Mosēs and Mosēs the philosopher he mentions were one and the same person. I repeat here the important parts of what Łazar writes: 'The blessed philosopher Mosēs and his enlightening and ignorance dispelling books' and at the beginning of the *letter* he says: 'I stayed in the winters in a cave with the most famous of all the clerics named Mosēs.' Please see Part II in connection with this subject.

I agree with Mahé that the 'dogmatic paper' in the *Book of Letters* (pages 163-71, Jerusalem, 1994) attributed to Mosēs is not of much help, being devoid of evidence in support of Mosēs' History. But the case of At'anas Tarawnts'i is different. At'anas is a chronicler of the sixth century and, besides mentioning Mosēs, he benefits from the History, against which he places the date 474. Mahé is certain that this date, too, is of no value, which is not good enough since he is unable or does not wish to explain what the date 474 represents. Anyone so certain of the veracity of their statement should then tell us why the year 474 is to be ignored, since any ancient document that bears a name and a date is bound to have historical value, otherwise why should a writer bother to place such a date for an author. Furthermore, this date tallies with that used by T'ovma Artsruni about Mosēs, i.e. 'he wrote our history starting with Adam up to the Emperor Zenon' (Zenon succeeded to the Byzantine throne in AD 474), it also agrees with Stephen Asołik of Taron's statement (p123) that the 'Philosopher Mosēs lived in the days of Giwt Kat'ołikos' (died AD 478).[47]

---

47. T'ovma Artsruni, *The History of the House of Artsrunis*, Classical Armenian edition with a translation into Modern Armenian by V. M. Vardanyan, University of Yerevan, 1978; see chapter 1.11 (pp 122-23).

Mat'evossyan, the writer of the 1989 article, explains many passages of chronological value, which At'anas has taken from Mosēs. Mahé does not mention these excerpts in the case of the date 474, and in denying the importance of this date he overlooks the decisive fact that simply mentioning the name of Mosēs as Mosēs Khorenats'i and adding to it *philisopa matenagir* (philosopher and writer) in addition to calling Mashtots' the same as Mosēs, Mesrop, in the second half of the sixth century, is more than sufficient evidence, which should have led Mahé to re-examine the various anomalies he thinks he has found and revalue the works of Carrière we have seen above, in which he has such an uncritical faith.

Mahé in his Commentary says that the only explicit references to Mosēs and his History are rather late, the earliest being that of T'ovma Artsruni of 905 (what T'ovma says about Mosēs of the time of Zenon Mahé ignores). He is wrong again since we have references to Mosēs in the Histories of Sebēos and Kałankatuats'i, both from the second half of the seventh century, as well as At'anas Tarawnts'i mentioned above and a host of literary evidence which we shall see in Part II. Most of the evidence for an earlier date for Mosēs we do not see in the commentaries of both Thomson and Mahé. However, Mahé's most remarkable statement is his claim that 'the Book I of Mosēs is modelled on the *Primary History* of the fifth century attributed to Sebēos of the seventh century' (yet, it is Sebēos who acknowledges Mosēs as his source!). I have mentioned that there is no such a document or oral tradition known as the *Primary History*, since it is wholly a scholarly invention which has also been used as the basis of further inferences; but there are the first two chapters of Sebēos' *History* replicating the pre-history of Mosēs which, unfortunately, remains unresolved by Mahé, Thomson and many others—see my study of the History of Bishop Sebēos (2007).

In his introduction, page 28 ('Décor et mise en scène'), Mahé refers to Mosēs' claim of 'occupying himself, night and day, with translations' (is this not what Łazar also said?) and asks whether Mosēs actually knew the Greek language, considering that he quotes Berossus, Polyhistor and Abydenus, names that would have been available to him after the translation of the Chronicle of Eusebius into Armenian. He adds that modern philologists, following A. Carrière, claim that Mosēs does not know any of these authors as his quotations are all second-hand. Mahé, repeating Carrière, should therefore tell us what were those books referred to by Łazar that Mosēs was busy translating (Armenian?)? He needs also to tell us how many authors of the sixth century he knows whose works have survived to our own time, besides the early sixth century Łazar, which I shall discuss in Part II, and At'anas from the end of the same century, since it is only such authors that could have confirmed Moses as the author of the History?

In Part II I shall discuss what Łazar writes about Moses. Scholars date Łazar's history to around 500 AD. I repeat here a few words written by Łazar about Moses: 'The blessed philosopher Moses ... His enlightening and ignorance dispelling books ... he devoted his life to such troublesome studies, day and night labouring for the enlightenment of the world of Armenians.' Is Łazar not confirming what Moses had written about himself?

In the introduction section above I outlined the difference between modern publication of a work and what the conditions must have been in the late fifth century. It was highly unlikely that another person would have known Moses' History until much later, say the seventh century, because the document was in the possession of Sahak Bagratuni, who died in AD 482, and most likely the History was not discovered for a considerable time (Moses, unfortunately, had not written his History in duplicate or triplicate!). At'anas is the first to confirm the existence of such a text in the second half of the sixth century. Sebeos and Kałankatuats'i followed during the second half of the seventh century— Sebeos being the bishop of the Bagratunis would have had personal access to the manuscripts owned by this house. Łazar's case was different: he does not know of a history, since these were being sent to Sahak Bagratuni chapter by chapter when ready, but, cohabiting with Moses, he would have known of the chapters and he would also have known of the translations that were being made during his stay of two years.

Mar Abas: a fictional character for Mahé

Mahé, on pages 38-39, remarks on the name of Mar Abas Katina, Moses' source for the many names of the Proto-Armenian kings. The claim is that this source 'belongs to the class of romantic fiction, similar to some Egyptian and Greek narratives', and his footnote 1 cites A. J. Festugière (*La révélation d'Hermès Trismégiste, I: L'astrologie et les sciences occultes*, Paris, 1950, pp 319-24), who claims that Moses had taken the fragments of his narrative and the names of his sources from Eusebius. Furthermore, on page 41 Mahé cites Carrière, who had said, like Khalat'yants', that Mar Abas is none other than Moses himself and that he is a fictional character. I have dealt with this subject above (pages 46-48) while discussing Thomson's stand. The remarkable part of such a claim by three erudite scholars is that Eusebius does not know and therefore does not record the names of the most ancient kings and the three exploits of Aram recorded by Mosēs, who explicitly tells us that this information comes from the book of Mar Abas Katina.

Mahé, on page 40, mentions Mosēs and his patron Sahak Bagratuni and remarks that these two are reputed to be real individuals, but 'such beliefs suffer from verisimilitude and according to Carrière suffer from a total untruth', since he places the History in the eighth century and claims it to have been written by a pretender who is addressing a distant descendant of Sahak Bagratuni. Of course, we are not given the name or any other details concerning this distant descendant of Sahak Bagratuni. However, as Mahé continues, 'on a less radical basis one notices that the identity of Sahak poses in all of its facets some problems, since it is known that the chronicler (Mosēs) had utilized the History of Łazar written circa AD 500.' The case of Łazar is discussed in Part II, and therefore we may ignore this remark which is an argument that has not been subjected to analysis, and thus, is not well reasoned as far as Łazar is concerned, for which I do not blame him, since none has given deep thought to the matter. I reiterate that it is Łazar that has benefited from Mosēs, as we shall see. We may also ignore Carrière and co., since readers are now able to study my works, *The Pre-History of the Armenians* (three volumes) and my commentary on the History of Bishop Sebēos.

Returning to the story of Mar Abas, on page 41, Mahé has further remarks concerning its veracity. He says that since Medes and the Babylonians in 612 BC had destroyed Nineveh and its archives, how could Mar Abas have benefited from these nearly 500 years later at the time of Arshak the Great of the second century BC. He does agree that the Babylonian archives in cuneiform were active during the time of the Parthians, considering that the great temple of Marduk existed and Berossus was its priest. But it appears there is a misunderstanding here since Mosēs does not say that Mar Abas consulted the cuneiform inscriptions of Nineveh but the Greek translations. Also, in this particular case I will give three examples and let the reader decide the truth of the claim concerning Nineveh which, incidentally, was ruined with its environs by Tigran the Great for the second time in the first century BC:[48]

---

48. Strabo, *Geography*, Loeb Classical Library, Cambridge, Mass. For Tigran's attack and destruction of Nineveh and Arbela districts, see vol. 5, p339, or Book XI.14.15. One will also find the reference in Manandyan (note 30 above), p149 (vol. I.II).

a) Troy was destroyed soon after 1200 BC and yet Alexander the Great visited it nearly 900 years later.

b) Mtsurn, city of Sanadruk in central Armenia, was destroyed before the middle of the fourth century (P'awstos in IV.14 confirms that at the time of Hayr Mardpet the place Mtsurk' was ruined and abandoned for a long time), and yet Mahé accepts that it had a philosopher named Mar Abas in the second half of the fifth century. However, the date of second half of the fifth century is wrong, since Sebēos' Mar Abas is a figure belonging to the end of the sixth century AD.

c) And finally, the Proto-Armenians after moving into Urartu used the city of Armavir (Argishtikhinili) for the next 400 years as their capital city. The excavations of last century showed a layer of destruction by fire,[49] which is also confirmed by the new name the Proto-Armenians gave to the city of Armavir, meaning 'the end ruined' (*arm* = 'end, edge, tip, point, extremity' + *avir* = 'ruined, destroyed').

On pages 41-2 Mahé tells us: 'Carrière had conclusively proven that Mosēs was an inventor and adds that Mar Abas was the source of Pseudo-Agat'angełos or pseudo-Sebēos.' Carrière never managed to conclusively prove his findings, unless one is more inclined to accept the word of one party and ignore all the other evidence available. Mahé does himself an injustice when he claims half-baked reasons as proof, particularly when he diminishes the potency of existing evidence to the contrary. Did Mahé or scholars sharing his opinion stop to think over the most practical reasons, the odds of Mosēs borrowing from the 'Life of Silvester', and so on, parts that did not exist in the Latin or the Greek versions of the works (apparently Mosēs does not even know that Latin and Greek versions existed)? Or did Carrière, as the other scholars of his opinion, know that the names of the ancient kings Mosēs had recorded were all real Hay kings, who had also claimed in their inscriptions to be Hays, in the countries of Aram, Tabal and Cilicia? I had shown above the contradictions prevalent in the works of Khalat'yants', Marquard, Akinian, etc, which Mahé had not noticed or if he had, he had kept quiet.

The similarity of Sebēos's first three chapters with the History of Mosēs leads to the conclusion that one directly derives from the other (Sebēos in his chapter 3 admits that he is following Mosēs), which in

49. R. D. Barnett, 'Urartu', in *Cambridge Ancient History*, vol. III, part 1, p364.

both cases have been partly ascribed to Mar Abas by Mosēs and Sebēos alike—and by scholarship when it suits them although those same scholars have at other times ascribed Sebēos' work to an Anonymous History and Mosēs' work to an imaginary individual. Here therefore is a question for Mahé and scholars who share his opinion: In paragraph five of chapter 1 Sebēos writes: 'I, Agat'angełos the scribe wrote on this stele with my own hand the years of the first Armenian kings, taking them from the royal archives at the command of the valiant Trdat', adding that 'you will see the list in its appropriate place'. True enough, we see the Parthian and the Armenian Arsacid king lists in the last paragraph of chapter 2 after the sentence 'these are the Arsacid kings who ruled over the land of Armenia…' But in Sebēos' History there is another name list (chapter 1, paragraph 7) that records Hayk, Aramenak, Aramayis, Amasia, Gełam, Harma, Aram and Ara Gełets'ik. The list is taken from Book 1, chapter 5 of Mosēs' History, wherein the longest line of Hayk's progeny taken from chapter 12 is quoted after Yapet' (Japheth). If one insists that this list derives from the Anonymous History, then where are all the other names in Book 1, chapters 12, 19 & 22 of the History? How could Sebēos pick just these eight names in the correct order as they appear in Mosēs' History, and give us an identical name list? Scholarship insists that Agat'angełos's inscription was the *Primary History*, but since the names of his kings are those of the Arsacids exactly how primary is this history? Furthermore, when one examines in detail the first chapter of Sebēos, one finds further evidence which establishes Mosēs as the original source (see Part IV, note 1 against my article 'Ara the Fair', where Sebēos's verbatim extracts from Mosēs are highlighted). The author of the alleged *Primary History?*, Sebēos, claims that Mar Abas copied in only circa AD 600 the names of the kings incised on the stele by Agat'angełos at Mtsurn, the palace of Sanadruk. In contrast, Mosēs mentiones a stele in the palace of Vałarshak at Nisibis, which was incised with the contents of Mar Abas Katina's discovery. (In both cases the inscriptions were those of names. In the case of Mosēs the names were those of the most ancient kings of Aram while the names of Sebēos were those of Arsacids.) Is it so difficult to realize that Sebēos is following Mosēs step by step but writing in his own style, introducing slight changes as an author in his own right might do so?

As for the so-called Primary History one might ask where do Agat'angełos, Mar Abas, Mosēs or Sebēos mention such a source? In which language was this source written? If the answer is 'oral source' then how could these cleric historians of different epochs have had access to the same source? What kind of date can the adherents of this theory place against such a source? Was this dubious Primary History known to all or it was the entitlement of a few writers of the early Middle Ages? Scholars who find it easier to distort perfectly viable ancient works instead of persevering in their studies in order to penetrate the true messages they contain, have not even grasped the simple logic that Sebēos' Agat'angełos could not have recorded the names of the kings who reigned after Trdat, if there was any truth in the claim that Agat'angełos himself inscribed these names on a stela by the order of Trdat the Great. Their inability to penetrate particular passages of Sebēos' History is perplexing to say the least, such as the first paragraph of the first chapter (unexplained until 2007's *The History of Bishop Sebēos*), the names of the five kings in the same chapter (unexplained until 2007), the name of the Sassanian king and the date of the excavations for the pillars (again unexplained until 2007).

Mahé mentions Firmilian of chapter 11.75 twice: on pages 36 and 45 of his Introduction. Firmilian I have explained above and on page 14 and the explanation of the chapter concerned can be seen in Part III.

On page 81 of his work Mahé tells us that Artashēs's horse jumping over the river like an eagle has been compared with Menua's horse called *'artsiv'* in the Urartian inscription. Again, not much thought has gone into this quotation either by Mahé or scholars who have expressed such a view with undisclosed insinuations, since we know that Armenians and the entire world knew nothing about Urartu, Menua or his horse until a hundred years ago! Was Mosēs able to foretell what the entire world would know only in the early twentieth century?

*

Part II
Understanding Khorenats'i's Chronology

In this part I shall examine the various historical and chronological anomalies that scholars have documented in Khorenats'i's History. I shall set out to explain and prove that such anomalies do not exist in the History and that most of these objections arise from the preconceptions, misunderstandings and unwillingness of such scholars to devote longer time to thinking and research, since it is far easier to follow the observations of a previous scholar. I shall also show that Khorenats'i is the enlightened old philosopher mentioned by Łazar P'arpets'i in his *Letter to Vahan Mamikonean*, and he is the author of the History, which was written and completed in the second half of the fifth century, AD 474. This section will again concentrate on what Mahé, Thomson and Toumanoff write, since their ideas derive from more than a century of scholarly commentaries and criticisms, of which they are the most recent commentators. On occasion, of course, I may also remark on scholars from the more distant past.

An important aspect of understanding the History of Khorenats'i is to reflect on the times in which it was written. We read of publication of a work and take it for granted that the original publication of an olden manuscript was the same as our experience in the present, which could not be further from the truth. Before the age of printing, when a work was published in the fifth to, say, the mid-fifteenth century, in most cases a single manuscript was written and, in Khorenats'i's case, it was sent chapter by chapter as they were written to the individual who had commissioned it. Under such circumstances it will be clear that the number of persons with direct access to such a work would be extremely limited and, in some cases, it may be just one. I should again stress that all too often it takes another writer whose own intact manuscript has reached us in order to acknowledge the existence of a second work. Sahak Bagratuni was killed in 482 and who would have thought of looking into his library, if he did have one, under such turbulent conditions? At'anas Tarawnts'i's manuscript took more than 1,400 years to be discovered, and that in a blighted state, which is precisely why Thomson and Toumanoff did not know of its existence when writing their commentaries. Another example is that of Kałankatuats'i's *History of the Alans*, which was known to exist in the eighth century but its contents remained unknown. When Anania Mokats'i Kat'ołikos, who had heard about the history, asked for a copy of it in the middle of the tenth century, he was refused.[1] These are the main reasons why the first acknowledgement of Khorenats'i's History that we know of was a century after its completion date, and this was only due to the fact that the acknowledger, At'anas Tarawnts'i, was requested to reform the Armenian calendar and he thus set out to search for works of chronological value.

The case of P'arpets'i was different. After his return from Byzantium in 470, where he had gone for his higher education, he stayed for two years with Khorenats'i in Siwnik', as he admits in a misleading fashion. He had seen how Mosēs was working on various difficult subjects. But, P'arpets'i did not know that what he was witnessing and reading, in addition to other translations, included also parts of the *History of the Armenians*, since what was written previously had already been sent to Sahak Bagratuni. P'arpets'i was therefore not in a position to acknowledge his colleague's complete work. It is in fact Łazar's misleading evidence in his Letter to Vahan Mamikonean and certain aspects of his History that is of utmost importance in deciding the period when Khorenats'i wrote his History, irrespective of At'anas Tarawnts'i, and so it is best to start this part with a discussion of Łazar.

Thomson in his commentary mentions the parallel literary sections between the Alexander romance of Pseudo-Callisthenes and the Greek works of the Jewish writer Philo, in addition to various borrowings from Gregory Nazianzenus, Gregory of Nyssa, Basil of Caesarea, Agat'angełos, P'awstos, the Ashkharhats'oyts' of Anania Shirakats'i, and so on. However, in the case of Łazar, on pages 50-51 of his Commentary,

---

1. M. Kałankatuats'i, *The History of the Albanians*. The translator V. Arak'elyan, at the beginning of his introduction, mentions that the history was known in the eighth century at its earliest, and was acknowledged from the ninth and tenth centuries onwards.

quotes events that are discussed differently by Mosēs. I find nothing unusual in such a case because if the two authors have consulted different sources it is obvious that their reports too will differ, Besides, it would be highly unusual to find an author writing in an identical manner to another or displaying the same expertise or knowledge.

The last entry of Thomson, concerning Book III.66 of Mosēs, says 'that he elaborates on Łazar's brief reference to Samuel's avarice'. Thomson's statement derives from the fact that he believes Mosēs to be a personality of the eighth century, whereas he was a contemporary of Samuel which means he would be better informed than Łazar.

I find it remarkable that Thomson does not quote the parallel (verbatim) excerpts in the History of Mosēs against those found in the History of Łazar P'arpets'i. He comments: '[Łazar's History] served Mosēs as a prime source for the troubled relations between the last Arsacid kings of Armenia and their Iranian overlords, until the abolition of the Armenian monarchy in AD 428.' Yet he does not mention that the events and the details discussed by Mosēs are far richer. He also says: 'Some of Mosēs' literary borrowings are...', then quoting three instances which actually amount to a single one, i.e. the description of Ayrarat and Karin ('Commentary', p50). However, 'some borrowings' is not adequate since there are many such parallels in these two histories, which I shall identify and discuss.

All the same, let us first try to establish an acceptable chronology for the movements of Łazar, based on what we know through his Letter, Armenian ecclesiastic custom and what other commentators have written. One aspect of the chronology must be known beforehand: Thomson highlights in his note 9 on page 250 that '(Łazar's) chronology in the letter is most unclear', to which I would add that Łazar intentionally misleads the reader in order to cover his footprints, since he knows he has not acted in good faith while a guest of Mosēs. He has plagiarised parts of the History that was being written at the time, without knowing that those parts belonged to a larger study, the History of the Armenians, hence he could not acknowledge the History (would he have acknowledged the History if he knew what he was plagiarising was a part of it?).

The case of Łazar P'arpetsi
Most likely, Łazar was born around 438-440. He mentions that he was older than Vahan Mamikonean and his brothers (Vahan's date of birth is accepted as 440—it should be a little later—and Łazar's date of birth

is given as 442 by a few scholars but should be before that of Vahan around 440 or thereabouts in order to agree with what Łazar says). He was educated together with the Mamikonean boys by Ałan Artsruni and others. According to what he writes in the fourth paragraph of his letter he must have been ordained by Ałan before AD 465, when he was sent to Byzantine territory in order to further his education. If Łazar was the son of wealthy parents and a civilian then perhaps he could have financed his maintenance and education while away from home. But this is most unlikely. Therefore, for an acolyte to be sent away for further education he had to have the sanction of the catholicos (this procedure has not changed). The conclusion is that Giwt Kat'ołikos agreed to his going away and took care of the necessary formalities and the finances, and that Łazar was about twenty-five years old when he left Armenia.

Łazar returned on 470, a date agreed on by most scholars. His first call in Armenia had to be to Giwt Kat'ołikos (this procedure too has not changed) with whom he stayed for a while. (An acolyte returning to his country could not please himself and go wherever he wished. Łazar's remark that he stayed with the Kamsarakan family after his arrival cannot be the whole truth.) It was Giwt Kat'ołikos, a fellow student of Mosēs, who placed Łazar with Mosēs in order to serve and gain experience. Łazar did not previously know Mosēs and I cannot accept that he chanced upon him in the course of his travels (if one is to accept what Łazar says, that in 484 he was cohabiting with Mosēs, then Łazar would be more than 40 years old; too old to serve and gain experience, and his meeting with Mosēs would lack an explanation as to how the two came together). Łazar stayed for two years with Mosēs sometime between 471 and 473, a period that coincides with the writing of the final chapters of the *History of the Armenians*, such as chapters 47 to 64 of Book III. It is evident that Łazar does not know the previous chapters, not even the very last one, 'The Lament', since he refers to it as a 'curse upon the clergy' (Thomson's translation, p265). Łazar's claim that he stayed with Mosēs for two years in Siwnik' (Thomson, p250) and that is where Vahan found him living with Mosēs is not true and is designed to mislead the reader, since it would give us the dates 484 to 486 by which time Mosēs had already become a bishop, died, was buried and had his bones thrown into the river.

Of course Łazar may have gone for a second time to Siwnik' but not to cohabitate with Mosēs. In the fourth paragraph of his Letter (page 188, line 2 of the 1904 edition, or Thomson's section 188, lines 2-3) he states that 'the Bishop of Siwnik' was acquainted with his life' (Thomson, p250) and yet he stayed with Moses whom he does not mention. Because, by 484-86 Moses had already been the bishop of Bagrevand, before Vahan was made a *marzpan* (AD 486), and passed away. Lazar conceals all these facts and his disclosures in his paper are rather naive.

It is possible that after 473 Lazar went to live with the Kamsarakans up to 478 (he must have been with Kamsarakans at the time of Vahan's apostasy, 476) which was the year Giwt Kat'olikos died. The next cathlicos was Mandakuni, who had Lazar helping him for the next few years. It appears that Lazar was at Valarshapat until 484, during the course of Vahan's rebellion and the battles of Akori (481), Nersehapat (482) and Charmanay (482). It was after 484 that he could have been in Siwnik' for the second time, if we accept what he writes in his letter.

Mandakuni's pontificate lasted at least ten years, if not twelve (the six years allocated by Thomson cannot be correct, since his long speech at the occasion when Vahan was made marzpan of Armenia in 486 represents his eighth year as catholicos). It appears that after Lazar left for Siwnik' in 484, Babken Ot'msets'i became Mandakuni's principle assistant. When Lazar returned as the dean of the monastery of Etchmiadzin after 486, he could not have cordial relations with Babken, since his presence would have threatened the latter's position. Lazar's flight to the city of Amid is usually dated to 490, but if we accept this date then it is clear that he would not have been able to finish the work he had started on the cathedral of Etchmiadzin, although such further details do not affect the immediate subject under discussion. Here I must mention that the only scholar who agrees with my dating of Lazar's stay with Moses to 471-473 is Archbishop Ormanian (he must know ecclesiastical custom since he was a man of the cloth)[2] but he makes no comment on Lazar's plagiarism or the verbatim extracts found in both Lazar and Moses.

We have looked at the period in which Lazar stayed with Moses, coinciding with the time the last chapters of the History the latter was writing, and the conditions under which Lazar had the opportunity to plagiarise sections of what was being written during his stay. This is therefore a good point to quote the many verbatim excerpts[3] found in

---

2.   Archbishop Malak'ia Ormanian, *Azgapatum*, Sevan, Beirut, 1959, vol. 1, part 1, §§ 327-331.

3.   See Part 1, Note 3 above. Buzantats'i on pages 8-10 provide a list of the verbatim extracts appearing in both Moses and Lazar. Some of his quotations were redundant and there were other phrases from various different parts that had been attached which I could not accept. This is the reason I have done my own sorting of the extracts, and the list given here represents my own conclusions.

both authors, which in fact represent only a part of Łazar's borrowings. As before, all the translations quoted are those of Thomson:

No.1: Movsēs iii.47: page 317, lines 8-9: *'Nshanagirs Hayots' lezuis.'*
Translation: 'Letters for the Armenian language'.
Łazar 1.10: page 14, line 2: *'Nshanagirk' hayerēn lezuoys.'*
Translation: 'Letters for the Armenian language.'

No.2: Movsēs iii.51: page 322, lines 15-17: *'Ew **metsari** i nmanē yoyzh;* **nakh vasn k'ajatohmik azgin Pahlawkats'**, **dardzeal ew zi aṙaji anhawatits'** argoy ew patuakan ts'uts'anē Astuats ztsaṙays iwr.'*
Translation: 'He was greatly honoured by him, first, because of his noble Pahlavik family, and second, because God shows his servants to be important and honourable before unbelievers.'
Łazar 1.14: page 23, lines 31-34: *'K'anzi **metsarēr** zna, **nakh vasn** azgakanut'ean aṙnn,* **ew dardzeal zi aṙaji anhawatits'n yargoy ew patuakan ts'uts'anēr** zsurb tsaṙays iwr Astuats.'*
Translation: 'For he respected him, first because of his lineage, and secondly because God shows his holy servants to be estimable and honourable before the unbelievers.'

No.3: Movsēs iii.52: page 326, line 5: *'zvaḷnjuts' gteal **sharagir taṙits'**.'*
Translation: 'The alphabet of letters that had been written down long before.'
Łazar 1.11: *'zvaḷnjuts' greal sharagirs taṙits'n.'*
Translation: 'to set in order the ancient written letters' (note that this translation is suspect).

No.4: Movsēs iii.56: page 332, lines 11-12: *'I nmin awur ew na anden I drann mardkanē nengeal satakets'aw.'*
Translation: 'On that same day (Shabuh) was also killed by the treachery of the courtiers.'
Łazar : 1.12: page 19, lines 9-12: *'I nmin awur ... andrēn I drann mardkanē dawov yark'unik'n satakets'in.'*
Translation: 'On the same day (his son Shabuh) was treacherously slaughtered in the palace by the courtiers.'

No.5: Mosēs III.59: page 338, line 17: *'Ew lerink'n li en ērēovk'*
kchłakabashkhiwk' ew orochaynovk'.'
Translation: 'The mountains are full of cloven-footed and ruminant
beasts.'
Łazar 1.7: page 9, lines 18-19: *'zhotseals ērēovk'n kchłakabazhniwk'*
ew orochaynovk'n.'
Translation: 'They abound with cloven-footed deer and ruminants.'

No.6: Mosēs III.63: page 347, lines 2-4, 6-7, 8-9 & 11-14 *'Ew ard*
part ē p'ok'r mi tanel t'erut'ean arnn ... ew och' anorinats matnel i
tsałr ew yaypanumn...Ayl na asē indz k'aw lits'i matnel gaylots'
zim moloreal och'khars ... zi et'ē ēr hawatats'eal t'agawori ařaji,
p'ut'ayi ew och' yapałēi ... k'anzi droshmeal ē awazanavn ...
t'ēpēt ew anařak ē, pořnik ē, ayl K'ristoneay ē, gichatseale ē
marmnov, ayl och' anhawat hogwov; zełkh ē varuk' ayl och'
krakapasht; tkar ē i kanays ayl och' tsařayē tarerts'.'
Translation: 'So we must endure for a while the man's faults... and
not hand him over to the lawless to be derided and mocked... He
said, heaven forbid that I hand over to wolves my erring sheep...
for if it was before a Christian king, I would be eager and would not
hesitate... For he has been sealed by baptism, even though he is
licentious, He is a fornicator, yet he is a Christian; he is dissolute
of body, yet not unbelieving in spirit. He is impure of life, but not
a fire worshipper. He is weak with women, but he does not serve
the elements.'
Łazar 1.13: page 20, line 37: *'Ew tareal vayr mi t'erut'iwn ařnn.'*
Page 21, lines 13-14: *'ew och' anōrinats' matnelov I tsałr ew*
yaypanumn ... tal zsowrb khorhowrd hawatoys meroy.'
Lines 32-38: *'indz k'aw lits'i matnich' linel ... zim hōti zmoloreal*
och'kharn matnel yaypanumn ... ayl droshmeal ē surp awazanin
... p'ut'ayi ew och' yapałēi.'
Page 22, lines 1-2: *'zi et'ē ēr hawatats'eal t'agawori ařaji.'*
Lines 15-18: *'zi t'ēpēt ew its'ē pořnik, ayl zknik' hōtin K'ristosi krē*
yandzin iwrum;
gichats'eal ē marmnov, ayl och' anhawat ew het'anos; zełkh, ayl
och' krakapasht; tkarats'eal ē i kanays, ayl och' tsařayē tarerts'.'
Translation: 'Endure for a while the faults of this man...
and not by handing him over to the impious, give the holy mystery
of our faith to derision and mockery. Far be it from me to become
a traitor and hand over the lost sheep of my flock for mockery. Yet

he has been sealed by birth of the holy font... I would hurry and not delay... if I had to bring such admonition before a Christian king...
For although he might be a fornicator, yet he bears on himself the seal of Christ's flock. He is polluted in body, yet he is not an unbeliever and a pagan. He is debauched, but not a fire-worshipper. He has a weakness for women, but he does not serve the elements.'

No.7: Moses III.64: page 348, line 6: '*ew na hrazharer bnav asel inch' ch'ar kam bari.*'
Line 19: '*yinēn och' inch' ēk' lselots' amenewin.*'
Translation: 'but he absolutely refused to say anything evil or good... but you will hear nothing at all from me.'
Lazar 1.14: page 23, lines 39-40: '*zi och' inch' lselots' ēk' yinēn yałags charakhōsut'eand aydorik ch'ar inch' ew kam bari.*'
Translation: 'For you will hear nothing from me, either evil or good, about this calumny.'

No.8: Moses III.64: page 349, lines 4-6: '*Vṛam aṛnul zt'agaworut'iwnn zArtashrē ... nuynpēs ew zmetsn Sahak ztunn Kat'ołikosakan unel yark'unis.*'
Page 349, line 19: '*et nots'a zBrk'ishoy omn asori.*'
Translation: 'Vram ordered Artashir to be stripped of his crown... and Sahak the Great [should be treated] likewise and the domain of the Kat'ołikos be confiscated to the court'
'and his name was Brk'ishoy a Syriac person.'
Lazar 1.14: page 24, lines 39-41: '*i pats' aṛnul zt'agaworut'iwnn yArtashesē, ınd nmin ew ztunn Kat'ołikosakani srboyn Sahakay yark'unis unel.*'
Page 26: lines 6-7: '*et nots'a zBrk'ishoy zomn anun ayr yazgē Asorwots'.*'
Translation: '(Vram) ordered that Artashēs should be deprived immediately of the throne, and likewise Sahak of the domains of the Kat'ołikos, and that he should be kept at court' [Thomson's translation of this line is doubtful, I think it should be 'and likewise Sahak, of the domains of the Kat'ołikos, be confiscated to the court'] .... 'and his name was Brk'ishoy a person of Syriac origin.'

Plagiarism by Łazar

Thomson knows well the History of Łazar—he has even translated the complete work into English (*The History of Łazar P'arpets'i*, Atlanta, 1991). Why therefore is it that he ignores all the verbatim excerpts quoted above? From the point of view of the reader, his negligence can be explained only in one way, i.e. disclosing all these excerpts while at the same time quoting what Łazar had written about Mosēs in his *Letter to Vahan Mamikonean* could have an adverse effect and place his theories in doubt. On pages 49-51 under the heading of 'Łazar' we are told how Mosēs plagiarised Łazar's History but did not cite his source. But in this very section one would have expected Thomson to tell us also about Łazar's comments on Mosēs. Instead we see a short paragraph on page 3 of his Commentary telling us what Łazar said about Mosēs the philosopher, which he ends with the words: 'But there is no suggestion in Łazar that this Mosēs had composed any historical work.' Of course not! How could Łazar, a novice acolyte placed in the care of Mosēs by Giwt Kat'ołikos in order to serve and obtain experience, know of a written History which Mosēs had already sent chapter by chapter to his patron, Sahak Bagratuni, unless Mosēs had bragged about it, which is out of question according to the description Łazar gives us, saying: 'while he [Mosēs] was still in the body, was yet continuously a citizen of the heavenly army.' The literary material taken by Łazar from Mosēs were from those parts that were being written at the time he was living with him. Therefore, Łazar could not know that these pages that were being written while he was living with Mosēs were a part of a whole history, and he did not disclose his source for the parts he had borrowed, but in his paper to Vahan used various means to cover his plagiarism, such as concealing the actual time he had lived with Mosēs (471-473), and giving the impression that Vahan Mamikonean found him in Siwnik' (486) while he was cohabiting with Mosēs, when in reality by that time the latter had already died.

So far, what I have written about Łazar and what will follow is based on reading the various manuscripts of his History, similar to all scholars before me, who have been involved in the explanation, the translation or the criticism of it. However, there is one point which concerns me, namely whether I have been fair to the person of Łazar P'arpets'i. This matter requires a thorough explanation and as far as I am aware none has involved himself in such a conundrum.

The manuscript of Łazar's Letter to Vahan Mamikonean, halfway down the sixth paragraph before the end, has a sheet or two missing. The sixth paragraph starts with a discussion of Mosēs the Philosopher, but after eight and a half lines it stops with four points, and the note for these four points says that here a sheet is missing (other manuscripts say two are missing). After these four points the next line again starts with four points and continues for another five and a half lines. The subject of these last five and a half lines is again Mosēs the Philosopher. My reasoning tells me that if prior to the missing sheet(s) the subject was Mosēs and the same continues after the missing sheet(s), then it is logical that the missing parts will also be about him. Another thought that comes to mind is why has Thomson in his translation of Łazar's History not directed attention to these missing sheet(s) with at least a note but is content to place in square brackets five points in each place (considering that in his introduction, in section 4 where such missing sheet(s) occur, he highlights the fact with his note 4). Of course, we will never know what was written on the missing sheet(s), but is it not possible that here Łazar had acknowledged the History of Mosēs or had come clean by admitting that he had plagiarised Mosēs' History?

Regardless of what were the actual contents of the missing sheets of the Letter, the surviving parts are sufficient to enable us to conclude that Mosēs wrote his History in the second half of the fifth century, and these two sources also date the time when Łazar lived with Mosēs, when one considers the fact that it is only Book III, chapters 47 to 64 of Mosēs that have their parallels in Łazar's History. Aside from the parallels indicated above, Łazar plagiarised entire excerpts and has recomposed them in his own style, such as paragraphs 1 & 4 of section 1.14. However, Łazar had no means of borrowing additional material from the previous parts of the History since these were not available since they had been sent to Sahak Bagratuni, Mosēs' patron, prior to the arrival of Łazar.

In his Letter, Łazar makes comments about Mosēs such as: 'the blessed philosopher Mosēs', 'his enlightening and ignorance-dispelling books', 'he devoted his life to such troublesome studies, day and night labouring for the enlightenment of the world of Armenians', and 'eventually, feeling ashamed they gave to the saint a "poisoned chalice" in the form of a worthless bishopric and silenced him' (this is a reference to Mosēs's advancement to the bishopric of Bagrevand, which took place a few years after Mosēs had finished writing his History). He adds that 'at the time of his death he left behind a written terrible curse against the leading clerics (this refers to the Lament (Book III.68) starting after 'Awake, Jeremiah, awake and lament'). There is an irony here since this worthless bishopric, granted to him a few years after he had written his

History, and which Łazar mentions, has acquired such an importance in the opinions of the sceptics that it has provided them with a basis for accusing Mosēs of being a Bagratid tool, boosting the Bagratid reputation and consequently showing a bias towards the Mamikoneans.

However, Thomson, Mahé and others say 'there is no suggestion in Łazar that this Mosēs had composed any historical work'. In that case, who was this Mosēs who was made a bishop and left behind a terrrible curse (the Lament)? Was there really another erudite scholar, a philosopher, from the fifth century named Mosēs and who occupied himself with such arduous works? It may not be concrete proof but we should not overlook the fact that concerning his studies Mosēs had described his occupation and health in Book III.65 exactly in the same manner as Łazar described him.

As we have seen above, Łazar had plagiarised Mosēs' History but only drawing on those parts that were being written at the time he was co-habiting the cave, since the previous chapters had already been sent to Sahak Bagratuni. We have also seen that the main extracts Łazar used fall between Book III in chapters 47 to 64. At'anas Tarawnts'i places the date 474 after the name of Mosēs Khorenats'i, adding the epithets of *philosopher* and *writer*; T'ovma Artsruni confirms this date by saying that Mosēs wrote his History up to Zenon's succession as emperor and Asołik (Stephen of Taron) records that the Philosopher Mosēs lived at the time of Giwt Kat'ołikos (p123).[4] This means that Mosēs could not benefit from Łazar's History, written around 500 by which time he had been dead for quite a few years, since Łazar, before fleeing to the city of Amid, knew how the remains of Mosēs were treated.

The important case of Łazar has been fully explained above, and I also discuss At'anas Tarawnts'i, Bishop Sebēos and Kałankatuats'i. There remains one final ancient manuscript from the late seventh century, called *The Anonymous Chronology* since it lacks an author's name, but is ascribed to Anania Shirakats'i by A. G. Abrahamyan (1940) and Fr B. Sargisian (1904). The latter published his findings with commentary at the Mkhit'arian's Press of Venice, and Abrahamyan in Yerevan, Armenia, but Toumanoff, Thomson and Mahé et al prefer to ignore sources such as these. The manuscript itself is a collection of chronological subjects deriving from Mosēs Khorenats'i, Andreas, Eusebius, Epiphanius and some minor writers. What is of interest for

---

4. T'owma Artsruni, *History of the House of Artsrunis*; see Book I.11 (p123). Stephen of Taron (Asołik Vardapet), *Universal History*, Yerevan University, 2000; see Part II, chapter 2, p123.

this study are the first three pages of the manuscript, which starts with ancient chronologists and the first name that appears is that of Mosēs Khorenats'i and a verbatim extract from his History, Book 1, chapter 4. Besides the first three pages there are also some interpolations from the History throughout the manuscript. Has scholarship not noticed this evidence concerning the date Mosēs lived and wrote his History?

The final point in this connection is to clarify why Mosēs uses the name Mesrop and not Mashtots'. We know from various writers, starting with the tenth century, that Mosēs was a nephew of Mesrop. Is there a more affectionate manner of demonstrating kinship other than calling one's uncle by his Christian name? However, it must also be pointed out that At'anas Tarawnts'i around the year 584 replicates Mosēs' chronology, confirming that the history was written by Mosēs, and, like Mosēs, he names the founder of the Armenian alphabet as Mesrop and not Mashtots'.[5] We find the same name used by Kałankatuats'i of the early second part of the seventh century,[6] but in his case he cites Mosēs as a source.

Objections and alleged incongruities

Some scholars, I am sure, may have considered the points and events outlined above but did not express any conclusions. Still, most would have been aware that there were chronological anomalies within the History of Mosēs which they could not reconcile with the second half of fifth century. Hence, they could not accept that Mosēs was an author from this period. Additionally, at the time when most of these scholars were operating nothing was known of At'anas Tarawnts'i and his manuscript. The chronological anomalies therefore forced them to move Mosēs from the fifth to the seventh, eighth or ninth centuries, which is not as bad as it sounds since the transposition is logical in view of the data available.

Therefore, it will be best to outline the six fundamental chronological incongruities, which appear in Thomson's *Commentary* (Toumanoff lists eight which Thomson has reduced to six). I should add that these incongruities have been noted since the last quarter of the nineteenth century and are not the inventions of Thomson or Toumanoff.

Thomson, prior to enumerating these six incongruities, has some uncomplimentary words directed towards Mosēs and his History, such as

5. A. S. Matevosyan, 'Movses Khorenats'i and At'anas Tarawnts'i's Chronology'; see note 4, p233.
6. M. Kałankatuats'i, *The History of the Albanians*; see 1.27 & 29 and 11.3.

'audacious', 'mendacious', 'faker', 'fraudulent', 'distorter', 'unscrupulous' and 'never be fully trusted'. I wonder, thirty years after the publication of his translation and commentary, whether Thomson would consider his past remarks proper? As I have said before, there is much in the History which Mosēs has written that he himself has not understood, particularly in the first book, and there is much more than that, which Thomson and others of his opinion have also not understood. Such remarks and condemnations can only be seen as premature—indeed, even my own words explaining different aspects of the History cannot be deemed as final.

The first incongruity

The first objection is directed to a section in 1.12 of the History:

> Mosēs [in Book 1.12] is the first Armenian writer to equate Siunik' and Sisakan. The latter term is first found in Syriac in the sixth century; in the seventh-century Armenian *Ashkharhats'oyts'*[7] it refers to a canton, not the whole province.

The section of the History referred to says:

> Here Sisak dwelt, and he filled the confines of his habitation with buildings. He called the land after his own name Siunik', but the Persians more precisely call it Sisakan. [Mosēs 1.12]

When in *c.* 588 BC the Hays entered Urartu and settled in various districts on the periphery of the country, in accordance with a predetermined plan agreed with the Urartians, the descendants of Sisak's ex-royal house settled to the east, south of Gełark'unik' and Lake Lychnides (Sevan). Like all the other ex-royal houses, such as the Manawazeans (deriving from Manawaz), Bznuneans (from Baz), Khorkhorunis (from Khor), Gełark'unik' (from Gełs), Kadmeans (from Kadmos), Angełats' (from Angeł), Shahunis (from Shakhu), the Sisakan district likewise was named after Sisak. At the time of Vałarsh I (AD 117-144), when 'reforms' were being introduced (see The Enigma of Mar Abas in Part IV), the royal house of the Sisakeans was reduced to a dukedom and the district renamed Siunik' (we do not know what Siunik' means, perhaps 'Place of Idols' since these were a feature of the capital

---

7. Anania Shirakats'i, *Matenagrutiwn*, Yerevan, 1979, p304; Thomson, p58; Toumanoff, *Studies*, p332.

cities of later Siunik'). Mosēs lived in a cave in Siunik' for a long time (confirmed by Łazar) and he knew the ancient division of the highland and the naming of all the districts through the book of Mar Abas. Is this clever and erudite scholar unable to pair the old Sisakan district with the new Siunik'? Does it have to take an outsider, a Syriac named Zacharias Rhetor of Mitylene (Chronicle, 554) of the sixth century, to tell the people of Siunik' what their land was called? Where might Zacharias have taken this hidden information from? Koryun calls Vasak 'Sisakan Vasak', prince of Siunik', (chapter 14), which means that Vasak belonged to a place called Sisakan, since by Vasak's time there was no more a Sisakan family. Perhaps over time Sisakan was reduced to a canton, but even then we have at least the reverberations of the name that had covered the whole district and it was not unknown, since even an outsider, a Syriac, knew of it.

The second incongruity

The second objection is directed to a section in 1.14, which reads:

> Mosēs knows of four Armenias. These four Byzantine provinces were not so organized until 536 AD (by Justinian).[8]

This particular objection involves a few sections of the History, which I quote below, in each case using Thomson's English translation:

> **A.** Mosēs (Book 1.14): (1) 'Moving to the west against First [Armenia] with forty thousand infantry and two thousand cavalry, he reached Cappadocia and a place now called Caesarea..... (2) Therefore to this day the Greeks call that area Proto-Armenia, which translated means 'First Armenia'..... (3) In the same way, from those regions as far as his own border he filled with inhabitants many uninhabited lands, which were Second and Third Armenia, and also Fourth. (4) This is the prime and true reason for calling the western part of our country First and Second, and also Third and Fourth Armenia'.

The first sentence (1) is obscure and translators (Thomson, Malkhazyants', Mahé, Minassian) have understood this in different senses. The text says

---

8. Thomson, p59; Toumanoff, p331; N. Adontz, *Armenia in the Century of Justinian*, Hayastan, Yerevan, 1987, p201.

'Ast yarewmuts sharzheal i veray'. In my opinion, a comma after *i veray* is missing from the text, and because of it, Thomson's translation is at fault in introducing within square brackets the word Armenia (Malkhazyants' translation is faultier still since it adds forty-odd thousand soldiers to the original fifty). The whole excerpt comprises three sentences, of which the first says 'Moved against the west', the second: 'with forty thousand infantry and two thousand cavalry of the first' and the last 'he reached Cappadocia, a place now called Caesarea'. This campaign involves the second battle of Aram. The first was against Mades and the Medians (the first campaign with fifty thousand). Therefore, the excerpt is telling us that this second battle with Payapis K'aałea involved the same army as that of the first, reduced by eight thousand, consisting from forty thousand infantry plus two thousand cavalry. In this sentence there is no mention of 'First Armenia'. This battle is described in Harma's inscription of Topada, which can be seen in *Pre-History Volume 2* (pp 154-162).

The second sentence (2) confirms that the region of Cappadocia around Caesarea was called 'First Armenia' by the Greeks. This is important in understanding the sentences that follow.

The third sentence (3) says that the rest of the lands up to the borders of Armenia were named Second and Third Armenia, and also Fourth. Scribal interpolation starts in this sentence. At the time of the battle there was not a country of Armenia, which precludes the divisions mentioned. But that is not of great importantance. The significant part of the argument is that as soon as a Third or Fourth Armenia is mentioned, the First Armenia is transferred automatically to the regions of Pontus Mountains and the Black Sea, dragging with it Caesarea and Cappadocia, which confirms that at the time the History was edited, or perhaps later, in order to make it an up to date textbook of history, much was added thereon. We notice the same interpolation, only in this case more obvious due to the manner of presentation, in the last sentence (4).

B. Mosēs (Book 11.8): After this he established the great principality of Tsop'k' in what is called Fourth Armenia, and also the principalities of the Apahunik', Manawazean, and Bznunik' from the same descendants of Hayk.

Prior to Tsop'k', in the same chapter Mosēs mentioned Angeł Tun, which is bang in the centre of this alleged Fourth Armenia, which was not mentioned. The Manawazeans and Bznunik' are mentioned and, again, are not qualified, but Tsop'k', which is the district name, is qualified as in Fourth Armenia. One wonders why. Mosēs says that these lands were named after the villages and districts, therefore after naming the district of Tsop'k' why does he qualify it with Fourth Armenia, and has nothing to say about the other houses he has mentioned? The Fourth Armenia here is an interpolation and a clever one at that, because the scribe or the editor incorporated a whole sentence of 'in what is called Fourth Armenia', which makes it difficult to notice the interference.

C. Mosēs (Book II.91): Therefore, Archilaeus, who had been appointed to the governorship of what is called Fourth Armenia, on being reprimanded by him [Aristakes] waited for an opportune day.

This is the most difficult sentence in which to detect an interpolation, because the Fourth Armenia has replaced the place name Andzit while the appointment of Archilaeus is rather mysterious—the Text does not tell us who had appointed him, the Greeks or King Trdat of the Armenians. However, if the name of the place is accepted as Fourth Armenia, then it becomes obvious that he was appointed by the Byzantines, in which case Aristakes could not reprimand him. If he was appointed by Trdat then there could not be a Fourth Armenia. All the same, this is a successful interpolation.

D. Mosēs (Book III.44): Khosrov's commander, Sahak the Aspet, marched against them, slaughtered many [of Vanandats'ik'], and made many others flee to Fourth Armenia. They did not rush to the land of Khaltik and take refuge among the Greeks, nor did they go to King Arshak, but they went for refuge to some brigands in Fourth Armenia on the Syrian borders.

This section too confirms that the Fourth Armenia, mentioned twice, is an interpolation. The Vanandats'ik' being brigands were made to flee, but they did not trust the Greeks and so they did not flee to the northern lands but south to Fourth Armenia. Here we have a contradiction, since Fourth Armenia too was a Greek land. If one says that at the time of the flight of the Vanandats'ik', chronologically speaking, there was a Fourth Armenia, he will only reinforce my argument, since Mosēs of even tenth or twelfth century could not mention it; he would have known of the date of the division of Armenia and the date of the flight of the Vanandats'ik', which means that the Third and the Fourth Armenias are clear interpolations.

Mosēs Khorenats'i could not have known of Third and Fourth Armenias, but as mentioned previously, his History had become a textbook soon after its discovery and continued to be the only authoritative history for the next fourteen hundred years. Scholars who have noticed various chronological anomalies have ascribed all of these to Khorenats'i without being prepared to take a deeper examination. Mahé does mention, however, that G. Traina has conclude that the matter of the Third and Fourth Armenias is an interpolation.

Finally, I think scholars who have pinpointed these anomalies in the History and held it against Mosēs have not used reasoning, but have accepted and followed the previous conclusions of various scholars and presented the same arguments in relation to the text as it has reached us. They may or may not agree with me, but the truth is that even if one removes Mosēs even to the tenth or twelfth century AD, he would still not have been able to use the place names of Third and Fourth Armenias for the simple fact that his history ends in AD 440. The Third and Fourth Armenias belong to the future with events such as the battle of Vardan (AD 451) or the Arab invasion of Armenia (AD 640). And certainly Mosēs of the fifth century could not know of events taking place nearly a hundred years after the point at which his history finishes.

The third incongruity
The third objection is directed to Book II.62, as follows:

> Mosēs refers to the territory east of Lake Van as Vaspurakan, a term used only after the partition of Armenia in AD 591. Not until the early eight century *Narratio de Rebus Armeniae* is Vaspurakan used to designate a province in the same sense as Mosēs uses it.[9]

The section in connection with the place name Vaspurakan says:

> King Tiran gave Erakhnavu the second rank and entrusted to him the care of the army of the east. The king also left his friend Druasp with Erakhnavu. Druasp was a Persian, related by marriage to the princes of Vaspurakan. [II.62]

9. Thomson, p59; Toumanoff, p331.

Vaspurakan is used in here as a place name, which has its roots in the early Parthian kingdom when the ruler used to keep a single son with him, the future king, sending the other offspring to a distant district, granting them apanage and lands in order to avoid palace intrigues and quarrels. We see the same principle in action in Armenia in the district of Ayrarat, when the Parthians (Arsacids) succeeded to the throne (AD 66). The term Vaspurakan could not be an invention of AD 591 during the late Sassanian period, since Strabo knows it and gives us the Greek form of it as Vasoropeda (*Basoropeda* = 'Border Land of the King'. *ba* = diminutive of *basileu*, hence *bas* = 'king's' + *oro* = 'boundary, limit, border' + *peda* = 'land').[10] M. Sprengling defines the word as 'Princely Heritage for Habitation' while W. Henning defines it as 'Crown Land'.[11] At the end all three definitions have similar sense.

Moses uses the word as defined by all the three authors mentioned above; in other words 'Druasp by marriage was related to the princes of Vaspurakan', which means Vaspurakan was the crown or king's lands where the royal princes lived. But Sebeos uses the word Vaspurakan with a double sense: on page 47 (chapter 12) he writes the phrase 'Vaspurakan Corps' with the meaning of 'the place of Vaspurakan where the Elite Corps is found or comes from', and on page 50 (chapter 16) he writes 'the Vaspurakan Censor', which means 'the official from Vaspurakan Nobility'. For this objection Thomson points to Toumanoff and the latter to Adontz, who in his study of 'Armenia in the Century of Justinian' has a truism on page 236: 'It would be ridiculous to conclude that late acknowledgement of a place is a proof of its non-existence in the past'!

Finally, it should be noted that Adontz, who is quoted by Toumanoff as his source via 'Armenia in the Century of Justinian', never mentions that Vaspurakan was designated as a separate territory in AD 591 by Justinian and only thereafter the name Vaspurakan came into effect. Toumanoff is wrong while Thomson, who does not quote a source, has not checked with Adontz in order to confirm the veracity of his statement. What Adontz writes on page 261 about Vaspurakan is as follows:

Turuberan was detached from Vaspurakan in the treaty of AD 591, when new borders between Byzantium and Persia came into effect. The same border line also detached Ayrarat from Vaspurakan.

10. Strabo, *Geography*; see vol. v, p325, Book XI.14.5, p325.
11. A. V. Mushelyan, *The Century of Movses Khorenats'i* (in Armenian), EPH Printhouse, Yerevan, 2007. The references are taken from Mushelyan's work.

Turuberan and Ayrarat have the same origins, similar to Fourth Armenia and Elevated Armenia. These last districts originated from the lands which in AD 387 had passed to the Byzantines at the time of the division of Armenia, when the Byzantines acquired the new lands.

Conclusion: if Vaspurakan had not existed for centuries prior, how could Turuberan and Ayrarat be detached from it in AD 591?

The fourth incongruity

The fourth objection is directed to a section in 11.65 as follows:

> Mosēs refers to the Khazars, not mentioned in other Armenian sources before the seventh-century *Ashkharhats'oyts'*.[12]

(I must confess I could not stop laughing when I read this quotation— Mosēs could never be first!) The section in connection with this objection states:

> Because in his days the hosts of the northern peoples united, I mean the Khazars and Basilk, and passing through the Chora gate under the leadership of their king, a certain Vnasep Surhap, they crossed to this side of the River Kura. [11.65]

Before starting on this subject I ought to correct another of Toumanoff's errors, which occurs on page 331 of his *Studies*. He says: 'In Book 2.65 Mosēs refers to the Khazars as at the time of the mythical First Arsacid King Vologases.' This statement is not correct since the alleged mythical king, the Parthian viceroy Vałarshak of Mtsbin, is the brother of Arshak the Great in Mosēs's History. Besides him the Armenians had two more kings of the same name, both belonging to the Arsacid dynasty. These were Vałarsh I of AD 117-144 and Vałarsh II of 186-198. In the History of Mosēs the reigns of Vałarshak of Mtsbin (Nisibis) and Vałarsh I are telescoped, but the reign of Vałarsh II appears in Book 2.65, which indicates that the Khazar and Basilk penetration of Armenia took place in AD c.198 (the date Vałarsh II died fighting them). Vałarshak of Mtsbin (died c.110 BC), the mythical king of Toumanoff's writing, has no role here.

---

12.   Thomson, p59; Toumanoff, p331.

In the History of Mosēs the northern tribes are mentioned twice. Of these the first names them as the Khazars and Basilk in 11.65 and can be dated to c.198 AD. The second does not mention the tribe names (III.9) but can be dated to c. AD.395. If there was no truth in this, Mosēs of the second half of fifth century could not have recorded the names of Khazar and Basilk and the name of their king, irrespective of what Toumanoff, Marquart and Thomson say. The history of these tribes roaming the countries to the north of Armenia is still obscure, since they had no writing system and their movements are not well documented unless they involved the European parts that Attila invaded. But Attila and his hordes did not go in a straight line to Europe without leaving destruction and misery spread behind them. For the Hun invasions of the Caucasus and further south, scholarship usually looks to the Persian, Armenian and Roman records, which are not as forthcoming as those of Europe suffering under Attila and some of the tribes connected with him. The multitude of the tribes to the west of the Caspian Sea or north of the Caucasus, prior to Attila's appearance in Europe, must have invaded the city and village communities to the south of the Caucasus many times, since fighting and plundering was their way of life. The case that the Khazars and Basilks are mentioned for the first time in the seventh-century *Ashkharhats'oyts'* does not prove that the names were not known previously (this work does not involve itself with invasions as it is purely a geographical catalogue). Arthur Koester says that 'circa 372 ... the Huns first started to move westward from the steppes north of the Caspian Sea' (p17).[13] One might question this statement since it does not cover tribes making forays to the south into other countries and then retreating north. He adds: 'Zacharias Rhetor of the mid sixth century refers to the Khazars. Other sources indicate that they were already much in evidence a century earlier, and intimately connected with the Huns; the Khazars had been under the Hun tutelage' (p21), and ' "Kagan" was the generic term for "ruler" among many tribes' (p51).

In 448 the Byzantine emperor Theodosius II sent an embassy to Attila (died 453), which included the rhetorician Priscus. Priscus informs of the Hun customs and habits in his narratives and mentions the people subject to the Huns as Akatzirs (the 'geographer of Ravenna' identifies them with the Khazars, as does Jordanes, the Goth historian; Ak-Khazars = White Khazars). *Chambers's Encyclopaedia* writes that about AD 350 the Huns were on the shores of the Caspian west, when the Alans

---

13.   Arthur Koestler, *The Thirteenth Tribe*, Pan Books, 1977.

were finally swept on to the Caucasus. The Huns and their Khazar subjects, passing through the Chora Pass, attacked Georgia and Armenia and the south in 395,[14] but prior to that in the second century the Alans, a Sarmatian group of people, had raided Georgia, Armenia and Cappadocia where the Greek historian and general Arrian fought them.[15] These extracts demonstrate that the names Khazar, Basilk and Hun were known prior to the seventh century, which neutralises the criticism of Toumanoff and Thomson. Furthermore, the Khazars are also mentioned by the seventh-century historian Kałankatuats'i in II.I: 'At that time news came to Shabuh II (AD 309-379) that the Khazars had burst through the Chora Gate and were invading the south.' But, unlike the certitude of Toumanoff, Thomson and others, I cannot insist that the invasions of Armenia at the end of the second century were that of the Khazars mixed with the Alans since no supplementary evidence exists except what Moses writes. That is good enough for me, since if one moves Moses to the eighth century then the names of the hordes may be familiar but not the details of their invasions and the name of their chief, Vnasep Surhap. But as I have indicated, the period under discussion is still ambiguous and hopefully this incongruity will in time be remedied.

The fifth incongruity

The fifth objection involves a section in III.18, as follows:

Moses knows of an Iranian advance into Bithynia. Only in the 604-629 war did the Iranians advance so far west.[16]

The section in connection with this objection says:

(Shabuh) entrusted Armenia to his friend Vałinak of Siunik', and himself pursued the Greek army. Arriving in Bithynia he camped there for many months, unable to do anything. By the sea he set up a column and placed a lion on top with a book under its feet.[17]

This objection does not require explanation, save to quote an extract from Ammianus Marcellinus (Loeb Classical Library, vol. 2, Book xxv.4.24, p515), which shows that the objectors have not done their

---

14.   John Man, *Attila*, Bantam Press, London, 2005, p112.
15.   Ibid., pp 73-74.
16.   Thomson, p59; Toumanoff, p331.
17.   Ibid.

research thoroughly (my italics): '... the threats of the Persians *which were soon brought into effect*, as they claimed everything as far as Bithynia and the shores of the Propontis (Sea of Marmara).'[18] The translator John C. Rolfe, adds that the whole story is told by Georgius Cedrenus in his *Chron. anno xxi Constantini* (p295 A f.), but it is regarded as apocryphal.

The sixth and last incongruity

The sixth (last) objection involves a section in III.46, as follows:

> Mosēs refers to two positions, *Presiding Prince* and *Comes*, in Byzantine Armenia; this reflects the position after Heraclius' victory over Iran in 629.[19]

The section in connection with this objection says (my italics):

> Thenceforth the Greeks appointed no more kings in their sector, *but the valiant Gazavon was the presiding prince of that area*, and the Greeks appointed counts as governors of their part of the country. [Mosēs III.46]

Thomson's translation betrays the influence of Toumanoff. The text of Mosēs nowhere says 'presiding prince', therefore the objection and mention of '*Presiding Prince* and *Comes*' is not valid but another scholarly invention, due to misunderstanding the Text, which says: 'but the valiant Gazavon was guiding the noblemen of those parts.' The veracity of my translation of the phrase is supported by the first paragraph of chapter III.48. I quote Thomson's translation with my corrections in square brackets (my italics):

> The Armenian princes [should be Nobles], seeing that the Greeks had not set a king over them and *considering it difficult to be without a leader decided of their own accord to submit to King Khosrov*. To this purpose they wrote him a letter in the *following terms* [terms should be changed to manner]:
>
> THE PRINCES' [should be Nobles] LETTER TO KHOSROV
> '*General Gazavon* and all the Armenian Nobles of the Greek sector, to our lord Khosrov, king of the region of Ayrarat, greetings.'

---

18. Ammianus Marcellinus, *History*, Loeb Classical Library, Cambridge, Mass., 2006; see vol. II, p515, or book xxv.23.
19. Thomson, p59, Toumanoff, p331.

We note Gazavon is a general and not 'presiding prince', which is also stressed in the sentence 'considering it difficult to be without a leader...'

*

The intriguing part of these baseless objections, so far as I am concerned, is the fact that they have been in force for the past 130 years. Each interested party, instead of trying to get to the bottom of the matter, has accepted the previous generation's opinions and has tried to add to the catalogue of anomalies or misunderstandings their own adverse views. We read in most of the criticisms that Mosēs does not know the Greek language or that what he knows is not up to standard. In the same breath in another section of such a work one reads that Mosēs has borrowed from Diodorus Siculus or another Greek writer, whose works were never translated into Armenian. Mosēs is occupied day and night in translations, as Łazar testifies, but what is he translating, Armenian into Armenian? Thomson says that Mosēs gives the impression of having higher education; in other words he is lying. Remarkably the same scholar calls him erudite, ingenious, etc. Mosēs says that he was sent to Alexandria for his higher education, a claim that is rejected by the sceptics, and yet we have a passage in a letter of Yovhannes II Gabelian (Kat'ołikos 557-574) in the *Girk' T'łtots'*, no. 45 (New Jerusalem edition, pp 210-220), which says: 'And similarly, those inspired vardapets and translators, who studied in Alexandria, and in other cities, have not added additional or new interpretations, and have not accepted or transmitted us.' Who then were these clerics sent to Alexandria?

In the *Girk' T'łt'ots'* there is the letter of Step'annos, bishop of Siunik' (New Jerusalem edition, 1994, Letter 89, pp 494-514), dated to *c.* 720, in answer to the letter of the bishop of Antioch, wherein the first part of the second paragraph derives entirely from Mosēs's History, Book II, chapter 74. The contents do not appear in Agat'angełos or any other historian of the fifth century.

Mosēs writes that the disciples of Mashtots' went to Constantinopole, which Koryun, one of the disciples and the writer of the biography of Mashtots', does not mention. The veracity of what Mosēs says is supported by the letter of Eznik (*Girk' T'łt'ots'*, Letter 4, in two parts, of the Jerusalem Edition, 1994, pp 28-29), another of Mashtots's disciples. How could Mosēs know such details if he was a seventh, eighth or ninth century personality? It should be added that even Eznik himself does not mention that their visit to Constantinopole was not sanctioned by the higher authorities, which Mosēs does.

The *Bazmavēp* of the Mkhit'arians of Venice, 1807 edition, has an article on pp 202-203 written by Fr S. V. Yazədjian, concerning a letter written by a certain Bagarat of Athens to his friend Suren of Armenia during the time of the Marzpans (AD 514-610). In this letter Bagarat reflects on the battle of Aram with Niwk'ar, the battle of Hayk and Bēl, the cemeteries where Bēl was buried and so on (my thanks to P. P. Kodjanian of the Mkhit'arians of Vienna for allowing me to have photo-copies of the article). I can accept that in those days people may have known of the battle of Hayk and Bēl and the activities of Aram. But from where does Bagarat obtain the name of Niwk'ar and the cemeteries unless he had studied the History of Armenians by Mosēs Khorenats'i? No other source mentions these names, not even Sebēos who has followed Mosēs's History for the first and third chapters of his own history (this fact demonstrates the futility of the efforts of various scholars to create two imaginary *Primary Histories*). The name of Bagarat sounds auspicious, and if my suspicion that he belonged to the house of Bagratids is correct, it may explain the whole episode, since Mosēs's manuscript was held by the Bagratunis. This brings me to the letter of Smbat Vrkan Marzpan (Bagratuni) addressed to the Georgian Kiwron Kat'ołikos (*Girk' T'łt'ots'*, letter 73, Jerusalem edition, 1994). In the third paragraph (p323) the following sentence occurs: '... there was within us *blood* [relationship] *and fraternity (ariwn ew harazadut'iwn i miji kayr)'*. Smbat Bagratuni died in 617, which is after At'anas Tarawnts'i discovered the history of Mosēs, thus meaning that he had access to the library of his namesake Smbat Bagratuni marzipan who died in 482, hence he has borrowed from the History the idiom *'ariwn ew harazadut'iwn'* created and made popular by Mosēs.

Procopius in his work *Buildings* refers to Arshak, the Parthian king of Mtsbin (Nisibis) in III.i.6 (Loeb Edition, vol. VII, p179), and quotes the name of his source as the History of the Armenians. Adontz claimed that this source must be Sebēos's History, which makes no sense as the latter wrote a hundred years after Procopius. Many have claimed that the source is Mosēs, in view of the fact that he is the only one who outlines the story of the Parthian conquest and the succession of Vałarshak as king over the great expanse south of the Armenian highlands, centred at Nisibis (Mtsbin). But the two names of Arshak and Vałarshak are not the same. In my study *The History of Bishop Sebēos* (pp 81-85, including note 16) I discuss this matter and come to the conclusion that the History of the Armenians mentioned by Procopius is the Book of Agat'angełos, which originally was very different to the hagiographic text we have at the present. Therefore I invite the reader to read my comments in *The History of Bishop Sebēos*, since I have not changed my position, irrespective of the case that I may be robbing Mosēs from a very important source of confirmation of around 560.

Yovhan Awdznets'i (Odznets'i, Kat'ołikos, 717-728) in his *Discourse against the Misbelievers* (*Chaṛ ənddem Erevut'akanats'*) on page 66 has a reference to the 'universally known Mosēs',[20] which I quote here both in Armenian and my translation:

> ... *ev kam or əst nots'anē, ev och' heṛi i nots'anē zmetsn imastasirats' ev zhṛchakealn ənd tiezers zter Mosēs; ork' ēin miangamayn aruestavork' t'argmanichk' ev ułap'aṛk'.*

> ... or with them some, who were not much far-off from them in time, great men of learning, and universally known master Mosēs. They were at the same time skilful translators and orthodox believers.

Who is this 'universally known master Mosēs' to whom Awdznets'i is referring in the early eighth century? How many such Mosēses do we know prior to the eighth century, who had been educated at Alexandria and translated or written such difficult but beneficial studies, which we can only guess at the present?

One matter that has intrigued me, and which still remains unsolved, is the period in which the History of P'awstos was written, as well as the writer's ethnicity and identity. These are important because most scholars are of the opinion that Mosēs had greatly benefited from this work without citing the name of its author. But P'awstos' history has the appearance of a compound document with no chronological structure and the language does not seem to be uniform. These aspects and some misunderstood parts of the work have given the impression that it was written after the middle of the fifth century, and that it is based on popular demotic tales which may be true. Still, the case remains debatable since such a conclusion is based on conjecture, irrespective of the case that this is the prevailing attitude of most of the scholars interested in the subject.

20. Y. Imastaser Odznets'i. *Yovhannu Imastasiri Andznets'woy Matenagrut'iwnk'*, Mkhit'arian Press, St Lazar, Venice, 1833, p66.

If we accept Malkhazyants's date of 470-475 as the date of the production of the manuscript it becomes obvious that Mosēs, while writing his own, could not have known of this history. My points above concerning publishing a work is just as pertinent in this case. Furthermore, the claim that P'awstos was one of the senior pupils of Mashtots' cannot be reconciled with the said date.

P'awstos's case has not yet been solved, and the claim that Mosēs has profited from his work is based on unfounded and wild speculation. Sadly scholarship has created such an intricate fable around the History of P'awstos that one can even accuse them for allotting a second place to basic down to earth considerations, such as when I read the explanation of the word *Biwzantaran*, I cannot help wondering which school of linguistics the inventors of the word had attended in view of Malkhazyants's explanation of the name 'Biwzantaran', with which, one notes, some scholars do agree.

To close this part of my study I should say a few words about the case of the 'Fourth Book' of Mosēs' History, mentioned by T'ovma Artsruni (p.122). It is well known that no such book has survived to our own times and we find no support for T'ovma Artsruni (Book 1.11) that Koryun, a fellow student of Mosēs, supports such a claim in his writings. I am of the opinion that T'ovma, or his editors, is mistaken in this matter, because the claim that Mosēs finished his History by the time of Zenon's accession to the throne of Byzantium in 474, or At'anas's identical claim mentioned above, does not allow the necessary time to write such a book. We have seen above that Łazar plagiarised from chapters 47 to 64 of the Third Book, which were written within the two-year period while he was living with Mosēs, that is some time between 471 and 473. After Łazar left, Mosēs wrote the last four chapters, numbers 65 to 68, and finished his Third Book and the whole History in 474. Between the date Łazar left and Mosēs finalised his History by writing the last four chapters of the Third Book, there is not sufficient time necessary for the writing of a whole new Fourth Book.

*

Part III

Some Explanations, Misunderstandings and Mistranslations

The Title of Book I

The title of Mosēs Khorenats'i's Book I is *'Tsnndabanut'iwn Hayots' Metsats''*, which Matkhazyants' translates into Modern Armenian as 'Genealogy of the Armenian Grandees' (*metsats'* literally means 'great ones), Thomson as 'Genealogy of Greater Armenia', and Mahé as 'Généalogie de l'Arménie Majeure', which has the same meaning as Thomson. All three translations carry the same sense, since a landmass, i.e. Armenia, cannot have a genealogy so the title refers to the leading noble houses who moved into the Highlands, settled and were living on the land, and the different interpretations do not play a great role in understanding the history.

The words *Hayots'* and *metsats'* are in the genitive plural and thus reflect the necessary grammatical agreement required by Classical Armenian. However, put together as a phrase, *Hayots' Metsats'*, they have the two meanings seen above: 'Greater Armenia' and 'Great Ones of Hays' (i.e. the noble houses). Therefore, the interpretations of both Thomson and Mahé are correct on grammatical grounds, and yet, on reading the first book and the initial chapters of Book II, one immediately realizes that the subject concerns the great noble houses and not the landmass known as Armenia, the habitation place of the Hays, nor the centrally situated city of Van or the Urartians (in fact Mosēs in his History does not mention Urartu or its people, even though he refers to the city of Van in connection with Semiramis, and once in the case of Slak' he expresses the view of not knowing whether he is a descendant of Hayk or the people before us). Judging from the contents of Book 1, the title translated by Malkhazyants' would be the most appropriate, particularly since Mosēs refers to Armenia not as *Hayastan* or *Hayots' Metsats'* but usually as *Ashkharhis Hayots'*—'The World of the Armenians'. It is one of the peculiarities of the language that *Hayots' Metsats'* can be translated or understood in two such different senses.

Khorenats'i makes clear the title of Book 1 in chapters 1 & 3 as follows (the translations are those of Thomson):

Chapter 1.1: We shall trace all the genealogies from father to son. Indeed I shall describe briefly but faithfully the origin and formation of all the Armenian noble families.

Chapter 1.3: To write the history of our nation in a long and useful work, to deal with the kings and the princely clans and families; who descended from whom, what each one of them did, which of the various tribes are indigenous and native.

This is exactly what the first book contains.

In chapter 1.29 Khorenats'i refers to *'Metsats' ew P'ok'unts''* which, this time, Malkhazyants' translates as 'Great and Minor Hayk' (Armenia)', while Thomson and Mahé give 'Greater and Lesser Armenia'. All three are correct. But, prior to this term Mosēs says that 'the king gathered (troops) from the confines of Cappadocia', which already covers the land of the later Lesser Armenia. This means that if *P'ok'unts'* is translated as Lesser Armenia, we have two odd readings: firstly, Lesser Armenia is repeated, and secondly, no such place was known at the time. What Mosēs is telling us must therefore amount to: '(The king) gathered the choicest fighters from both the Greater and Minor Nobilities, in addition to those from the confines of Cappadocia, Georgia and the Alans.'

Chapter 1

In connection with the request of Sahak Bagratuni, Thomson inserts his note 4, which says: 'Cf. 1.3 for Sahak as the supposed first patron of any Armenian historical work.' Looking to chapter 1.3 we discover that Sahak's request is for a history in the Armenian language 'from the beginnings of our nation up to his present'. The *Histories*, which were written earlier than Khorenats'i's such as Agat'angełos[1] and P'awstos, involved short periods corresponding in the main to their contemporary times.

Still on the same subject, Thomson's note 2 for chapter 1.3 comments: 'But see 1.8, for Vałarshak's supposed interest in the Armenian past.' His observation is correct since Vałarshak, the Parthian king of the Atropatene, was the first to be interested in the past history of the Hay (Armenian) people, and it was because of him that Mar Abas Katina wrote the oldest history concerning the Hays, a fact of which Khorenats'i is aware, since Mar Abas is his main source for Book 1. It appears Mosēs uses Mar Abas' composite work as a source, as all the other sources, and never reflects that it is different from the others, since it deals with solely Hay ancient history.

Chapter 2

Khorenats'i in this chapter writes about the genius of the Greeks and their translations of the literature of various nations into their own language. He mentions Ptolemy Philadelphus (285-246 BC) and repeats the old tradition current in his own time concerning the Septuagint, for which see Josephus' *Antiquities of the Jews*, Book XII.2.

Khorenats'i also mentions Berossus, the Chaldaean scholar, who in the third century BC wrote the Assyro-Babylonian history following the Babylonian cuneiform inscriptions. Both Mahé and Thomson say that Khorenats'i has taken the name from Eusebius' Chronicle—I have discussed this subject in Part 1, and see section 1.14 and chapter 3 below.

Chapter 3

In this chapter Khorenats'i bemoans the unscholarly habits of the ancestors compared to the literary works and the histories written by other nations, which serve as sources for enlightenment and knowledge of what has been achieved in the past. However, he does concede that there were records of the succession of the noble houses and records of the temples and their schools. Toumanoff states that the fact that 'temples and temple-states were found in Armenia and that some of them had archives and written records, presents nothing unexpected' (*Study*, p105, note 160). Thomson in his note 3 (p69) says that 'Mosēs makes much of archives supposedly kept in Armenia' and cites

---

1.   It is plausible that by the time of Mosēs, Agat'angełos' manuscript had already been edited by Koryun, since Mosēs does not borrow any subject from it that we cannot find in the present book by Agat'angełos.

Toumanoff, as above. But what Toumanoff says and Thomson insinuates are not the same, which indicates that Thomson is expressing an opinion but at the same time displaying a healthy attitude, making this known to the reader of other views. Mahé in his note 2 for this chapter adds that 'Mosēs ignores that Tigran the Great had instructed Metrodore *Misorhomaios* (hater of Romans) to write the history of his reign', which is something of which Mosēs is not aware—in fact Mosēs ascribed most of the deeds of this king to an earlier Tigran (Sakawakeats') of *c.* 560 BC.

Concerning the Temple Records, I must add here that my *Pre-History Volume 3* contains translations of the Kululu Lead Strips, which are the Temple Records from the eighth century BC. Such records do not stop in this period but continue with whatever script was available at the time, such as Greek or Aramaic, as highlighted by Mosēs in his History.

In his note 2 for this chapter, in connection with Khorenats'i bemoaning the unscholarly habits of the ancestors, Thomson says: 'But see 1.8, for Vałarshak's supposed interest in Armenian past.' I have discussed Thomson's notes under chapter 1 but here I shall add that what Khorenats'i says about the negligence of the ancestors compared to the literary works of other nations highlights the fact that it took a foreign king, Vałarshak, to initiate research and the writing of the first history of the Armenians by Mar Abas Katina, which confirms that Thomson's observations are quite justified in this case.

In his note 7 for the same chapter, he expresses the opinion that the '*Primary History* is earlier to what Khorenats'i writes'. In my study of Sebēos' History I have conclusively proven that there was no such *Primary History*, and the whole thing is an unfeasible scholarly invention.

Chapter 4

Khorenats'i says that Berossus, Alexander Polyhistor and Abydenus think differently and are not in keeping with Christian teachings and, in particular, with his own convictions. In their notes to this chapter, Mahé, Thomson and Malkhazyants' repeat the view that the names of these three individuals derive from Eusebius' Chronicle. The scholars themselves explain and ascribe various episodes found in Khorenats'i's history to Eusebius and are correct in most cases. However, Mar Abas Katina has benefited from the very same sources 400 years earlier than Eusebius; in fact they do not even believe that Mar Abas Katina could have been such an exceptionally rich source of information for Khorenats'i. In Part 1, I have shown that the two names of Berossus and

Abydenus were an inseparable part of Book I of the History—otherwise, there could be no names of the ancient Hay kings of Aram, which do not derive from Eusebius and who does not record such names. I have shown in my *Pre-History of Armenians* that the names given by Mosēs besides being all real could only derive from the Assyro-Babylonian sources, for which see my study of Mar Abas Katina in Part IV (these are the same names that scholars had ascribed to Khorenats'i's imagination). The third name, Polyhistor, may or may not have derived from Eusebius. I do not have any tangible data to prove otherwise.

Chapter 6

In this chapter Khorenats'i writes about various stories he has heard and collected in connection with the biblical accounts of the flood and the origins of mankind. Since these stories are not in complete harmony with the bible's narrative he decides to consult the Sibylline Oracles, in which he clearly places an unusually high faith.

In fact Khorenats'i states that now he will happily begin to present his account from his beloved and truthful Sibyl, daughter of Berossus. Thomson's translation of this part says: 'But now I shall be happy to begin my present account (quoting) from my beloved Sibyl, Berossus, who is more truthful than most other historians.' In his note 4 (page 78) he adds: 'The passage attributed to Berossus is based on the Sibylline Oracles.' When I read Thomson's phrase 'Sibyl, Berossus' I assumed the flawed presentation was due to a printing error (the Harvard University edition has many typographical errors). But Thomson's comments could not have been based on a mere printing fault. I considered then whether he had not understood what was written about Sibyl in the phrase '*i Biwroseann Sibylleay*'. This idea, too, was soon dispelled, since Thomson correctly translated '*i Skayordvoyn Paroyr*' as 'Paroyr son of Skayordi' (chapter 1.21), and the phrase '*i Mavrinea*' as 'by Martine' in his translation of the History of Bishop Sebēos (volume 1, chapter 44, p104).[2] One is left therefore with the conclusion that Thomson is not favourably disposed towards Mosēs and his History and so has no qualms over corrupting it.

Khorenats'i's text has '*i Biwroseann Sibilleay*', which means 'of the Berosian Sibyl', which can only be translated as 'Sibyl belonging to or by Berossus'; in other words 'Sibyl, the daughter of Berossus', which Mahé translates correctly as '*la Sibylle, fille de Bérose*'. Khorenats'i while studying abroad read or heard that the Palestinians called Sibyl the daughter of

2. R. W. Thomson & James Howard-Johnston, *The Armenian History Attributed to Sebēos*, in two volumes, Liverpool University Press, 1999.

Berossus, a fact confirmed in Pausanias' *Description of Greece*, Book x.xii.8, (Loeb edition, vol. 4, p437). As Pausanias says: 'There grew up among the Hebrews above Palestine a woman who gave oracles and was named Sabbe. They say that the father of Sabbe was Berossus, and her mother Erymanthe. But some call her a Babylonian Sibyl, others an Egyptian.'

Khorenats'i quoting from *Oracula Sibyllina* writes: 'Before the Tower and before mankind became multilingual, but after the voyage of K'sisut'ros to Armenia, Zruan and Titan and Yapetost'ē were the rulers of the world; these seem to be Sem, Ham and Yapheth.' The Greek version in Book III.110 (p55)[3] says: *'Kai basileuse Kronos kai Titan Iapetos te'*. It is notable that in writing Yapetost'ē, Khorenats'i's transcription of the name does not agree with the Greek original. A few scholars, such as A. von Gutschmid, have concluded that Khorenats'i did not possess good knowledge of Greek. Mahé remarks that Khorenats'i's Yapetost'ē is bad Greek, but he is unsure whether the fault lies with Khorenats'i or this is an ancient translation. Thomson says that Khorenats'i's Yapetost'ē is the Greek *'Iapetos te'*, which means that in transcription he has joined the *'te'* postposed enclitic to the name and at the same time has replaced the Greek *t* with the Armenian *t'*, which, as a rule, is equated with Greek *th*. Thomson is right in claiming that the enclitic has been joined to the name. We can also note that the Armenian manner of spelling the name of Japheth is with a *t'* whereas the Greek name is spelled with *t*, which Mosēs has transcribed correctly as *Iapetos*, which will not agree with the orthography in Armenian. It is possible that, in order to get over the anomalous orthography, he incorporates the Greek enclitic *te* to the name with a *t'* and armenicises the name, which from our present point of view is incorrect and unnecessary.

The following paragraph begins with a description of how the world was divided between Zruan, Titan and Yapetost'ē, but Zruan then prevailed and ruled over the others. Zoroaster, the magus and king of the Bactrians, *'who is (also king) of Medes'*, had claimed that Zruan was the original and the father of the gods. The phrase *'who is (also king) of Medes'* has not been understood—the nearest translation is that of Malkhazyants': 'Magus Zoroaster of the Bactrians, who is the king of the Medes.' Thomson's translation has: 'Zradasht, the magus and king of the Bactrians, who are the Medes.' And Mahé's translates it as: 'Le mage Zêradacht, roi des Bactriens, c'est-à-dire des Mèdes.'

3. *The Sibylline Oracles*, revised edition 1973, translated from the Greek by Milton S. Terry, AMS Press, New York.

The next paragraph describes how the sister of these three, Astłik, managed to bring about an agreement between them, which required every male born to Zruan to be killed, so that he could not continue to rule through his progeny. Some sons were saved and sent to the mountain called 'Diwts'nkēts'' to live. Mosēs says that this mountain is now called Olympus. Malkhazyants', Thomson and Mahé etymologise Diwts'nkēts' as 'thrown out, rejected', which is on grammatical grounds correct but sensewise rather confusing. I cannot find a logical basis for such a word and its proposed meaning; instead, in my opinion, the scribes had perpetuated an orthographic error by changing the last 'e' of the word to 'ē', thus completely changing the meaning of the word. The compound should have been *'diwts-ənd-kets''*, meaning 'the place where gods dwell', which is exactly what the gods do on Mount Olympus. The children of Zruan are sent to Olympus for safekeeping, but if they were rejected and thrown from the dwelling of the gods, the Titans would kill them. I wonder whether Khorenats'i had derived his information from Herodotus 1.56, which describs the 'move of Dorus, the son of Hellen, to the tract at the base of Ossa and Olympus, which is called *Histiaeôtis*, from where he was expelled (thrown out) by the Cadmeans'.

I find the next paragraph rather puzzling for I do not see any benefit deriving from it so far as the history of the Armenians is concerned. But the paragraph after it gives us the contents of oral traditions, which, as it is said, many villagers retell. Thanks to Mosēs we too are in the know, irrespective of the fact, as Mosēs himself says, whether we believe in it or not. The source of the story is one David, learned in philosophy, who declares: 'Old men, when I was among the Greeks studying, one day the discussion turned to questions of geography and the division of the races. The wise Olympiodorus (his teacher) talked about unwritten tales and added that there used to be a book about K'sisut'ros, which cannot be found anymore.'

The story etymologizes three place names in Armenia, the mountain of Sim and the districts of Tarawn and Tsrawnk'. The last two are implausible etymologies, and as it is stated, they derive from demotic tales of the *gusans*. The case whether Olympiodorus, a philosopher of Athens?, would have known these etymologies or not is not significant since it adds nothing to our knowledge, except perhaps in providing ammunition for the sceptic. Nevertheless, Khorenats'i mentioned the name K'sisut'ros in chapter 1.4, and in the present chapter he confirms that the reciter of the present story is Olympiodorus, and in chapter 74 of Book II he repeats the name of the same philosopher. This insistance and the consistency of what he says can only indicate that there indeed were such stories circulating. Readers may not agree, which Mosēs had already anticipated, since he finishes the chapter by saying that whether 'these stories are true or not does not concern us, I have only mentioned them so that you are informed'.

In the same chapter we have another tale, which has not been understood and therefore the translations are wanting. The tale is not important for Armenian history, but it does show how deep was Khorenats'i's learning. All the same, any misunderstanding here should be put right. The story says (my italics): 'The same Tarban dwelt for a few days on the borders of Bactria, and one of his sons remained there. For in the eastern regions they call Sem Zruan, *and the district is called Zaruand up to now.*'

Mahé has no remarks on Zaruand, while Thomson has notes 16, 17 & 18 for this excerpt. These three comments demonstrate the fact that Thomson has not understood what Mosēs is saying. In Note 16 he says that 'Mosēs implies that Bactria is on the eastern border of Armenia', and to support this claim, which is a complete misunderstanding, he adds "cf. the Bactrians who are the Medes" (a classic example of supporting one misunderstood sentence with another). On page 96 I had explained the latter misunderstanding as 'who is (also king) of Medes'. As for the present sentence 'Bactria is on the eastern border of Armenia', one has to read again, Thomson's own translation above, 'for in the eastern regions they call Sēm Zruan'. Mosēs does not mention Armenia, and the place under discussion is Bactria, which we know to be in the east, not bordering east of Armenia.

In note 17 on Sēm as Zruan, Thomson says: 'Mosēs equates Kronos with Zruan and then with Sēm: see above note 4.' What Thomson is telling us is that Khorenats'i in the first place has equated Zruan with Kronos and now he is equating him with Sēm. This is certainly wrong. We have seen above that Khorenats'i quoting *Oracula Sibyllina* says: 'Zruan and Titan and Yapetost'ē, the rulers of the world, which equates with Sem, Ham and Yapheth.' The name of Kronos has nothing to do in this chapter (this will be mentioned in the following chapter 7, in a different context). It is Thomson alone who equates Kronos to Zruan in his note. Furthermore, in note 18 Thomson continues: 'Zaruand, a district in south-eastern Armenia, see Hubschmann AON, p338'. Thomson is piling up the misunderstandings. While it is true that there was a district known as Zaruand in the southeast of Armenia, the subject is not Armenia as mentioned above but Bactria, which with its outlying districts was also known as Zariaspa, where one of the sons of Sēm, Zruan, remained. Zariaspa in Armenian usage becomes Zaruand!

Chapter 7

Kronos is mentioned for the first time in this chapter and is equated with Bēl and the biblical Nimrod. Khorenats'i also adds that Hephaistos was the first man of the Egyptians. Besides these sentences other subjects are also mentioned, until the following rather ambiguous sentence (Thomson's translation):

> To this bear witness the order of the Egyptian dynasties and the sum of years from the dynasty of the Shepherds to Hephaistos, in agreement with the Hebrews; that is, from the times of Joseph up to Sem, Ham and Yapheth.

I am surprised that none of the translators have offered any explanation against this misleading long sentence because as it stands it would imply that the Shepherds were earlier than Hephaistos and that Joseph was earlier than Sem, Ham and Yapheth. In reality Khorenats'i's original words would have been: 'from Hephaistos to the dynasty of the Shepherds and from Sem, Ham and Japheth to Joseph.'

Chapter 8

This chapter starts with the rebellion of the Parthians, the conquest of Mesopotamia and the death of Antiochus of the Macedonian dynasty. This preparatory beginning of the chapter does not derive from Mar Abas Katina, which Khorenats'i makes clear by adding the uncertain phrase of 'they say'. The chapter introduces Mar Abas, who will write the first and the oldest history of the Armenian people.

The Parthian king, Arshak, makes his younger brother Vałarshak king over Armenia in the city of Nisibis, and places under his rule the lands of Syria, Palestine, Asia, all of Anatolia and T'etalia (All these countries lie to the west of Nisibis) and from the Sea of Pontus (Black Sea) to the place where the Caucasus runs into the Western Sea (as the Caspian is called, which would be from the point of view of the Parthians) and Atropatene (these places lie to the northwest and east of Nisibis). Thereafter, Vałarshak sends the learned Mar Abas Katina, a Syriac versed in Greek and Chaldaean languages, to his elder brother Arshak with a letter asking him to allow his envoy to examine the archives.

Here we have three problems, foremost of which is the matter concerning the historicity of King Vałarshak and his rule over Nisibis. Khorenats'i has made Vałarshak king over Armenia and the first Arsacid, which is incorrect (but see 'The Enigma of Mar Abas' in Part IV), because at the time Armenia was under the rule of the Artaxiad dynasty. Nisibis, where Vałarshak was to rule, lay outside to the south of Armenia, and therefore it becomes clear that Vałarshak became viceroy over Atropatene, which had in the main a population of Armenians comprising Kadmeans, Gordyene and Mygdonians. The last two had migrated from Paeonia to these parts in the fourth and second centuries,[4] and were indicated by Khorenats'i as the people of the house of Kadmos (Kadmos derives from the old Assyrian toponym Kadmukhi). Khorenats'i writes about the role of Mar Abas Katina and his history, which is true and verifiable, as we will see later.

The second matter concerns the archives at Nineveh. Was there such an archive? In order to answer this question we must first think about Khorenats'i's sources and the manner of his writing and not expect modern precision if our intention is to uncover the truth. Sceptics have no interest in such matters, for them what is written represents reality, an attitude that leads them most of the time to the wrong conclusion as seen in their various interpretations in Parts I & II above. For the case here of the existence of archives the answer is an emphatic yes. But where were these to be found needs explanation. It appears Khorenats'i's source had indicated Nineveh, which we now know was incorrect, as it should have been Babylon. There are many such instances in Khorenats'i's history, therefore, when Khorenats'i says Nineveh or Babylon we must accept it as Mesopotamia or Assyro-Babylonia. In support of this claim see in this chapter the part where Khorenats'i says: 'He (Arshak the Great) killed Antiochus, the king of Nineveh', which we know was Babylon. Or, in chapter 1.11: 'The messenger returned to Babylon', which actually was Nineveh where Sargon II had his seat of government. Scholars who do not believe Khorenats'i should take note of what other writers have said about the Mesopotamian archives concerning the Assyrian and Babylonian histories, as we shall see later.

The third problem is the country name of T'etalia. We do not know exactly where this place was. Following the list of the countries mentioned to the west, the only place that might equate with T'etalia is perhaps Thessaly in Greece, which cannot be considered due to the fact

---

4. Strabo, *Geography*, Loeb Classical Library, Harvard University Publication, Cambridge, Mass., 1988; see vol. III, p363; vol. V, p319; vol. VII, p231.

that there are many other places in between Anatolia and Thessaly. Unless, of course, that Valarshak had learned that the original homeland of the Gordyeneans and the Mygdonians lay in the central Balkans, in which case Thessaly would border these. The other alternative is the T'etalian land, mentioned in the histories of Armenian writers. This place, besides being opposite to the geographical order of the countries mentioned, is far away and indicates Bactria, which means there are other countries in between. Also, the lands of this T'etalia, which would be established in the future as the kingdom of the K'ushans, are to the east of Parthia and under the rule of the kingdom of Arshak the Great, the elder brother of Valarshak of Nisibis. Thomson thinks that T'etalia is in the direction of Bactria and quotes Marquart's *Eranshahr* and the K'ushans of Elishē and Sebēos. At the time of Valarshak the Yueh Chi, the Tocharians, were just about arriving in these parts (the merging of these tribes produced the K'ushans), therefore the kingdom of the K'ushans was not yet established—this would take place in AD 60. This is discussed in my study *The History of Bishop Sebēos*.

One last point to be made is the fact that Thomson in this chapter translates Atropatene as 'Azerbaijan', which is tantamount to corrupting the text. Besides, at the time of these events there was no such place name. The northwest of Iran was only called Azerbaijan well after the Arab conquests while the Azerbaijan of the twentieth century, to the south of the Caucasus and on the western coast of the Caspian Sea, has nothing to do with its historical Iran counterpart, except to reflect the homogeneity of both peoples associated with the regions.

Chapter 9

This chapter starts with the letter of Valarshak to his elder brother Arshak the Great. The letter and practically whole of the chapter appears to be the imaginative composition of Khorenats'i. The second part of the chapter, which starts with the heading 'The Beginning of This Book', is about the book that Mar Abas found containing the names of the ancient Hay kings in a translation from Chaldaean to Greek. This information derives from Abydenus, who had also recorded the kinglists of various other countries according to Eusebius.[5]

---

5. Eusebii Pamphili, *Chronicon Bipartitum*, in Greek, Latin and Armenian, Mkhit'arian Press, St Lazar, Venice, 1818. Eusebius does not give the king-list of the Hays (Mar Abas had taken these directly from Abydenus; otherwise we can find no explanation for the names we have), which is understandable, since in the Assyro-Babylonian records they are presented as Hati and never indicated as Hays.

However the manner the second paragraph of the section 'Beginning of the Book' is written presents certain problems since it starts with 'in the beginning of which, he says, were Zrvan, Titan and Yapestot'ē' (*'Oroy skizbn leal asē zZruann...'*), which should have been the continuation of the first paragraph after a comma, if it was in connection with 'This Book'. A new paragraph cannot start with the word *oroy* (the genitive of *or*, a relative pronoun) if it is referring to the same subject just discussed. Thomson and Mahé do not discern the problem even though they provide the correct grammatical translations, whereas Malkhazyants' translates the phrase as it stands, ignoring the anomalus and ambiguous manner of writing, which is not the only one in the history. This can be explained in two different ways: either from interference early in the life of the manuscript due to misunderstanding, or it is a referral to the *Oracula Sibyllina*, Book i, lines 357-60, and Book iii, lines 120-26, on the impious plan of building a tower which aroused the anger of gods and a fearful divine wind blew scattering the construction.

In my opinion, this relative pronoun starting a new paragraph refers to the latter case, which was mentioned in the previous chapter 6. In other words the heading of this section plus the first paragraph of two lines are the total sum of information about the 'This Book' section.

The last two paragraphs again derive from *Oracula Sibyllina*, but Mosēs has composed these in his own style and added Hayk, Aramaneak and so on, which as he confirms derive from the book of Mar Abas' history inscribed on a stele. Thomson's note 6 on this chapter says: 'in Gen. ii there is no mention of wind, but see Eusebius', etc. Thomson is insinuating that Mosēs' source is Eusebius. It is true that Eusebius in his Chronicles mentions the historians Alexander Polyhistor, Castor, Cephalion, Diodorus and so on, and these historians do mention, as Oracula Sibyllina, the Tower of Babel and the 'wind blowing' but none mentions the names of Zrvan, Titan and Yapestot'ē.

Khorenats'i says that 'Vałarshak had part of the contents of Mar Abas' history inscribed on a stele'. This sentence may well have given the idea to Sebēos for the incised stele he mentions in chapter 1 (paras 2-4) of his history.

In the final paragraph of this chapter the names of Yapetost'ē, Merod, Sirat' and Taklad are quoted, which Khorenats'i interprets as Yapheth, Gomer, T'iras and T'orgom. For the names of Merod and Sirat', Carrière says that these are anagrams of Gomer and Tiras. I doubt whether such anagrams were made 1,500 years ago.

Chapter 10

With this chapter starts the history of the Armenians. So far, the narrative has involved the origins of mankind and various beliefs, which may not be of interest to the present generation but they were of utmost importance for the people at the time this work was written. Additionally, the preparatory beginning makes one feel, without so saying, the superiority of the Christian religion and prepares the ground for the intended narrative of the history of the Armenians, which starts with Hayk.

Hayk participated in the building of the Tower of Babel. Bēl, taking advantage of the prevailing conditions of the time, imposes his tyranny on nations. At the time Hayk, living in Babylonia, would not submit to Bēl and therefore, after the birth of his son Aramaneak, he leaves Babylonia for the northern regions for the land of Ararat in the Kashiari range with 'his sons and daughters and sons' sons, martial men about three hundred in number'. Hayk builds a house at the foot of the mountain and gives it to Kadmos, the son of Aramaneak. After this Hayk again leaves for the northwest for an elevated plain which he calls Hark' and builds a village and names it after himself Haykashēn. We shall see later that the deeds of the 'other Haykak' of the third name-list (1.22) have partly been ascribed to Patriarch Hayk.

Under this chapter and in connection with Aramaneak being the firstborn, Thomson has placed his note 4, which says: 'But in 1.12 Mosēs says Aramaneak was begotten after the confrontation with Bēl', and under chapter 12 he has placed note 1: 'But in 1.10 it is said that Aramaneak was begotten before the battle with Bēl.' Thomson creates an incongruity in this simple story where there is none. Mosēs says (Thomson's translation): 'Hayk refused to submit to Bēl and after begetting his son Aramaneak in Babylon he journeyed to the land of Ararat', and in chapter 12 he can only be referring to the same event when he writes: 'after living a few more years he beget Aramaneak in Babylon, as we said above.' Neither of these statements refer to a battle or confrontation but we know through chapter 11 that the battle between Hayk and Bēl took place after Hayk left Babylon against the wishes of Bēl. Khorenats'i has made it clear that the birth of Aramaneak took place in Babylon before the battle with Bēl, which took place in Hayots' Ts'or east of Lake Van, in other words Armenia. Thomson (and Mahé) is highlighting an ambiguity which is of his own making. Besides, it is obvious that after 1,500 years from the time this history was written scholarship in general has understood nothing of the real meaning concealed within the complicated composition of this story.

According to Khorenats'i, Hayk was the original and eponymous ancestor of the Hays (Armenians), therefore he derives the epithet Hay from Hayk. Aramaneak is his firstborn and Kadmos the firstborn of Aramaneak. Hayk leaves Babylonia after his firstborn, Aramaneak, and yet he has a grown-up grandson Kadmos and many sons, daughters and grandsons who follow him to the country of Ararat, where he builds a house and presents it to his grandson, Kadmos. The story is chimerical and to the present reader may not make sense, and so one has to pose the question how could a polymath and a philosopher write such a story? It is remarkable that scholarship has accepted this as legend and it appears that none has tried to discover why such an implausible account is given for the origins of the Hay people. It is also of note that Khorenats'i himself does not challenge the contents of the story and, like a good narrator, reproduces the parts found in the book of Mar Abas Katina and embellishes it up with features he has collected from oral traditions, a fact that he admits in the same chapter by saying 'this verifies the old unwritten tales'. He does not understand the concealed meaning of the story yet he instinctively appreciates the historicity of it.

When Khorenats'i refers to Nineveh, Assyria and Babylon he usually means the Assyro-Babylonian countries, south of Armenia. Hayk lived in the southeastern corner of Assyria in a place called Kuluman, but Khorenats'i's account has it as Babylon, because the unruly biblical Tower of Babel was built there when the mixing of tongues took place according to the story and the Bible. What we have here is the mixture of a true story written by Mar Abas Katina, and imaginative writing by Khorenats'i, based on religious belief and oral stories in order to prove the authenticity of the Bible. In other words here we have a composite work.

In Assyro-Babylonian history, Hayk's name was Eshpai → Esh-Hay = 'Ass Hay'. The ass part of the name was given to him because he was a giant of a man, brave and extraordinarily strong. This name was changed to Hayk, deriving it from the Armenian autonym of Hay, in the early Classical era or by Mar Abas, since the popular memory of the Hay people had a vague retention of the meaning of the word Hay as a giant or titan, which Strabo confirms,[6] that Pelagonia in the Balkans (the first settlement lands of the Hays after they separated from the Indo-European conglomerate) was the country of the Titans. Later, in the

6. Strabo, *Geography* (Loeb edition, vol. iii, p363, or Book vii, p40), where it is stated that the Titans were called Pelagonians, which was the first settlement area of the Hays, probably at the end of the third millennium BC after their split from the Indo-European multi-tribal conglomerate.

first decade of the fifth century AD, during the Armenian translation of the Bible, Hayk was equated with the constellation of Orion but at no time was he ascribed divinity.

Mosēs writes that Hayk was in Babylon (1.10) but is unable to give us the true reason why. For a cleric of the fifth century with an uncritical faith in the Bible, he makes Hayk one of the participants of the Tower of Babel, a connection which again spoils chronology but establishes the Hays in the Middle East of the 25th century BC. It is a historical fact that Hayk was living in Mesopotamia as an exile,[7] but not in the manner Mosēs describes. To confirm the event and know the reason why Hayk was in Babylon (this should be Assyria) is a comparatively simple task, provided one first of all establishes the identity of Bēl. Therefore, the question must be posed of how many Summerian, Agado-Babylonian or Assyrian kings have died in foreign countries and in battle. The answer is two, of which only one died in battle, Sargon II of Assyria. The other was Sargon's grandson Esarhaddon, who was taken ill and died on the way to Egypt. Therefore the Bēl of the story is Sargon II of Assyria.

Hayk's actual habitation was Zapkaka ($z \rightarrow$ emphatic prefix + *ap'* $\rightarrow$ 'palm of hand', therefore *zap'* = 'palm', *kiaka* $\rightarrow$ *kia* = 'life' + *ka* = 'there is', hence 'Palm-sized Place Where There Is Life'), which later, in Roman times, was known as Kiaka (*kia* = 'life' + *ka* = 'there is', hence, 'There Is Life'—the original *zap'* has been dropped), north of Melid and west of the curve of the river Euphrates. It appears that Sargon II of Assyria in one of his previous campaigns against Tabal (708 BC), when he built five fortifications on the borders of Urartu, moved some of the population of the village of Zapkaka to Assyria and settled them in the southeastern corner of the country, the furthermost point from Zapkaka.

With regard to the district of Hark' in the Manawazean lands, to the north of Lake Van, and the village of Haykashēn, Khorenats'i is right in giving us the name of Hayk, but unfortunately he ascribes the name to Ēshpai, the Patriarch Hayk, and not to the true Hayk recorded in his name-list 3 as a contemporary of Cyaxares, as we shall see in chapter 1.13. Due to this mistake, the date of the entry of the Hays into Urartu is by more than a hundred years too early and the parts of Armenia mentioned do not yet exist. In other words at the time of Hayk (Ēshpai) there was not a country by the name of Armenia; Hayk belongs to the end of the eighth century BC (Bēl's [Sargon II's] death falls in 705 BC), whereas the

---

7.   H. G. Wells in his *The Outline of History* (Garden City Publishers, New York, reprint of 1930), I think relying on the story of Hayk being in Babylon, makes the Armenian people Semitic, who acquired an Aryan language; see p240 & note 1.

entry of the Hays into Urartu falls on *c.* 588 BC, when they were called Armenians, i.e. 'People of Aram'. Also, the district of Hark' is directly to the north of the first house Hayk built, which he presented to his grandson Kadmos, from where, if one travels northwest as Khorenats'i indicates, one ends up in Zapkaka and not in Hark'. The ethnic names Hay and Armenian were exclusive to the Indo-European core that entered Urartu, but after the assimilation of the two nations the Urartians too were called Hay and Armenian.

In support of these explanations there is a letter numbered 129 in the Kuyunjik Collection addressed to Sargon II by his plenipotentiary, a man called Mannuki-Ninua, which says:

> Regarding the people of Zapkaka, of whom the king my lord has written, I shall inquire. I have seen where they go out and in. Send (thither). Now they have departed from the house of Dalta. They have entered into the city of Kuluman tribe with their kinsmen (and) dwell (there)... On account of the city of Zapkaka they have besought me.

The translator of this letter, in his commentary, says that Kuluman was a loyal Assyrian city, near the southeastern borders and Zapkaka apparently belonged within Armenian territory.

My explanation of this story is based on Assyrian history and inscriptions. Kadmos represents Kadmukhi where the Proto-Armenians had just one king named Dati.[8] He is made the son of Aramaneak, which confirms that there was only one Hay king of Kadmukhi, therefore in this country (representing the grandson) the Hays were not successful and for that reason it was not as important as Aramaneak, the son, where the Hays had many kingdoms. We also notice that Kadmos has not been allocated progeny which again confirms the singularity of the Hay kingdom in Kadmukhi.

The birth of Aramaneak, the first born, points to the establishment of multiple Proto-Armenian kingdoms in the country of Aram, since Aramaneak means the 'Circuit of Aram Country' (*Aram + maneak*). Mosēs' making Hayk the primogenitor from which the ethnonym Hay derives is not correct, since the Hay kingdoms of Aram country start 280 years before Hayk, which Mosēs does not know. Therefore, the true

---

8.　D. D. Luckenbill, *Ancient Records of Assyria;* see chapter XIII, §718. The third campaign of Shamshi-Adad V.

story that Hayk, after the establishment of Hay kingdoms in Aramaneak, together with his family and followers, escaped from Assyro-Babylonia to his abode is a true story told in the ancient manner of perpetuating oral history.

As a final word about this chapter, I confirm that the story of Hayk and his battle with Bēl (unaware of the king's name the story quotes the name of the supreme god of Babylon) has always been in circulation in Armenia, since it is an interesting story—this is confirmed by the translation of the Bible, wherein Hayk was equated with the constellation of Orion. The elders used to tell such stories to the children, which also served as a means of perpetuating the glorious parts of the past.

Chapter 11

This chapter is all about the battle between Hayk and Bēl and what happened after the death of the latter. Khorenats'i again has taken from Mar Abas the bare facts and dressed it up in his usual manner. Though there are a few mistakes in his account, due to the fact that he believes there was a Hark' district and an Armenia at the time and uses in his narrative place names which all belong to a period much later than the said battle.

He says: 'Hayk came to the edge of a lake whose waters are salty and contains small fish.' Malkhazyants' and most scholars have equated this with Lake Van and the small fish with the sprat (*taṛekh*). Hayk 'halted on an elevated plain to the right of a stream of water', whereas Bēl 'on the left of the water on a hill', which is usually equated with the River Euphrates. The site of the battle Hayk called 'Hayots' Dzor', a place to the southeast of Lake Van, and the place where Bēl was slain was called 'Gerezmank'', but Hayk 'embalmed the corpse of Bēl and ordered it to be taken to Hark' and to be buried in a high place', adding: 'Now our country is called Hayk after the name of our ancestor Hayk.' As explained above this should be the opposite way around where Hayk derives from Hay.

The salty water cannot be Lake Van, the site of the battle cannot be Hayots' Dzor since Bēl was not buried there, nor can the embalmed corpse be taken to Hark'. All these places are in later Armenia, which at the time of the battle and the slaying of Bēl were the heartlands of a strong Urartu.

According to Babylonian Chronicle no. 1,[9] 'in his seventeenth year

---

9. A. K. Grayson, *Texts from Cuneiform Sources, Vol. V: Assyrian and Babylonian Chronicles*, Chronicle 1, p76.

Sargon marched to Tabal' in order to apprehend or do battle with Eshpai (Hayk). There was a battle wherein Sargon was killed and the Assyrian army dispersed, as is inscribed on a fragment of Assyrian tablet which says: '(The king) went against Eshpai, the Kulumean, he was killed, and the camp of the king (dispersed).' The township of Zapkaka was to the extreme east of Tabal. If Hayk marched south from Zapkaka together with the Proto-Armenian forces of various city-states (Hayk collected all his sons), than they would have passed west of Lake Hazar with salty waters and the battle is bound to have taken place in Commagene by the waters of the Euphrates. Sargon's corpse was buried on a high place, which can only be the mountain of Nemrut in Commagene (Kummukh), where the princes of the country had been buried since immemorial times[10] and for which reason it was known as Gerezmank' ('Cemeteries'). This is the same Mount Nemrut (there is another one west of Lake Van) where Antiochus I of Commagene (69-34 BC) built his monumental burial tumulus.

Hayk embalming the corpse of Sargon and taking it to Hark' is Khorenats'i's own addition, the same as the site of the battle to the southeast of Lake Van, Hayots' Dzor, but the embalming may be true—after all Sargon was a great king. It appears though that Isaiah (14:4-20) does not agree with this view. He does not name the king but there can be no doubt that he is writing about Sargon, as not many Assyrian kings died away from their country. Another king to have died abroad was Esarhaddon on his way to Egypt when he was taken ill. What Isaiah writes is interesting: he starts with 'you will take up this taunt against the king of Babylon' (this should be Assyria, although at the time Sargon was king of both countries), and ends with 'may the descendants of evildoers nevermore be named'.

Chapter 12

This chapter, in my opinion, is Mar Abas Katina's masterpiece. At first sight it may look like an odd collection of names and a simplistic narrative, but it takes only a few questions and a little reasoning to discover how this old-fashioned manner of presenting a story has in it hidden messages that conceal the history of the Proto-Armenian movement into Urartu in the year 588 BC (this date is based on calculations from Khorenats'i's data). In fact, however, the whole story and what is hidden therein was beyond the understanding of Khorenats'i

---

10.   Seton Lloyd, *Ancient Turkey*, Guild Publishing, London, 1989, p73.

himself and has remained unexplained up to the present. In 'The Enigma of Mar Abas Katina' in Part IV the Battle of Hayk and the various noble houses are explained in detail.

The story tells us that Hayk confirmed his bestowal to Kadmos of the first house he had built and ordered him to live there. Hayk went to Hark' district and lived there until his death. After Hayk's death his firstborn son Aramaneak left his brothers Manawaz and Khor together with Baz, Manawaz's son, in Hark' and, collecting the rest of his host, moved northeast. Manawaz settled in Hark' and the district became known after him as Manawazean, Khor named the north of Lake Van after his own name as Khorkhorunik', and Baz named the lake and the lands to the northwest of it as Bznunik'. Aramaneak lived on a plain between the mountains (Ararat and Aragats), of which according to Mosēs the old mountain he called Aragats after his own name. After his death, Aramayis, his son, built a house by the banks of a river and called it Armavir and named the river Eraskh after his grandson Erast. Aramayis sent his son Shara north to a nearby fertile plain, which became known as Shirak. The second son of Aramayis, Amasia, lived in Armavir and named the mountain Masis. Amasia for his two sons, P'arokh and Ts'olak built two great houses and these were named after them P'arakhot and Ts'olakert. Gełam was the third son of Amasia, and he begat Harma in Armavir. Gełam left Harma in Armavir and moved northeast, to the edge of a lake where he built a house and called the lake and the district Gełark'uni, but the mountains Geł. Here he begat another son named Sisak, to whom he gave the greater part of his possessions. Sisak named his domain Siwnik', which the Persians call Sisakan. Gełam, returning to the plain, founded a house and named it Gełami, which name was later changed to Garni after Garnik, his grandson. Harma, the son of Gełam, after few years begat Aram, after whom all nations call us Armenians but the Persians and the Syrians call us Armenik, which has the same meaning.

From this chapter I have left out Ordunis and Varazhnunis and the river name Hrazdan as these belong to later periods and were inserted in this chapter by Khorenats'i. I have presented only the framework of the chapter, which, in my opinion, corresponds to what Mar Abas originally wrote.

It is important to note that in this chapter the various houses that are being established are patriarchal houses (*nahapetut'iwn*), some of which, towards the end of the second century AD, became dukedoms. Toumanoff does not differentiate the designations patriarchal and dukedom, which is another reason for his many erroneous conclusions,[11] which Thomson and Mahé cite and, it seems, they accept Toumanoff's conclusions. Additionally, some of Thomson's notes to this chapter are unacceptable. His note 6 states that the earliest references to Hayk are to be found in the *Primary History* and in Shirakats'i. No! The earliest reference can be found in the Armenian translation of the Bible, for which Thomson gives the correct references; and it should be noted, for the last time, that there is no such a thing called *Primary History* but that it is a scholarly invention (see my study *The History of Bishop Sebēos*).

Thomson's note 7 is in connection with the opposition between the Armenians and the Chaldians (Urartians), which is also highlighted by Mahé but who cites Grousset, 1947. Thomson cites three references from Xenophon's *Cyropaedia*, of which the first two quotations are wrong and the third is incomplete. The full references to the *Cyropaedia* should be Book iii.1.34 and 2.4 (Loeb Edition), besides, Xenophon's remarks concern a period of 180 years after the times under discussion.

Thomson's note 9 says that '(the name of) Erast is unattested, presumably Mosēs' own invention'. He cannot be blamed for this, since at the time of the publication of his translation the name Erast was unattested—see the name in 'The Enigma of Mar Abas Katina' in Part iv.

Thomson's note 12 says: 'This is the mountain perhaps known to Strabo as 'Masius'. The mountain name Masis (Ararat) is an Armenian creation and has nothing to do with the mountain range Strabo calls Masius, which, according to his description, was the name of the present Mardin Dağları. As for a possible confusion with Nekh Masik' (Sipan), this is not possible since Sipan is to the north of Lake Van. Mahé cites the *Primary History* and tells us that 'Masis was named by Marsiak and not by Amasia' (see *The History of Bishop Sebēos*).

Note 15 is in connection with the equation of Sisakan and Siwnik', a subject I have dealt with in Part ii. However, I shall outline here an abridged account as it is pertinent. Khorenats'i writes that Gełam granted the greater part of his estate to his son Sisak. The lands comprised from the lake to the east where the River Araxes descends to the plain, which became known as Siwnik' after his name. In chapter 14

---

11.   C. Toumanoff, *Studies.* Toumanoff ascribes to the Manawazeans, Ortunis and Bznunis an Urartian origin (pp 216 & 218), which destroys the precedence of the patriarchal system of the Hay interlopers, and he never considers the unusual land titles of Hark' and Son, which is bound to influence his conclusions of later events concerning these houses. The case of the extinction of these houses is not well researched and, in view of the scarcity of the sources, can only have conjectural value. Mosēs has only a line about it in Book iii.2, whereas P'awstos is more forthcoming (Book iii.4).

'the defence of the East was entrusted to the Sisakeans', and in Book 11.8 we find that 'at the borders to the east where Armenian speech ceases he appointed Sisakeans prefects' and that 'Aṛan, a descendant of Sisak, inherited Albania'. From these quotations it is obvious that the east of Armenia was called Sisakan as it was in the possession of the patriarchal house of the Sisakeans. All other districts under a house were called after their name, such as Manawazeans after Manawaz, Gełark'unik' after Gełam (see 'The Enigma of Mar Abas' in Part IV for a full account), Shahunis after Shakhu, Angełats' after Tork' Angēł, and so on. Therefore the lands occupied by the house of Sisak could not be called anything else save Sisakan in those days. But these lands at the time when Khorenats'i was living there were known as Siwnik'. The question is this: was a person of the stature of Khorenats'i unable to make the connection that the old Sisakan was his present Siwnik'? Was this correlation of Sisakan and Siwnik' a secret kept from the population of Armenia of the time? Does it take a Syriac, Zacharias Rhetor, to tell the Armenians for the first time about this? If the correlation of Sisakan with Siwnik' was not in existence in Armenia before the time of Zacharias, how could he have known of it? Furthermore, why should Mosēs not know of this correlation of Sisakan and Siwnik' considering that he was actually living in a cave in the same Sisakan/Siwnik'? I think the objection that Thomson, Toumanoff, Adontz et al bring against Khorenats'i in this particular case to prove that he was not a historian of the fifth century is but academic nitpicking.

Note 20 concerns Aram. Thomson says that in Genesis 10.22 the descendants of Aram represent the Syrians (Aramaeans). The revised standard edition of the Bible in English says: 'The sons of Aram: Uz, Hul, Gether and Mash.' There is no mention of the Syrians but the same reference in Josephus (*Antiquities*, I.vi.4) says that 'of the four sons of Aram, Ul (Hul) founded Armenia'. Hul must be the abbreviated form of Hulmeru known also as Qulmeru, Kullimeri in Assyrian and Gełimar in Armenian.

On the same subject of Aram and the appellation Armenian, Mahé asserts in his note 12 that: 'The Armenians call themselves Hay and the Georgians name them Somēkhi. Contrary to Khorenats'i's belief Persian Armina does not correlate directly with Aram.' First I will do away with the Georgian name Somēkhi, which signifies an inhabitant of the region of Suhmu, and suggests that this region may have been the place where the Proto-Georgians for the first time met the Hays.[12] Naram-Sin of

---

12. I. M. Diakonoff, *The Pre-History of the Armenian People*, translated from the Russian by Lori Jennings, Caravan Books, Delmar, 1984; see pp 104, 126.

Agade was the first to record the country name of Aram circa 2200 BC, and it indicated the southeastern regions of Anatolia. Proto-Armenians inhabited Aram from 1200 to 588 BC and when they entered Urartu, they were called Armenians, which means the people of Aram. It appears a similar epithet was given to the Semitic tribes of Sutu and Akhlamu, the forerunners of the Aramaeans, after they settled in southern regions of Aram circa 1200 BC.[13] The Aramaeans were the first to call the Hays *Arminaia*, followed by the Persian's *Armina* and the Greek's *Armenoi*. The word Armenian is thus used by non-Armenians since it does not exist in the Armenian lexicon. The Armenians call themselves Hay, an exclusive self-appellation of which few non-Armenians are aware. The correlation of Armina and Aram can be explained as follows: T'orgom is the father of Hayk; in otherwords Teg-aramah of the Hittites is the place where Hays lived and called themselves *T'orgomian azg* (the Aramaeans of Aram country acquired their name by living in the land of Aram—see what is written about Sutu and Akhlamu above). In time the name of the city became known as Tog-armah, and that is how it appears in the Bible. The form Tog-armah indicates that the second 'a' of the ancient name Aram, had already been dropped by the time the Proto-Armenians moved into Urartu. That is the reason for the appellation Armenian instead of Araminian.

Khorenats'i gives us three name-lists. The first is in this chapter and is headed the 'Generations descended from Hayk', the second is found in chapter 19 as 'The Agreement of the Genealogy of our Nation with Those of the Hebrews and Chaldaeans', and the third is in chapter 22 as 'The Order of Our Kings and Their Number'. We shall see lists 2 and 3 below. However the present list (list 1) and the list in chapter 19 (list 2) are inseparable because the names are interrelated. For instance, Gełam (Sulumal) of list 1 is the son of Vstamkar (Khelaruata) of list 2. Garnik (Sangara) is mentioned in list 1 whereas the king previous to him, Kaypak (Katuwa), is in list 2. The same is repeated in the case of P'arokh (Larazamasa) and Hrant (Khalparutiya). In list 1, we have Baz (Sastura) as a son of Manawaz (Muwazisa), but they belong to different city-states. Sisak (Kikki) is an older king of Tabal than Aramayis (Tuwatis), Amasia (Asatuwatimaza), the son of Aramayis (Tuwatis) in the list, is far older than his supposed father, and Gełam (Sulumal) and Harma (Wasusaramimasa) are contemporaries yet the former is the father of the latter in the list.

---

13. R. T. O'Callaghan, *Aram Naharaim*, Pontificium Institutum Biblicum, Rome, 1948; see especially p95.

In this first list there are further anomalies. The names Aramaneak (Circuit of Aram), Kadmos (Kadmukhi) and Aram (Aram country of south-eastern Anatolia) do not represent persons but are geographical names. Erast (Astir) is mentioned for the second time as Ara the Fair. And finally, the list is not complete because Tork' Angeł (Tarkunazi) is missing and it will only be added to the list of Hayk's generation in chapters 23 and 11.8.

At this point one might ask why these country names are presented as persons, which, sadly, Khorenats'i accepts as such and makes a fuss of it, particularly of Aram. This is the simply most ancient manner of perpetuating oral history and we shall see that all the anomalies in this chapter are intentional and not the result of ignorance or defective narrative.

The word Aramaneak means 'The Circuit of Aram (land)' and derives from *Aram + maneak*. Therefore, the country name of Aram is the same as the Aram of Aramaneak, where the Proto-Armenians settled after migrating from the Balkans. And the word Kadmos is the name of the country of Kadmukhi, south of Shubria and Lake Van, in between Assyria and Urartu, on both sides of the Tigris, with its main city of Khubuskia (in the future Kadmukhi would become the settlement area of the Mygdonian Proto-Armenians). The remaining names are those of various kings of various city-states.

The story makes Hayk the 'Father of the Armenian Nation', and yet he was not even a king but a chieftain, the only one who battled with the Assyrians and with the help of the Proto-Armenian city-states prevailed. Thus he liberated his people from the yoke of the Assyrians and became the 'father' of the nation. While Hayk was in Babylon his son Aramaneak was born, which means that while Hayk was in exile the Proto-Armenians established their city-state kingdoms within the circuit of the country of Aram. This is when Hayk flew from Babylon. Aramaneak had a son named Kadmos who was given the first house his grandfather Hayk had built. This means that there was a one-off Proto-Armenian king in the country of Kadmukhi, which we now know had the name of Dati of Hubushkia,[14] who lived at the time of Shamshi-Adad v (823-811 BC). The Proto-Armenians did not make much headway in Kadmukhi, therefore the kingdom could not have been all that prominent (this is the reason Kadmos [Kadmukhi] is made a grandson and a son of the Circuit of Aram), which is also reflected in the fact that Kadmos had no progeny.

14. See note 6 above.

Of course, the chronology is completely wrong. Hayk himself belongs to the end of the eighth century BC (the battle of Hayk and Bēl falls on 705 BC), whereas the first Proto-Armenian kingdoms in Aram start with the tenth century (see 'The Proto-Armenian Kingdoms' in Part IV).

List I appears to be enigmatic. Why is it that these names have been selected as the progeny of Hayk and none of the others in list 2 (chapter 19), who just as any other are the descendants of Hayk? The answer lies in the fact that each name of this first list has somehow been represented in future Armenia, as a city, lake, river, mountain, district or patriarchal house, irrespective of the fact that the names and the places named after them do not perfectly correlate. Therefore, if we select only those who represent patriarchal houses or later dukedoms from list I, we end up with the following: Manawaz → Manawazeans, Khor → Khorkhorunis, Kadmos → Kadmeans, Baz → Bznunis, Shara → Shahunis, Gełam → Gełark'uni, Sisak → Sisakeans, Tork' Angeł → Angełats' Tun. These are the original members of the Ostan Organization who, after prevailing in the battle against the Medians led by Niwk'ar Mades, settled on the periphery of Armenia, except for Manawaz, Khor and Baz who were left in Hark'. The dispersion of the Proto-Armenians completely surrounded the fallen kingdom of Urartu, whose forces, or rather the remnants of it, may have joined them in the fight against the Medians.

At the time the Proto-Armenians entered Urartu, they did so as a united force from various city-states, which were the branches (Ostan) of the nation. But the people of Kummukh and Cilicia abstained. Ostan (*ost* = branch + *an* = collective suffix) was obviously selected as a collective name for the Proto-Armenians of various city-states. Khorenats'i knows that the ancient patriarchal houses were known as Ostan, and he explains the fact in Book II.7.

I have stated that this chapter is the masterpiece of Book I. My opinion is based, besides all the explanations given above, on the fact that it describes the entry of Hays into Urartu as clearly as possible a thousand years after the event. In order to understand it fully one has to forget Patriarch Hayk, whose battle with Bēl took place over a hundred years before the events of this chapter. One must also forget Patriarch Aram and replace both, Hayk and Aram, with Haykak of chapter 22, and ask the question: why is Aramaneak (i.e. the people of the Aram country) all the time on the move until he settles in Armavir? The people of the *Circuit of Aram* (Aramaneak) after battling with Medo-Scythian forces enter the country en masse. The Manawazeans, Khorkhorunik' and

Bznunik' stay in Hark' whereas the remainder press on with their wanderings to the northeast, some settling around Armavir, while Gełark'unik' carries on to the northwest of Lake Sevan, the Sisakeans taking over Siwnik' and Shara goes to the north to Shirak (this is a reference to the Gusharids, a branch of Shahunis). The whole saga could not have been any clearer, indeed this is an impressive and true description, particularly when we consider that it is by word of mouth that it has reached Mar Abas or Mosēs. The other remarkable part of the story is that the Shahunis of Tsop'k', Angełats' house of Ingilene (they were in the west and did not need to take part in the migration) and the Kadmeans of Nisibis (see above where it states 'Hayk confirmed his bestowal to Kadmos of the first house he had built and ordered him to live there') are not part of this wandering since they settled in the western and southern parts of the Highlands and had parted from the incoming mass of Hays some time previously.

Chapter 13

This chapter and the one following describe Aram's wars. Khorenats'i does not know who were the kings responsible for these wars and quotes the name of the country. He presents the last war of the Proto-Armenians of the Aram lands as the first. The other two wars of Aram, described in the next chapter, are historical facts and are the deeds of individual kings around the middle of the eighth century BC, for which I will produce evidence; but this first war of the beginning of sixth century BC, as described in this chapter, is a collective deed of the combined forces of the various city-states of the Hays of the country of Aram under the label of Ostan, and there is no outside evidence in support of what actually took place. Therefore in this particular case we have to rely on a combination of what Khorenats'i says, the political situation in the Middle East at the time and circumstantial evidence.

The chapter has the heading of 'Aram's War against the People of the East'. Aram was hard-pressed by the nations around him and therefore he collected an army of 50,000, comprising archers, lancers and warlike men. He met the Median soldiers led by Niwk'ar Mades, who had devastated the borderlands to the east and *held his compatriots in servitude for two years* (this is an outstanding revelation, it is a pity that Mosēs does not understand it). In a sudden attack at dawn Aram slaughtered the enemy forces and captured their leader Niwk'ar Mades. He took Mades to Armavir and nailed him to the wall for all to see. This is the essence of the story, the remaining parts of the chapter are those of Khorenats'i's own graphic presentation. This however does not mean that he is inventing history; on the contrary, he is repeating from other chapters topics that he thinks are relevant to the subject of this chapter, such as in chapter 5 where he makes Aram and Ninos contemporaries. He is repeating in this chapter, in a slightly different manner, that Ninos was a contemporary of Aram and adding that Ninos had in his mind the memory of rancour with regard to his ancestor Bēl's death at the hands of Hayk, which is a reference to chapter 10.

In this account of the war there is no mention of the Urartians, and it is made clear that Aram was trying to clear the Armenian plateau from the Medians led by Mades, who clearly had at the time the command of his Scythian forces in additon to the small Median army.

In 591 BC Cyaxares, the king of the Medians, marched against Lydia. The war with the Lydians lasted for six years, ending in 585 BC. The Median forces did not pass through Urartu, irrespective of the opinions of a few historians—it was still an independent country under the rule of Rusa III (610-590 BC). In fact, after this Rusa there was another, Rusa IV (590-588 BC), who reigned for a very short time. Marching against Lydia, Cyaxares could not afford to leave an enemy, i.e. Urartu, even a weak one, behind his lines. To thwart any action by Urartu, he took the precaution of placing a small army under the leadership of Mades, the son of Bartatua (Protothyes), who with a combined force of Medo-Scythians was to attack Urartu and thus remove any danger to the Median main force in the west of Anatolia.[15] Mades subdued most of Urartu and destroyed the kingdom of Van, which is ascertained from various archaeological excavations in Armavir, Bastam, Karmir Blur, Ch'avushtepe, Kef-Kalesi and Toprak Kale.[16] Khorenats'i says that Mades occupied the country for two years, which is the reason for my dating Aram's attack and the Armenians' move into Urartu to 588 BC (the start of the Lydian war 591, plus two years for Mades's domination of Urartu and a little time to take into account the Proto-Armenian preparations).

The Proto-Armenian forces never fought with Urartu; on the contrary, it appears that it was the surviving Urartian aristocracy that had requested the help of the Aram city-states and had agreed to share their land with them. This is the reason for the spread of the Hays (Proto-Armenians) in the periphery of the country, leaving the Urartians all around Lake Van, except the north and a small part of northwest.

---

15. Diakonoff. On p93 it is stated that the Medes could not have left Urartu in the rear while starting a major war to the west of it.
16. Barnett, *Urartu*, p364.

Urartu remained an independent country[17] and, judging from the later migrations of Hays and their settlement places, one can assert that the Hays never impinged on Urartian lands. However, this fact is also the reason that we know nothing of Urartu from the inception of the kingdom up to the time of the discovery and decipherment of their cuneiform inscriptions as recently as the early twentieth century.

As already detailed Aram took the captured Mades to Armavir (Van was the capital city of the Urartians where Aram could not go) and nailed him to the wall. The northeastern part of Urartu had a great number of Proto-Armenians, perhaps more than 120,000, taken there by Menua, Argishti and Sarduri II, kings of Urartu, in the course of the ninth and eighth centuries BC, plus those of voluntary migration. We know that the patriarchal houses of Gełarkuni (the Melitinian Proto-Armenians) and Sisakeans (the Tabalians including Togarmah) settled in the northeast of Armenia, by the Hay colony already existing there as the uprooted people of Melid mentioned above, and this area became the most densely populated of the time. Therefore Armavir as the new capital city of the Hays was a natural choice and it continued to hold the same status well into the second century BC. However, according to the archaeological discoveries mentioned above, Armavir was one of the cities destroyed by the Median army. Remarkably the name Armavir confirms this fact, since it means 'End of It Ruined' (*arm* = 'end, point, edge' + *avir* = 'ruin, destroy, spoil', hence *Arm-avir* = 'end/edge of [the city] ruined'). Starting with Armavir, all the future capital cities of Armenia have been in the northeast of the highland (except for a short time Tigranakert due to political reasons), even after the assimilation of the Urartians. Because Armavir was on the northeastern borders of Armenia, the statement of 'Aram's war against the people of the East, *in order to free his kin from the rule of foreigners*' does not make sense, but it is perfectly understandable if we consider the large population of Hay colony of Uelukuni (so named at the time of Sarduri II—the same as Hay Gełark'uni), dislodged from the kingdoms of Melid and Tabal at the end of the ninth and eighth centuries BC. It is this colony of Hays that under Mades and his army suffered the rule of the foreigners. This explanation also confirms that the Hays' entry into Urartu had not yet taken place, and Aram's attack on Mades was the beginning of the widespread penetration. It makes it clear that the starting point of the Hays is the country of Aram, the eastern borderlands under Mades of the story is

17. Xenophon, *Anabasis*, translated by Rev. J. S. Watson, George Routledge & Sons, Manchester, 1894; see Book IV, ch. III.4.

Urartu and not Armenia east of Armavir (there was no half of Armenia to the east of Armavir). Now the whole affair makes full sense, and it will be in agreement with what exactly took place. Khorenats'i's statement was correct but, unfortunately, he does not reflect on it and he does not know that the *kinsfolk* of Aram for the past two hundred years prior to the battle had settled in lands to the west of Lake Sevan (Lake Lychnides), and had built the fortifications of Erebuni in 782 BC besides naming the land Gełark'unik' in the time of Sarduri II. If Mosēs had reflected on what he had written about Tigran Sakawakeats' in chapter 24—'extending the borders of our country and establishing them at the extreme limits of our habitation places in antiquity'—perhaps he might have realised that the 'places in antiquity' indicated the countries of Aram, Tabal and Cilicia and the *kinsfolk* of Aram was the existing colony of Hays in northeastern Urartu.

To confirm that Aram represents a country and not a person or leader of the Proto-Armenian forces, we have at our disposal two places and one personal name: Hark' district within the Manawazean lands, the township of Haykashen, and Haykak, a contemporary of Cyaxares.

Of all the kingdoms in the country of Aram, the one at Gurgum, that of the dynasty of Manawazeans, with the capital city of Marash, was the oldest and the most revered. In fact, the first and the oldest inscription we know of originates from Marash, and is the work of its first king, P'aṛokh 1, belonging to the beginning of the tenth century BC (the P'aṛokh of Mosēs' name-list of chapter 10 is the second king of Marash of the same name). The last king of Marash was Mutallu, who was dethroned by Sargon II of Assyria in 711 BC. However, the ex-royal family, as in the case of all the other city-states, continued to be responsible for the population of their city-state. It appears that the population of Marash comprised mainly of Proto-Armenians. Therefore, at the time when the Proto-Armenians agreed to help Urartu, they also had an agreement between themselves in order to divide the allotted lands between the various ex-royal families—in other words each ex-royal house knew exactly where they were to settle. The agreement of all these ex-royal houses was given the name of *Ostan*, i.e. the branches of the Proto-Armenian ex-royal houses of Aram, indicating the various city-states. It is not surprising that the patriarch of the ex-royal house of Marash, named by Khorenats'i as 'Haykak the Other', was to lead the entire force of the united Proto-Armenian city-states and those remnants of the Urartian army that were available at the time. The leading family became known as 'The Fathers', which means leaders, seniors, chiefs and so on, and for that reason alone the Manawazean district to the north of Lake Van became known as Hark', land of the 'Fathers'. A township was founded and it was named Haykashēn after Haykak, the patriarch of the house of the Manawazeans, who was a contemporary of Cyaxares. Khorenats'i is correct in his assertions such as that Hayk settled in Hark' and that Haykashēn was named after him, except that he ascribes all these to Patriarch Hayk, which means that a telescoping of the deeds of the two Hayks have taken place.

Thomson's note 2 says that 'the account of Diodorus Siculus concerning Ninus subjecting the Armenians and so on, is the basis of Aram's exploits' and he cites Markwart, Khalat'yants' and Ługasyan (yet the books of Diodorus were not available in Armenia and Mosēs, according to the same scholars, did not know Greek). Before answering this note I must state that the names of Ninos (Shamshi-Adad i or v) or the Armenian king Barzanes are non-existent in actual history. We know about Khalat'yants' unending and absurd quotations and it is disappointing that Thomson joins him. Diodorus in Book ii.i.8 mentions Ninus and his invasion of Armenia, there is no mention of a battle and capture of Barzanes. As for the capture of the Median king Pharnus, Diodorus writes that he and his family were captured and Pharnus was crucified. These facts render Thomson's reference citing Khalat'yants', or any of the other two scholars, rather absurd as the two stories have nothing in common that one may safely accept as similar. In history, for example, there are many such events when the captured king is either nailed to a wall or crucified. I discuss one such event in the following paragraph.

Thomson's note 4 quotes from the Bible (Judges 4.21) as a basis for Aram's nailing Mades to the wall (although in the previous paragraph he says that the story is an adaptation of the account of Diodorus Siculus ii.i.8). Well I shall quote here another such episode that has come down to us from the first quarter of the tenth century BC, which is much older than the times when the Bible was written. My quotation is from the oldest inscription deriving from the land of Aram and belongs to King P'aṛokh i of Marash (see above). Inscription Marash viii, line 6: '*CITY a-naia i wami mi kami za*' (in the view (*a-naia*, the Modern Armenian verb is *nail* = 'to look, to see') of the city, to the stone (*i wami*, the ancient *wam* has become *vim* and under Iranian influence *vēm*) I nailed him (*mi kami za*, Modern Armenian 'to nail' is *gamel*)—the full inscription can be seen in my *Pre-History Volume II*, pp 113-15. This quotation makes it clear that such punishments were routine in the ancient world and the Bible does not have exclusive rights to it nor do the Assyrians, Babylonians or the Romans, all of whom practised it.

A final comment on this chapter concerns Malkhazyants' note 53, which explains the name of Mades as 'the Median'; this interpretation is surely based on the phonetic similarities of the two names and is wrong.

Chapter 14

This chapter has a long heading, the important part of which says: 'The Fight with the Assyrians and with Payapis K'aałea and about Caesarea and the First and Other Armenias'.

In Armenian *Asurerēn* (the Assyrian language) and *Asorerēn* (Syriac/Aramaean) have always been confused, which we also see in the heading of this chapter and all the translations. An Assyrian is called *Asorestants'i*, whereas a Syriac or Aramaean is called *Asori*. But the fatherland of both is called *Asorestan* (Assyria or Syria); *Asorik'* has been used to denote the land of the Syriacs and refers only to Syriacs. The heading of this chapter should have said 'The Fight with the *Aramaeans...*', since the Assyrians did not have a god by the name of Baal-Shamin (Barsham), and the translators, knowing this fact, should have been more precise, particularly, when Mosēs at the end of paragraph 2 makes the affair crystal clear:

> Aram marched against [Asorestan] Assyria [should be Syria], where there was another wrecker named Barsham ruining the country and severely taxing the people. Aram opposed him in battle, slaughtering many of his men and Barsham himself. Barsham was worshipped for a long time *by the Aramaeans/Syriacs as god*.

Khorenats'i in his description of this battle is correct in all details except, as mentioned before, he considers Aram's expedition starts from Armenia, and so he writes that Aram chased Barsham through Korduk' (Gordyene) to the Assyrian (*Asorestani*) plain, which should be understood as the plain of Syria, where the battle took place. This battle with the Aramaeans (not Assyrians) occurred around the middle of the eighth century BC and was between the kingdom of Arpat of Mati'ilu and Carchemish of Havanak (Kamana). Both parties were at those days, inhabiting Aram. Khorenats'i does not know the names of the combating kings and quotes, in the case of the Aramaeans, the name of their god Baal-Shamin and, in the case of the Hays, the country name of their habitation, Aram.

This is a historical event to which Khorenats'i is referring. The war between Kamana (Havanak) of Carchemish and Mati'ilu of the Aramaean city-state of Arpat is described in Kamana's long inscription of Cekke (see *Pre-History Volume II*, pp 101-107). According to the inscription, Mati'ilu attacked and occupied the city named Kamana belonging to Carchemish, and had imposed taxes on the population; the inscription says *'pawa susu ta'* ('person imposed tax' – *susu* is the *susuni* of the later period) and adds *'misu na'* ('he was getting fat' – *misu na* literally 'he becoming meaty' = 'fat'). However, Aram's lancers did not kill Mati'ilu as Khorenats'i says. When attacking and burning the temple of the city, Mati'ilu suffered burns which proved fatal, as in the inscription 'it was the gods who killed him'.

The second war of Aram took place simultaneously in the west of Tabal, which might have been near Caesarea. The opponent in this case was Payapis K'aałea, who is known in history as Bar-ga'ya of KTK—the KTK, according to Diakonoff, stands for the Kaska people.[18] History and the long and damaged inscription of Topada describe this war in detail and relates that it was Bar-ga'ya who first attacked the Proto-Armenian lands in Tabal, which prompted Wasusaramimasa, Khorenats'i's Harma, to retaliate. Harma's inscription says *'The king of Parzuta attacked my city… With the double the size of his army I went to fight and destroy his kingdom, which made me famous'* (see this inscription in *Pre-History Vol. II*, pp 155-162). Unfortunately the inscription has lost much of its contents due to damage suffered by the stele, but we know the outcome of the war, since Harma lived for many years after his victory and executed this stele, which is also confirmed by what Khorenats'i writes, but we do not know whether Bar-ga'ya was killed or escaped. Khorenats'i does not know that this was one of Harma's wars and ascribes it, again, to the country of Aram as a person and makes Harma the Father of Aram, which means 'the leading king of Aram'. Also, Khorenats'i is of the opinion that Aram marched from Armenian highlands to First Armenia by Caesarea in order to fight Payapis K'aałea. All the same, his knowledge of the three wars described in chapters 13 and 14 and many other aspects of Proto-Armenian history leaves one awestruck, and wondering at how he managed to get hold of these true events after 1,200 years from the time they had taken place.

History tells us that Mati'ilu, who attacked a city of Carchemish in the south and Bar-ga'ya, who attacked Tabal in the north, had signed a

18.   Diakonoff. In connection with KTK, see pp 75, 87, and note 234, p173.

treaty,[19] which was obviously designed for a simultaneous attack on the Proto-Armenian lands in the north and south within a pincer movement, otherwise the treaty does not make sense, considering the distance between Arpat and Parzuta or the Aramaeans and the Kaska people.

In the third paragraph of this chapter there is an obscure sentence, which can be understood in three different senses: '*Ast yarewmuts sharzheal i veray* arajnoyn ch'oriwk' biwrovk' hetewakazōrov ev erku hazar hetselovk'.*' Malkhazyants' has translated this phrase as '(adding) on the first 40,000 infantry...', but it appears he was not completely satisfied since his note 54 against the translation of the phrase, which says that that is how he has understood it, but Emin and Stepanē have ignored the phrase. However, his translation of Aram adding 40,000 soldiers to the 50,000 he already had while fighting in the east gives a figure of 90,000, which is an impossible number even for the combined kingdoms of Tabal and the rest of the Proto-Armenian city states. Crucially, the text does not contain the word 'to add'. The French translation by Mahé says '(moving) against the first [adversary] with 40,000'. Here Mahé is following Minassian (see his note 2 under this chapter) and in parenthesis he adds the word 'adversary', which according to Minassian represents the Titan Payapis K'aałea. Mahé's translation is nearest to the truth while Thomson's says: '(moving to the west) against First [Armenia] with 40,000 infantry'. Thomson introduces in paranthesis the word Armenia, which is incorrect since the subject is not Armenia but the enemy of the west with whom Aram decides to do battle. I have discussed this subject in Part II under the Four Armenias. Here I shall just repeat that a comma is missing after the phrase *i veray*, where, in my quotation above, I have placed an asterisk in order to make it obvious. With this comma it becomes clear that 'Aram has moved against the west' with '40,000 infantry and two thousand cavalry of the first'; the first was in the east with a number of 50,000, which means that Aram has reduced his force by 8,000.

Khorenats'i writes:

After the war Aram appointed governor for the district a person named Mshak and ordered the inhabitants to learn the Armenian language. Mshak built the city of Mazhak (Caesarea Mazaca); for this reason the Greeks call the district First Armenia.

Khorenats'i's Mshak ('Cultivator') is the Mugallu (*mug* → *moz* =

---

19.   J. D. Hawkins, 'Neo-Hittite States', in *Cambridge Ancient History*, vol. 3, part I; see p402 and related notes in connection with the treaty of Mati'ilu and Bar-Ga'ya.

'progressed, mighty' + *allu* —> *alu* = 'affable', hence 'Affable Progressed Person') of the Assyrian inscriptions. Khorenats'i is right that Mugallu extended his authority to Tabal (Caesarea), where the inhabitants were all Proto-Armenians. The name Mshak given to this king is of great interest since it does not appear in any of the name-lists. Khorenats'i's name highlights the case that Caesarea part of Tabal was instructed by Aram to learn Armenian, and so the appointee governor is given the name Mshak, meaning 'Affable Cultivator', i.e. cultivator of people, a teacher. Against this the Assyrian name highlights the case that this king, while ruling in Melid and Togarmah, extended his authority to include western Tabal and Caesarea, thus he was named Mugallu ('Affable Progressed Person').

In the same paragraph there is a rather baffling statement which concerns the habitations of the Proto-Armenians in Aram. Khorenats'i writes: 'The Greeks call this area "Prote Armenia", which translated means First Armenia'. S. Yeremyan says that 'this "First Armenia" has nothing to do with the division of Armenia Minor and the western parts of Armenia Major.[20] It is only a reference to the first habitation places of the Armenians.' Yeremyan is certainly correct but offers no supporting evidence besides contradicting this statement with further conjectures concerning Arme Shubria, etc, which is not an issue here. A few lines down the paragraph Khorenats'i mentions that 'these uninhabited places were filled with people and thereby were called Second and Third and also Fourth Armenia', which further complicates things since Fourth Armenia was within the highlands and inhabited with Hays—see Part II where I have discussed the matter of the various Hayks (Armenias).

The important and final statement of this chapter says: '(Aram and his deeds) were not recorded in the original books, but as Mar Abas Katina relates, they were collected by some unimportant and unknown men from ballads and are now found in the Royal Archives.' This does not however state where these archives were situated. Fortunately, as seen above, the deeds were recorded in the hieroglyphic inscriptions but not the name of Aram.

Thomson's note 3 for this chapter is about Sisakan, which has been discussed in Part II. Note 4 states: 'Payapis K'aałea, not attested elsewhere'—I have shown above that Payapis K'aałea is the Bar-ga'ya of history and that Khorenats'i's Barsham is Mati'ilu.

Note 5 is rather involved. It concerns the sentence wherein Aram instructs the inhabitants of Western Armenia to learn the Armenian

---

20. S. Yeremyan, *The History of the Armenian People*, vol. I, Academia, Yerevan, 1971, p233.

language. It says *'usanel zkhoss ev zlezus'*, which Thomson has translated as 'to learn the Armenian speech and language'. Malkhazyants' has translated this as 'to learn to speak Armenian'. Both of these translations are correct, though Thomson's efforts are more loyal to the literal meaning of the sentence, and he is also correct when he says 'the "s" after *khawss* and *lezus* may be the first person demonstrative suffix', but his second alternative, that of *s* being the 'accusative plural marker' in this case is wrong. *Khawss ev lezus*, meaning 'our speech and our language', in this particular case being an idiomatic phrase, adds a kind of flair and emphasis to the story, and means no more than 'the Armenian language'. Thomson mentions, 'Grigoryan (Hay Barbaṛagitut'yun, p51) who takes up the second alternative mentioned above as an indication that various dialects were recognized by Mosēs'. Adjaryan exhaustively discusses this subject in *History of the Armenian Language* (vol. II, chapter 27: 'The Time of the Emergence of the Dialects', pp 362-439). Besides, *lezu* means 'language/tongue' and not 'dialect' for which the Armenians have the word *barbaṛ*.

Thomson's note 6 concerns the name Mshak: 'Otherwise unattested, he is Mosēs' fanciful eponymous figure for Mazaca.' We have seen above that Mshak/Mugallu was a real person and is confirmed by the inscriptions of Esarhaddon and Ashurbanipal of Assyria.[21]

Note 7 is all about the 'four Armenias' which has already been discussed in Part II but it will be helpful here to rehearse my argument briefly. The sentence says: 'This is the reason for calling the western part of our country First and Second, and Third and also Fourth Armenias.' Khorenats'i's History was edited and updated during the seventh or eighth century, hence the words 'and Third and also Fourth' must be later interpolations and alien to his language and manner of writing. The same interpolation has been repeated, but further down in the text where the scribe being more careful has managed to give it an authentic appearance, dividing it into two separate groups: 'First and Second' and 'and Third and also Fourth.' The question arises of why and how any writer, particularly Khorenats'i, who has written a great history according to the very same scholars who pinpoint this matter, might place Caesarea in Cappadocia next to First Armenia and in the same paragraph places it in the Pontus or Black Sea? These Third and Fourth Armenias derive from the Byzantine emperor Justinian's reorganization

---

21. Luckenbill, *Ancient Records of Assyria*. See §781 where Ashurbanipal says: 'Mugallu, king of Tabal, brought a daughter, the offspring of his loins, with a large dowry, to Nineveh, to serve as my concubine, and he kissed my feet.'

of Armenia in 536. Khorenats'i does not know Justinian nor of his reorganization of the provinces. The conclusions of Mahé, Thomson, Toumanoff, Adontz et al are completely unfounded in this case.

Mahé and Thomson, in both their notes 8 to this chapter, write about Khorenats'i's sources: 'Mosēs is ambiguous on the origin of his information about early Armenian traditions and reinforces his sources in oral tales by elaborate accounts supposedly drawn from written archives.' Here I think Mahé and Thomson are partly justified since the archives mentioned by Mosēs lack any sort of explanation to satisfy modern scholarship as to where, in what language and under whose order. In my opinion, in this particular case it is a reference to the archives of Vałarshak of Nisibis, which start with Mar Abas and includes stories procured by him from obscure individuals (for this complex subject see 'The Enigma of Mar Abas' in Part IV). These traditions are not found in the ancient histories of Mesopotamia written in Greek, something which Khorenats'i acknowledges.

As indicated above, Aram was the name of the country of Hay habitation and not a person as Mosēs has it. Therefore one will not find valorous deeds ascribed to him, nor a record of his name in history, which makes it obvious that the name and many deeds of valour ascribed to Aram derive from the ballads or the poems of the gusans. According to Mosēs such information about the past was collected by anonymous persons, which Mar Abas allegedly studied and placed in the archives of Vałarshak the Parthian of Mtsbin (Nisibis).

We should also examine the case of Aram from the angle of the sceptics, which is necessary to help reach an acceptable conclusion. Mar Abas went to Assyro-Babylonia to study the archives and sort out information about the Hay people of those days comprising the population of Mtsbin (Nisibis) and its surrounds. Having in mind what was said above, that history does not record a person by the name of Aram, one is bound to suspect the validity of what Mosēs says. We now know, and the situation has not changed since the time of Mar Abas, that the Assyro-Babylonian inscriptions or any other history written in Greek that has reached us are bereft of any reference to Aram, the patriarch of the Hays.

If we halt our analysis at this stage, as most scholars have done, then the apparent contradictions would force us to conclude with Thomson et al that what Mosēs writes is a fiction and that he himself is an unreliable inventor of history. It is therefore important that we examine the contents of the book of Mar Abas, which we know through the

History of Mosēs. Mar Abas tells us the ancient names and battles and many other events that took place about a thousand to fourteen hundred years before the time of Mosēs and about 450 to 850 years before the time of Mar Abas. It also tells us of events that took place after Mar Abas' time as far in the future by 350 years which clearly could not be the work of the original Mar Abas of c. 130 BC. We can only explain this anachronism by accepting that the book of Mar Abas was rewritten around 350 years after his time and that much new material has been added thereon. Besides, his manuscript could not have lasted to the time of Mosēs 600 years later. I hope it has now become clear that some time between the second to early third centuries AD the manuscript of Mar Abas was renewed and edited, and this editor added much new material (for more, see 'The Enigma of Mar Abas Katina' in Part IV).

Chapter 15

The historical facts concerning the following four chapters, 15 to 18, are completely mythologized and much has been added from the writings of Ctesias, which can be seen in Diodorus Siculus. Here it is conjectured that Ctesias is also the source of Mar Abas Katina, either directly or via the histories of Cyrsilus of Pharsalia and Medius of Larisa or other writers in Greek whose works have not survived. In other words, the facts have been veiled in myth, names have been changed and events have been invented. Therefore, in order to understand what Mosēs is saying and to compare it with the modern accepted history, it is important to know what each person involved in the history of the chapters 15-18 represents and the explanations of their names:

1. **Ara** is also known as Ara the Fair. He was the king of Carchemish (c. 785-770 BC), was the great-grandson of Garṇik (Sangara) and was known as Astiruwa (Erast-oga). Note that the syllables of Ast-ir have been transposed and become Er-ast. The *'oga'* (*uwa* → *oga*) ending of Astir-uwa means 'person, soul, being' and is a titular ending of names reserved for rulers. And finally Ira, the diminutive of Astir, has become Ara in later times.

2. **Ninos** is the Assyrian king Shamshi-Adad V (823-811 BC), however, most of the time this king is portrayed as Shamshi-Adad I (1813-1781 BC), perhaps the real founder of the Assyrian kingdom.

3. **Semiramis** (Sammuramat) is the Shamiram of the Armenian history. She was the wife of Shamshi-Adad V and mother of Ninuas. Much has been written about her, particularly by Greek writers,

however there appears to be no compelling reason to believe that she acted as ruler of Assyria after the death of her husband.[22]

4. **Ninuas**, also known as Zameses by Khorenats'i, is Adad-nirari III (810-783 BC) of Assyria, the son of Ninos and Semiramis, who was a minor when his father died.

5. **Kardos**. This is the epithet of Arayan Ara. The name Arayan Ara belongs to later period. In Proto-Armenian he was known as Yarairaisa (→ *yar-ira-sa* = 'Attached to the Thinker/Just'), which has become 'Ara belonging to Ara'. The epithet Kardos (→ *kard-os* = 'Sharp Speaker') means erudite, wise, sage, well-versed, etc. In the Proto-Armenian inscriptions there is such a reference to him in Carchemish A24, line 3.3, wherein he is called 'the learned person'.

6. In chapter 20 the son of Ara the Fair, the twelve-year-old, is called **Ara**, which should be Kamana or Havanak of Khorenats'i's writing mentioned in chapter 14 above.

7. **Zoroaster**. The Iranian prophet of the sixth century BC, who founded the Zoroastrian religion and was the author of the *Gāthās*. Zoroaster is the Greek form of Zarathustra.

Chapter 15 starts with Ara the Fair becoming king a few years before the death of Ninos. In fact Ara was possibly not even born when Ninos died. Ara was the great-grandson of Sangara (Garnik) whose death may have occurred in the forties of the ninth century. After Sangara there was an intermediate period. It may be that Ara was a young prince in the eighties of the eighth century. We know from the inscription of Ilapikasa ('Attacker and Smasher of States') of Körkün that he had to fight for the throne (Ilapikasa says 'when my father, Azina ['The Fiery'], was ruler he supplied soldiers to Astiru for his struggle for the throne'—line A3), which was his legitimate right, but we do not know who comprised the opposition. It may be that the Hurrians of Carchemish were still discontent with the Hay rule of the city-state—after all, prior to the Hays the Hurrians were in power. The last Hurrian king was Ura-Tark ('Great Thunder') who gave the throne to his daughter and her Proto-Armenian son-in-law Suhis (*suhis* → *yoyis* → *yoys* = 'hope') at the beginning of the tenth century BC.

The case of Semiramis, her dissolute and lascivious personality and her desire for Ara is no more than a good yarn, which was told, usually by an elder, to an audience in a summer's night gathering of neighbours and

---

22. A. K. Grayson, 'Assyria', in *Cambridge Ancient History*, vol. III, part 1, 1982, pp 271-272.

children. I do not know whether Mar Abas extracted this tale directly from Ctesias, who is also the source of Diodorus Siculus, or he followed other Greek writers. Diodorus (Book 11.13.4) relates that Semiramis, 'choosing out the most handsome of the soldiers, she consorted with them and then made away with all who had lain with her'. It may well be that this theme was taken out (not from Diodorus who wrote his History after Mar Abas) and modelled on Ara who died young, which is again borne by the Körkün inscription, where in line A2 it says '*hati sa na manu[k] ha*' ('he died young', *hati* = 'expired', *manu* is *manuk*, 'young'). However Ara (Astir) did not die in battle but in the plague of *c.* 770 BC, which is confirmed in the inscriptions of Yarairaisa (Kardos, Arayan Ara) Carchemish A6 & A15b. The inscription in line 2 relates:

zi hawa za na pina hi nu ha a-sati.
since this breath (*hawa* > *hag* = 'breath' = 'person') due to that old (*za na pina* —➤ *hin* = 'old') disease with us (*hi nu ha*: *hi* the root of *hiwand* and *hiwandowt'iwn* = 'illness', *nu ha* = 'with us') expired (*a-hati* = 'did expire').

The same plague had travelled to Tabal where it also claimed the life of king Tuwatis (Aramayis) in around the same period, which is confirmed by Ruwas, the prime minister of the kingdom (inscription Kululu I). It is notable that Ara the Fair of this story is the father of Kamana (Havanak) of Carchemish who fought with Barsham, as we have seen in chapter 14 above.

Thomson in his note 4 says: 'The derivation of Ayrarat from Aray is Mosēs' own fancy.' This conclusion is wrong since the district name had derived from Aray long before Khorenats'i. When the Proto-Armenian names of the generation of Hayk (see chapter 12 above) were being recomposed in Classical Armenian around the end of the second or early third centuries, such unviable etymologies were ascribed to them on purpose, as we have seen.

In note 6 to this chapter Thomson confirms that *vernatun* means 'upper chamber' and he also knows that *tanisn* (Modern Armenian *tanik'*) is 'roof', and yet he translates, just as Mahé, '*i vernatann aparanits*' as 'on the roof of her palace'—the excuse being that P'awstos in v.36 has a parallel to this in 'Mushel is placed on the roof of a tower'. Semiramis' intention is to keep Ara's corpse in a secret place away from watchful eyes and not to expose it to the view of the people by placing it on the roof of her palace.

The story of Ara and Shamiram also appears in Sebēos' History.

Mahé believes that Sebēos' source is the *Primary History* and yet no such history exists. Instead Sebēos has followed Khorenats'i, which may also be deduced from the verbatim sentences and phrases he has used (see Part iv, 'Ara the Fair', note 2).

Chapter 16

Practically the entire chapter is taken up with Semiramis' building of the city of Van, a palace and diverting rivers etc. A similar description, though far more detailed, is to be found in Diodorus Siculus' account of the building of Babylon by Semiramis in Book ii.7-9, which Diodorus ascribes to Ctesias. Van existed much earlier than Shamshi-Adad or Semiramis, and was the capital city of Urartu. It appears that Mar Abas had taken the idea from what Ctesias had written, which Khorenats'i, taking the basic information from Mar Abas, embellishes it in his usual manner. In reality our ancient writers and the entire world up to the end of the nineteenth century knew nothing concerning the Urartians (this matter has been explained in *Pre-History Volume 1*), with the exception of Khorenats'i's remarks that when Hayk settled in the plateau there were other people spread about the country, and his inability to decide whether Slak Słkuni was a descendant of Hayk or belonged to those prior inhabitants (ii.8). However, by the fifth century AD, the Armenians knew of the existence of the city of Van and the various rock inscriptions in cuneiform. These inscriptions of the monarchs of Urartu are ascribed to Semiramis, though some of them are older than her reign and others later, which shows how little the Armenians knew of Urartu and related matters. It is possible that various stories were in circulation in the Armenia of Classical times, since it is unlikely that Khorenats'i himself would have invented all the details he describes.

Chapter 17

In this chapter Khorenats'i writes about Semiramis having her summer holidays in Armenia, while entrusting Zoroaster with the running of her government. This is a fiction Khorenats'i has acquired from various Greek writers. At the time of Semiramis there was no Zoroaster—it would take another century or so until his birth. It is notable that he is called 'Magus', an epithet that belongs to the third-second centuries BC when the Greek and Iranian commentators connected the name Zoroaster with Western. Iran and thus created a false continuity from Zoroaster to the Magi.

At the end of this chapter Ninuas, the son of Semiramis, kills his mother and takes over the running of the government. But Diodorus (Book II.20), quoting Ctesias of Cnidus, says that Semiramis turned the kingdom over to Ninuas and disappeared, having lived 62 years of which 42 were as reigning monarch of Assyria. The whole story makes a good read and shows how Khorenats'i was misguided by the Greek and Iranian authors, since what the Greek and Iranian authors had written also found its confirmation in the local oral stories circulating during his time in Armenia.

Chapter 19

Khorenats'i starts this chapter with the words: 'Putting everything in order, I shall expound to you in this book the greatest men and ancestors of our nation.' The main theme of the chapter is the name-list of the ancestors, which he will be taking from the book of Mar Abas Katina, as there is no other source he can turn to. His phrase 'putting everything in order' is a reference to Eusebius. From Eusebius he took the names of the Hebrew patriarchs starting with Isaac, the son of Abraham, and the names of the Chaldaeans (and Assyrians), after Ninuas, down to Sardanapalos, 'which are arranged and exactitude is assured, or almost so'. The last phrase 'or almost so' is a reference to his own correlation of the Hay names taken from Mar Abas with those arranged by Eusebius, since he is not one hundred percent sure of his own exactitude. Of course, the arrangement of Eusebius is erroneous, but Khorenats'i does not know that and shows great faith in this work. As for the names of the ancestors taken from Mar Abas, these are all correct, except for a couple of instances of repetition, but the order in which they have been placed is completely wrong. As mentioned above, there are good reasons for this arrangement but even this does not justify the chronological and dynastic mistakes. All the same, weighing up the information and analyzing the names of the Proto-Armenian ancestors, one is awestruck by the veracity of what Khorenats'i writes.

In this chapter it becomes clear that Khorenats'i's Ninos is Shamshi-adad I, Semiramis his wife and Ninuas his son. The confirmation of this wrong chronology derives from the sentence: 'At the time of Ninuas the days of Abraham came to an end.' This statement is correct so far as the times of Shamshi-adad I and Abraham are concerned. But since Semiramis was the wife of Shamshi-adad V at the end of the ninth century BC, it is clear that the story is linked to the Bible which, again, spoils the chronology relating to the Hay people and their leaders, and proves a telescoping of the times of Shamshi-adad I and V, particularly, when in the name-list the Hebrew patriarchs start with Isaac, the son of Abraham.[23]

The seventh name of the list of Hebrews is that of Joshua. Khorenats'i says that it was at the time of Joshua that the Canaanites parted for Libya and that one of their princes, the honourable K'ananidas, came to Armenia. Furthermore, he adds that the Armenian king Sur was a contemporary of Joshua. We have seen that Shamshi-adad first belonged to the end of nineteenth century BC, and the Biblical tradition places Joshua to the end of the fifteenth century BC. Also, according to Classical tradition, the Phoenicians from Tyre founded Auza in Libya (the whereabouts of this city is not known) in the first half of the ninth century BC. The death of the Proto-Armenian Sur (meaning 'Sharp/Sword') of Kinalua in Unqi belongs to the early second half of the ninth century BC—the last two dates correlate. In Armenian, Joshua is written as *Hesu* and Jehu is written as *Heu*. If one eliminates the '*s*' of *Hesu*, obviously one ends up with *Heu*, who, according to biblical tradition, belongs to the first half of the ninth century BC. This matter of one single letter shows how things can change due to carelessness. Heu and the Proto-Armenian Sur were contemporaries, and it was during their era that the Phoenicians founded their outpost Auza, which was earlier than Carthage but more than two hundred years later than the founding of their first outposts Cadiz in Spain and Utica in Tunisia.

On chronological grounds the arrival of K'ananidas in Armenia is not possible, but it would make sense if he had moved to one of the Proto-Armenian city-states of the time and then his progeny moved to Urartu together with the Proto-Armenians. The same reason, that there was not an Armenia in his time, would preclude Sur.

The Armenian name-list starts with Ara, the son of Ara the Fair. We know the names of Ara the Fair's (Astir) sons through inscription Carchemish A7 and there is no one named Ara. In fact the Ara and the Havanak (Kamana) of Khorenats'i are the same person, which means that in this particular case there is a repetition, and the same person has been recorded under two different names. The same applies to Haykak who is also mentioned as Arnak, while Baz of the first Haykid list is the Bazuk of this list.

After the name of Zarmayr Khorenats'i offers the note that he was

23. Moses' greatest chronologically incorrect decision occurs at the beginning of Book 1, chapter 1, where he states that 'he will begin his history from where the Church Fathers have done', which means he will link the Proto-Armenian history to the Bible. We now appreciate that he could not have done otherwise since he was a devout cleric with no other sources available to him.

sent to Troy by Tewtamus, king of Assyria, with the Ethiopian army and there was killed. This is another of the enigmatic stories written by Ctesias and reproduced by Diodorus Siculus (11.22). The Assyrians never had a king by the name of Tewtamus who, in the *Iliad* of Homer (11.843), is the Pelasgian patriarch of Larisa. Homer does not mention East Ethiopians or their king Memnon (king of Susa), which we only find in *The Fall of Troy* by Quintus Smyrnaeus (Book 11).

In Part 1, I dealt with the subject of the Proto-Armenian names. I have placed a list of the kingdoms in Part 1v, which records all the names and dynasties as well as explaining the meanings of the names in the article 'The Enigma of Mar Abas Katina'. The two names of this chapter that need explanation are those of Anushawan and Skayordi. We shall see the first in the next chapter and the latter in chapter 21.

Chapter 20

The substance of this short chapter is partly correct on historical grounds, but the names have been changed and additional material appears to have been added. Khorenats'i writes: 'Semiramis called the son of Ara the Fair after his father Ara, who was twelve years old when his father died.' The true story is that Astir (Erast, Ara the Fair) died young and at that time his eldest son Kamana (Havanak) was twelve years old. The hieroglyphic inscriptions confirm this and additionally illustrate in relief Yarairaisa (Kardos or Arayan Ara), the chief minister of the time, leading the youngster Kamana (Havanak) by the hand to the temple to be crowned.

The final sentence of the first paragraph is enigmatic: 'They say of him that he (young Ara or Kamana) died in the war together with Semiramis' *(Ara merani ənd Shamiramay i paterazmin)*. Thomson and Mahé translate the phrase as 'died in war against Semiram' which, in my opinion, is wrong. In this case the *'ənd'* preposition has the sense of 'together, conjointly' (Nor Bargirk' Haykazean) and so Malkhazyants' translation of 'died in the war together with Shamiram' is correct.

Khorenats'i continues by quoting Mar Abas Katina: 'Ara dies in the war together with Semiramis, leaving a male child ... named Anushavan, who was dedicated to the cult of the plane trees of Aramaneak *in Armawir*'. This sentence should have finished with the word 'Aramaneak'—the addition of 'in Armawir' (in italics) is either due to an interpolator or to Khorenats'i since the 'plane trees of Aramaneak' means 'the plane trees in the circuit of the land of Aram', which cannot be transported to Armawir. The reader will see from the list of kingdoms (Part 1v) that Anushavan was the son of Mshak (Mugallu) and had nothing to do with the dynasty of Carchemish, to which Ara (Kamana/Havanak) belongs.

The third and last sentence of this chapter, again, has a certain substance of truth in the story it outlines, provided that we change the name of Zameses to Ashurbanipal (668-627 BC) of Assyria. Khorenats'i says 'Anushavan endured Zameses' scorn', which would make sense if the latter becomes Ashurbanipal. In fact the Assyrians even erased part of his name from their inscriptions, and when Anushavan died in a palace fire, Ashurbanipal claimed that it was divine retribution for his sins against Assyria. The name of Anushavan means 'Without Memory and a Place to Rest'; because he died in a palace fire he had no resting place (i.e. tomb), which means he would have left no memory behind. The explanation of the name by Adontz, Adjaryan and others as 'Immortal Soul', deriving from the Zend-Avesta *'Anaoshō urvān'*, historically does not follow since at the time of Anushavan's rule of Tabal and Melid there was no contact with the Medians, Parthians or Persians.

Clearly following Adontz and Adjaryan, Mahé in his note 1 for this chapter also explains the name Anushawan as 'Immortal Soul' or 'One Who Possesses Immortality'. He adds that Ara, the father, had become immortal, thus a relationship may be seen between the two—this part can be ascribed to Mahé's imagination. Of course, we now know where these fictions derive from. Even Ara the Fair, the father of this alleged Ara, never achieved immortality, but was dumped into a well when his body started to stink. Is Mahé identifying Ara with Er, the son of Armenius of Plato's *Republic?* I know many writers have claimed that Er of Plato's writing was an Armenian—miracles never cease! The truth is that scholars of more recent times have expounded and elaborated the demotic tales, which are but entertaining stories, and thus have conferred godship on Hayk, Ara the Fair, Tork' Angeł and others. Such claims have no place in historiography, and it is remarkable that our source Khorenats'i never ascribes godship to any of the names mentioned.

Khorenats'i finishes this chapter with the words: 'It would be too much if we were to write all the acts and histories of the men mentioned above.' This last sentence refers to the name-list of chapter 19, which is important to know in order to understand the difficult first paragraph of chapter 21.

Chapter 21

The first paragraph of this chapter is badly written, and is very difficult to translate. I find the existing translations unsatisfactory as these are apt to give the wrong impression—the translators have understood the substance but their writings do not reflect the true picture. Malkhazyants' interprets instead of translating what is written, Mahé's translation is similar to that of Malkhazyants', while Thomson is more loyal to the text, which makes his version as vague as the contents of the said paragraph since he does not explain that the sentence refers to chapter 19. The sense of the paragraph is as follows: 'the last of those [Proto-Armenian grandees, listed in chapter 1.19], who lived in the time of the Assyrian kingdom, which had come down from Semiramis or Ninos, was our Paroyr, in the time of Sardanapalos.'

The last sentence of this first paragraph confirms that the destruction of the Assyrian kingdom took place at the time of Paroyr: 'He (Paroyr) gave no little help to Varbak the Mede in seizing the kingdom (of Assyria) from Sardanapalos.' This is exactly what history used to say up to the nineteenth century. However, we now know that the statement is incorrect in the case of Paroyr and Sardanapalos, who is also called Tawnos Konkoḷeros, the last two names represent Ashurbanipal (668-627 BC). At the time of the fall of Nineveh (612 BC) Sin-shar-ishkhun, the second son of Ashurbanipal, was king. The very last king of Assyria in exile, in Harran and later Carchemish and back to Harran, was Ashur-uballit. With regard to Paroyr, the Proto-Armenians never had a king with such a name. The meaning of the name is 'Par to Which' and has the sense of 'Par [a city, the later Misis, the Armenian Mamestia in Cilicia] to which [kingdom returned at the time of Skayorti]'. The phrase in the text says *'or i Skayordwoyn Paroyr'*, which means 'Paroyr born to Skayordi'. It is remarkable that Khorenats'i, or any other writer up to the present with the exception of Kaḷankatuats'i,[24] has not understood the sense of the phrase correctly. If one reads *'or i Argishtwoyn Erebuni'* ('Erebuni born to Argishti') one would understand that Argishti had founded the city of Erebuni, which is the same expression as that of Skayordi and Paroyr.

Skayordi's name does not appear in any Proto-Armenian or Assyro-Babylonian inscriptions, but we see his father's name, that of Ishkallu (Ska-aḷu), in the inscriptions of Esarhaddon of Assyria (see this name in Part IV, 'The Enigma of Mar Abas Katina'). Varbak is the Cyaxares of the Medians, who was responsible for the destruction of Nineveh in 612 BC. The Babylonian army was late in arriving and most probably did not see any action, irrespective of what Eusebius writes.

---

24. Kaḷankatuats'i, *History of the Albans*, book III, chap. 15, p31.

It is impossible for us to express a firm opinion about the 'four rhapsodies' that Khorenats'i mentions, or about the 'wisest of wise men', except speculate. If this wise man was David Anyałt' and the four rhapsodies were his epic history concerning Tigran (Sakawakyats' or the Great?) then the contents will involve later times.

The last paragraph of this chapter has not been understood, and each of the translators Malkhazyants', Thomson and Mahé have changed the contents and explained it as they think fit, which has nothing to do with what the text actually says: 'In the previous chapters we had blamed our ancestors' unscholarly habits, the same is the case here.' This sentence refers to chapter 3 wherein Khorenats'i censured the unscholarly habits of the ancestors. He adds that these habits have not changed and that the same is true even in this case. And he brings the example of Nabuchadnezzar's father, whose deeds were written down by the supervisors of the Chaldaean Annals. Then Khorenats'i adds: 'Since our own people did not think of doing such a thing, these [names and deeds of our ancestors] remained recorded in the latters (*mnatsin nshanakeal i verjinsn*), which has been erroneously translated as 'in recent times have their deeds been recorded'. The word 'latters' is a reference to the Chaldaean Annals, which describe the deeds of Nabopolassar, the father of Nabuchadnezzar, and, while doing so, their records also name the deeds of the Hay Grandees which, as Khorenats'i emphasises, remained in the archives of the Chaldaeans (the 'latters'), until the time of Mar Abas. Further down Khorenats'i explains that 'the Chaldaean, Assyrian and Persian archives contain the names and the deeds of our ancestors, who were prefects, governors and satraps appointed by them', which is the reason for their names appearing in their archives (the archives of the Chaldaeans). It should be emphasized that Khorenats'i is talking about the acts and histories of the Hay Grandees and not only their names, which Mar Abas had sorted and brought with him to Vałarshak at Mtsbin. It is remarkable how true are Khorenats'i's remarks in this last paragraph. Of course, the conclusion is that Mar Abas Katina's book is the first history of the Armenians written in Greek or Syriac, and that Khorenats'i himself is the first person to have written the history of the Armenians from the beginning up to his own time. Mahé in his note 7 mentions that Biwzandats'i and Minassian (1991, p290) correct the text and claim that these acts were never recorded in archives. Having read Biwzandats'i and Minassian (1991, 66.4-6, p290), I cannot fault the fact that their conclusion and the explanations given do not agree with the sense of what Khorenats'i says.

Mahé in his note 1 claims that Paroyr was the Scythian Partatua who fought the Assyrians in 674 BC and he cites Russell, 1987, p30, and Diakonoff, 1984, p91. It appears he has overlooked the fact that Khorenats'i is discussing the period 612 BC, the fall of Nineveh, and what has taken place 62 years earlier (which would make Partatua a hundred plus years old?) cannot have any bearing on the matter; furthermore, Partatua was not alive in 612 BC since his son Mades had succeeded him. I also do not agree with academics who discuss Paroyr as a person since no such person existed. We do not have direct evidence whether Skayordi did exist, but we may infer firstly from his unusual name of 'Son of Ska' (the name Ska as Ishkallu is recorded by the Assyrians) and secondly from the fact that his son Syennesis (Pachoych) is the next king of Par (Misis or Par, later Armenian Mamestia) in Cilicia, and he is one of the vassals of Cyaxares who took part in the peace treaty with the Lydians in 585 BC on behalf of the Medes together with Nabuchadnesser of Babylon.

Chapter 22

Khorenats'i starts this chapter by saying that he intends to record the names of our great men down to the rule of the Parthians while lamenting his fate that he lives during the reign of foreigners, whose names he will also record alongside those of the Hay kings. The names he lists are those of the kings of the Medes who, according to Khorenats'i, are contemporaries of the Armenian kings mentioned, which cannot be true, with the exception of Haykak paired with Cyaxares. The last four names of the Median kings appear to be in order, but, as indicated above, the correlation with those of their Armenian contemporaries are incorrect.

The Armenian list starts with Paroyr, son of Skayordi. There is no king bearing such a name, despite efforts to find a derivation from the Iranian. The next five names of the Proto-Armenian list belong to the various states within Cilicia, which I have shown in 'Kingdoms', Part IV. The next name, that of Haykak, belongs to Marash while the last two names, Eruand and Tigran, belong to Armenia proper.

The following sentence is ambiguous: 'But now I, living during the reign of foreigners, shall set forth the order of the kings of our nation alongside theirs.' The word 'foreigners' is an acknowledgement of the foreign rule of Armenia by the Sassanians of his time, yet he is not quoting the names of their kings but those of the kings of Media against the Proto-Armenian names in this chapter. Therefore 'living during the reign of foreign kings' has a dual meaning here. First of all it indicates his present time, namely Sassanian rule after the fall of the Arsacid kingdom in AD 428, and secondly it indicates a relationship between the kings of his present, the Sassanians, and those of the past, the Medians; in other words, both the Median and the Sassanian kings belonged to various Iranian tribes of Persia.

Thomson in his note 2 for this chapter says: '... the phrase foreigners is not of much help in dating Mosēs; it could mean Sassanian rule or Muslim rule from the late seventh century.' Thomson (as well as Mahé) has overlooked the crucial fact that Khorenats'i does not record any Islamic names against the phrase 'foreigners and alongside it the names of our kings' but the names of the Median kings, who are as Iranian as the Persians. Foreigners, in Khorenats'i's present terminology, could never mean the Islamic rule of Armenia which belongs to after the middle of seventh century (the first Arab attack on Armenia was in 640 AD).

The second paragraph quotes the famous appeal of Jeremiah in 51:27 (Thomson's reference is wrong), which says: 'Summon against her (Babylon) kingdoms, Ararat, Minni and Ashk'enaz.' Compare this with the Armenian version—'Command the kingdoms of Ararat and the band of Ashk'anaz'—where Minni is not mentioned because the next line 28 mentions them as the Medes. From this quotation Khorenats'i concludes that Ararat represents Armenia and that at the time there was a kingdom of Armenians, which cannot be supported by historical facts. Jeremiah belongs to the time of the fall of Jerusalem (587 BC) and the Destruction of the Temple (586 BC) by the forces of Nabuchadnezzar of Babylon. The event belongs to the same period when the Proto-Armenians entered Urartu and were poised to settle down in its various districts. Therefore at that time, since there was no Armenian kingdom, Jeremiah's 'Kingdom of Ararat' can only mean Urartu. The band of Ashk'anaz indicates the Scythian hordes and the kingdom of Minni is that of the Medes. Nevertheless, it must be pointed out that up to the end of the nineteenth century, history and Jeremiah's appeal were in agreement with what Khorenats'i writes.

In the list of the Cilician kings, after Paroyr, we have Hrach'eay, of whom Khorenats'i says that he was so called because of his shining face and fiery eyes. This description is absolutely correct since Hrach' means 'Fiery Eyes' (*hur* 'fire' + *achk'* 'eyes') and his Proto-Armenian name in the Assyrian inscriptions was Sandasarme, and so it has nothing to do with the Iranian *Frāch'ya* (there are a number of original Armenian names which, ignoring their derivation and meanings, have been ascribed by scholarship to Pahlavi due to either similarity of phonetics or transcription, e.g. Arbak/Urballa). Khorenats'i adds that this Hrach'eay requested and received a Hebrew captive, Shambat, from Nabuchadnezzar. I suspect his source for this information has confused various issues, and it is not possible for us at the present to solve the mystery. It is a fact, however, that Hrach'eay was a contemporary of Ashurbanipal and not of Nabuchadnezzar, and that he was never a king in Armenia. Since Khorenats'i originates the clan of Bagratunis from the said Shambat, it is important for the history of the Armenians to resolve this issue, which at the present appears to be impossible to do so, even though in the Bible, Nehemiah 7:59 in the Register of the Exiles, i.e. the people returning from Nabuchadnezzar's captivity back to Jerusalem, there is a name Pochereth-hazzebaim which the Armenian Bible transcribes as P'ak'arat' Sabayim. Therefore I suggest that we accept on faith what Khorenats'i says, since the other muddled-up idea from Sebēos does not make sense.

To this latter point we may also add the opinion of Toumanoff who prefers the ideas of Sebēos and yet derives the Bagratunis from the Orontids, making them of Iranian extraction. Scholarship has labelled Khorenats'i a 'nationalistic' writer and he is also accused of glorifying the Bagratunis since he was their bishop (see Bagratunis versus Mamikoneans in this part under chapter II.81 below). It has not been considered that he wrote his history prior to becoming a bishop, nor that a nationalistic writer wishing to glorify his patron would of all the choices available to him make the Bagratunis of Haykid origin, the highest honour he could bestow on them. In fact Khorenats'i, addressing his patron, states that 'some unreliable men say, out of fancy and not according to the truth that the Bagratunis descend from Hayk', adding the caveat 'do not believe such foolish words'. Mahé in his note 7 and Thomson in his note 9 express the opinion that: 'Mosēs is attacking the older claim found in the *Primary History* (Sebēos, p9) in which a local origin (from P'arnawaz) is ascribed to the Bagratunis.' In my *History of Bishop Sebēos*, however, I conclusively show that there were no such *Primary Histories*. Sebēos' first chapter is paradoxical and seriously flawed and the P'arnawaz of Khorenats'i is a different person (third name of the list of this chapter) and belongs to Cilicia of the ninth century BC. In fact, Khorenats'i could not have known of Sebēos (the latter follows the former's history) and the phrase 'unreliable men' is in the plural.

The other Haykak of this list was the chief patriarch of Marash, as mentioned above. It appears his deeds have been ascribed to patriarch Hayk, the slayer of Bēl, and to patriarch Aram as early as the time of Mar Abas Katina or even earlier, since Khorenats'i writes nothing about Haykak. In reality he was the leader of the Proto-Armenian forces that entered Urartu and fought with the forces of the Medes under the generalship of Mades. His people under the name of Manawazeans of Marash settled centrally to the north of Lake Van, a township was founded or renamed after him as Haykashēn, and the district became known as Hark' (land of the Fathers, i.e. 'leaders'). Khorenats'i is the only source to write the story of the Proto-Armenian move to Urartu, their battle with the Medes and their settlement areas, and even the name of Haykak. Unfortunately, all these deeds and much more he has ascribed partly to Hayk and partly to Aram.

The last short paragraph of this chapter is corrupted. There has been a concerted effort by various scholars to set it right. Unfortunately their efforts still remain wanting. In my opinion, this corrupted paragraph should read: 'For I say that the later Eruand and Tigran (last two names of the list) from these (meaning the whole list of names) were so named, and hopefully, the time being not very distant, someone would recall their names' (see also chapter 29 below). Khorenats'i is aware that the last two are not indigenous Armenian names, but since they have acted as kings of the land he expresses the hope that some people might recollect the names, because they are not so far removed in time as all the previous names.

Chapter 23

This chapter starts with the name of Tigran, the son of Eruand Sakawakeats', as the ninth king of the Armenians, but stops short of any detail, which will be expounded in the next six chapters. The main subject is Sennacherim and his two sons, Adramelek' and Sanasar.

Khorenats'i says that more or less eighty years before the reign of Nabuchadnezzar the two sons of Sennacherim (704-681 BC) killed him and fled to Armenia. Our Skayordi settled Sanasar in the southwest (this is a strange claim since Skayordi in 612 BC helped Cyaxares and between Cyaxares and Sennacherim's death there are some 69 years) near the borders of Assyria. Ardamozan dwelt to the southeast of the same area, and, according to Mar Abas Katina, the Artsrunis and the Gnunis descended from him.

Khorenats'i is more or less correct when he says eighty years before Nabuchadnezzar, since Sennacherim was killed in 681 BC and

Nabuchadnezzar's accession to the Babylonian throne was in 604 BC. However, he is wrong when he mentions Skayordi as king of Armenia since at the time of the slaying of Sennacherim there was no such a country—the whole country was known as Urartu—although it must be stated that Skayordi's father Ishkallu was the ruler of Tabal more or less at the time of the death of Sennacherim, which makes me think whether there is a telescoping of the times of father Ska-alu and the son Ska-ordi.

The Bible records the affair twice (11 Kings 19:37 and Isaiah 37:38), but both times states that the two sons escaped to the country of Ararat. The Armenian version of the Bible in iv Kings 19:37 states the country of Ayrarat, and Isaiah 37:38 has Armenia. Josephus, too, mentions the affair in Book x.1.5. Besides these references Esarhaddon, the succeeding son of Sennacherim, in his inscription records that 'A firm determination 'fell upon' my brothers. They forsook the gods and turned to their deeds of violence' (Lukenbill, §501) and adds 'to gain the kingship they slew Sennacherim, their father' (§502) and 'they fled to parts unknown' (§505).[25]

In the Bible, the names of the brothers appear as Sharezer and Adrammelech. As seen above, in the first instance Khorenats'i writes Adramelek' as in the Bible, but a little further down the same name is written as Argamozan which, according to Malkhazyants', is a corruption of the name. I have my doubts about this claim, since the information of Khorenats'i derives from Mar Abas Katina, who in his turn extracted it from the works of Abydenus (Abydenus is also Eusebius' source, who offers the name as Ardumuzan, cf. Thomson's note 5, p112), which was based on Assyro-Babylonian sources, some of which have been quoted above. H. F. W. Saggs says that the individual is now identified as Arad-Mulissi and the Biblical name of Adrammelech is a corruption of it.[26]

According to Khorenats'i the houses of Artsruni and Gnuni descend from Adramelek', but according to Toumanoff they were descended from the Orontids. Toumanoff's writings are highly persuasive but regrettably in my opinion this work (*Study*, 1971) is flawed: the beginning is based on false premises and throughout there are many errors. Writing about dukedoms and precedence Toumanoff gives us some lists, of which table I (pp 223-4) shows 15 out of 64 princely houses as Orontids and none as Haykid. His table II (pp 226-7) shows out of 50

25. D. D. Luckenbill, *Ancient Records of Assyria*, see §§ 501, 502, 505.
26. H. W. F. Saggs, *Assyria*, Sidgwick & Jackson, London, 1984, see p103.

princely houses of the Arsacid period 12 Orontids but, again, none of Haykid origin. His table III (pp 227-8) shows out of 42 post-Arsacid princely houses 10 Orontids and no Haykids. Is Toumanoff writing about the Hays, the people who gave their language to the country and became known as Armenians, or some other country? What Toumanoff fails to take into account is that an organised system existed within Proto-Armenian society while they inhabited the country of Aram for 600 years, and that this organisation consisted of advisers, minor vassal kings, heads of cities and villages answerable to the chief authority of the kingdom, the great king (there are a few Proto-Armenian examples in the inscriptions translated in *Pre-History Volume II*, such as Sultanhan pp 166-72, Kululu II, pp 177-9, and Porsuk, pp 180-2). This system was still in place when the Hays entered Urartu and settled in predetermined central and peripheral lands and became known as the ancient ex-royal houses, which in the course of the second to third centuries AD, under Arsacid rule, were reorganised with the title of dukedoms for themselves and their descendants. Such facts negate Toumanoff's invented theories. Finally, as far as the origins of the Artsrunis and Gnunis are concerned, there are many additional reasons in favour of what Khorenats'i writes, which are more likely than what Toumanoff proposes.

The last short paragraph of this chapter is in connection with the house of Angeł who, according to Khorenats'i, descended from a certain Pask'am, grandson of Hayk (in Łukasean, no. 10, 1913, this name is Haykak). Malkhazyants' and Mahé translate the name correctly as it appears in the text, but Thomson follows Toumanoff and Adontz and translates it as Angł, which in my opinion is a corruption. Thomson, as a translator, should adhere to the spelling of Angeł as it is found in the text, as should Adontz, Toumanoff and all the other scholars who have changed the name. The least they could have done was to reflect on the editions of the Zohrapian and Bałtatlian Bibles, which they freely quote, and ask how a vulture might be equated with Nergal, the god of the Underworld and pestilence, since in their definition Angł means 'vulture' (also 'lugs, earrings'). But, there may have been some justification in equating Angeł, in the sense of 'inglorious/disgraced', with Nergal, who was expelled by the assembly of gods (hence disgraced), although I doubt whether Sebēos, whom they supposedly follow, would have known anything about such matters when he invented his nonsensical equation of Angeł = god. Sebēos himself and all the writers up to his time, such as Agat'angełos, P'awstos, Khorenats'i, P'arpets'i, write about the place and princes of this important dukedom as Angeł Castle, Angeł Tun and Angełats' Ishkhan. Why is it that these scholars corrupt the name with no knowledge of the facts, such as who actually was Angeł and why was he called so? For the adjective *angeł* the *Baṛgirk' Haykazean* offers three definitions: a) the opposite of beautiful, b) ugly, and c) inglorious/disgraced (*unshowk'*). Because of his physical appearance, described in vivid terms by Khorenats'i, scholars past and present have concluded that Angeł means ugly, whereas the man involved was called so for being inglorious. No one has considered this alternative or made an effort to find out the truth (Karst, *Mythologie*, pp 64-9 may be the exception, see Toumanoff's note 96, p300). The Tork' part of the name of Tork' Angeł is discussed in Part IV.

Chapter 24

This chapter is devoted to the personality and the deeds of Tigran, the son of Eruand Sakawakeats'. We do not know much about this Tigran, except from what Khorenats'i writes and what Xenophon had written in his historical romance *Cyropaedia*. The deeds ascribed to this Tigran are those of Tigran the Great of the Artaxiat dynasty. Somehow Khorenats'i has mixed the two Tigrans. The information that such a person existed at the time of Cyrus derives from Mar Abas Katina, but the deeds ascribed to him are those of Khorenats'i's own confused composition relying on traditions.

Clearly Eruand Sakawakeats' and his son Tigran could not belong to the Orontid dynasty of Armenia. Having the same name does not automatically relate them to the Orontid dynasty starting after *c.* 401 BC. According to the information given by Xenophon and Khorenats'i, Eruand must have belonged to *c.* 570 BC, and, as his name implies (Sakawakeats'), he was short lived; his untimely death must have fallen *c.* 560 BC when his elder son Tigran took his place. The accession of Cyrus to the throne of Anshan occurred in 558 BC, and his defeat of Astyages and capture of Ecbatana in 550 BC. Cyrus was the chief general of Astyages prior to his accession to the throne of Anshan, which gives credence to Xenophon's claim that Cyrus, as the chief of staff of Astyages, went to recover the tribute Eruand had held back, and while thus occupied he also borrowed additional money for himself for his future plans. Cyrus had to be on friendly terms with Tigran, the successor of Eruand, since such a friendship would facilitate his future plans. So far we have a few details, which are also described in the next two chapters, from which such inferences can be made, but the main question still remains unanswered: who were these

Eruand and Tigran, presented as kings of Armenia, but whose names do not belong to the Armenian language? In fact these would be the first names of Iranian provenance on the soil of Armenia. This question can only be answered conjecturally since we know nothing about Eruand and what are purported as the deeds of Tigran are actually misrepresentations.

While Cyaxares was involved in the west of Anatolia the Proto-Armenians entered Urartu (*c.* 588 BC), fought with the Median army under the leadership of Mades and settled in predetermined districts of Urartu. It appears the plans of Cyaxares, both in the west and towards Urartu, had gone awry. However, the war with Lydia came to an end in 585 BC when the main Median army returned to its base and possibly was on the point of attacking Urartu when Cyaxares died (584 BC). Astyages, the son of Cyaxares, succeeded to the throne and it must have been in his time that the Medes successfully overran the whole of the Armenian plateau and entrusted its governance to a prominent Iranian prefect known as Eruand. Khorenats'i, at the end of chapter 21, confirms that the ancestors of the Armenians were the prefects, governors and administrators of the Chaldaeans, Assyrians and the Persians. It appears, and this cannot be much of a guess, that Eruand and his son Tigran, being Iranians themselves, were aware of the political foment taking place within the Persians of southern Iran, hence the friendly disposition of Tigran towards Cyrus and the holding back of tribute from Astyages. The conclusion of this line of reasoning must be that both Eruand and his son were neither Proto-Armenians nor Urartians, but foreign governors. They may have tried to take advantage of the political situation in order to create for themselves an independent kingdom, but what they achieved, at the end, was to replace the Median rule with Persian after 550 BC. The whole affair also reveals why neither the Proto-Armenians nor the Urartians managed to create an indigenous kingdom until the Artaxiad period.

In this chapter while writing about the deeds of this Tigran Khorenats'i has a very revealing sentence, which actually appertains to Tigran the Great of 95-55 BC: 'He extended the borders of our country up to the edge of our habitation places in antiquity.' Khorenats'i does not realize that he is actually confirming that prior to Urartian highlands the Proto-Armenians inhabited southeastern Anatolia, the countries known as Tabal, Cilicia and Aram. After the name of this Aram (not a person), he again confirms that the Hay people were named Armenians ('people of Aram') on entering Urartu.

Chapter 29

This chapter is the climax of the story of Tigran Sakawakeats'. Tigran manages to save his sister and a full-blown battle with the Medians starts. At the end Astyages is killed and Tigran is glorified.

The chapter starts with the words 'After this he says'. Thomson has placed his note 1 against this phrase and justifiably asks who is 'he'? Is it Mar Abas Katina, *The Web of Chries* or the *Four Rhapsodies*? Mahé begins the chapter with the words 'After this the author says', which again is uncertain: who is the author? Malkhazyants' note 82 for this phrase says that it is not certain as to who is this 'he' and quotes Step'anē whose translation 'says the historian' is just as imprecise. Malkhazyants' is of the opinion that the story derives from the *Four Rhapsodies* and *The Web of Chries*, in which case why the phrase 'he says'?

In my opinion what Mahé and Step'anē write is ambiguous but Malkhazyants' and Thomson's conjectures may be partly correct if we accept the *Four Rhapsodies* and *The Web of Chries* as sources. Khorenats'i usually lets us know when the information derives from Mar Abas Katina, such as 'After these the same chronographer continues' (chapter 9), 'Continuing his narrative' (ch. 11), 'After this many things are related in the book' (ch. 12), 'Now the historian tells of this wonderful fact' (ch.12), 'Yet as Mar Abas Katina relates' (ch. 14). However, in the case of other or mixed sources Khorenats'i uses different phrases such as 'Hayk, he says' (ch. 10), 'As the storyteller says' (ch. 25) and 'After this he says' (ch. 29).

I have said above 'if we accept the *Four Rhapsodies* and *The Web of Chries* as sources', but how can we do this given that we know nothing about the contents of these two sources? Some scholars have written on the subject but such writings are conjectural, nothing more—there may have been such sources but as our knowledge of them amounts to nothing, we must drop the matter.

Chapter 30

This chapter starts with the words 'This too is told', which means the source is, again, oral tradition. Tigran settled his sister in the city of Tigranakert which he had built and named after himself and which, together with the surrounding lands, he orders to be her appanage. Khorenats'i repeats the phrase 'he says' and continues with 'the nobility of those regions called Ostan is descended from her as a royal line'. This information too derives from oral sources, but in this case there is at least one aspect of the information that hold veracity since it reflects on the antiquity of the Ostan, which, during the time of Khosrov Kotak, the Arsacids and other up and coming dukedoms used for their own purposes. The subject of Ostan is repeated by Mosēs in greater detail in Book II.7, therefore I shall discuss it under that chapter—bearing in mind in *Pre-History Volume I* I have already written on the subject in detail (pp 170-92). Suffice to say here that Khorenats'i is the only individual who has some idea of what Ostan stood for. Thomson's note 3 says that 'it literally means "royal land" or "royal city"', but he is not the only one to conclude thus, since after Khosrov Kotak exterminated the 'house of the Fathers', the Manawazeans, and the 'house of the Sons', Bznunik', he usurped the 'title', which from that period onwards acquired a different sense.

Next, Tigran 'settles queen Anoysh (the chief wife of Astyages) with her sons in the place the debris of the great mountain landslide ends'. Thomson's translation of this sentence is off the mark.

Khorenats'i then quotes ancient songs of balladeers. These are much older than his history but fortunately they are understandable with the exception of one, which is composed in a masterly fashion although some have claimed it to be a corrupted version of an ancient poem. This particular poem has not been understood because it contains compound words which various scholars have considered to be loans from the Iranian and explained them differently. All such explanations make no sense and, tellingly, those of Thomson, Mahé and Dowsett are completely off the mark. The survived three lines of the poem supposedly say: 'Queen Sat'enik had great longing for the tender wine leaves and lettuce' or 'vegetables from the embroidered pillows (or cushions) of Argavan'. Adjaryan dates these two lines of a poem to 180 BC. In my opinion, thanks to Khorenats'i, this is one of the oldest of poems that has reached us. The line 'Queen Sat'enik with her great longing' has hints of erotic undertones and it is generally accepted that she had fallen in love with Argavan, which renders absurd the 'tender vine leaves, lettuce, vegetables or embroidered cushions' explanations of the unknown words, unless, as some scholars have suggested, we are dealing here with two thousand-year-old allegory and magic. I do not think so. The poem is the work of a top-class bard, whom we will never know, and it is perfectly understandable provided one does not expect the same language as that of Khorenats'i's time. As mentioned this poem is much older, and so far as the language is concerned, it still has traces of Proto-Armenian and is devoid of Iranian loan words (a point the translators should have realized), and so one should adopt a more down-to-earth approach and think in terms of purer Armenian language and basic root words. Below is provided a full explanation of the poem.

Mosēs Khorenats'i has preserved for posterity these two lines of an ancient song in his History of the Armenians—these may have been part of a long poem and it is plausible that other bits of songs preserved in other parts of his History also belong to a single whole. Here I shall examine only these lines concerning Sat'enik. The other partially preserved songs are: Artashēs' battle with the Alans (Book II.50), the brideprice of Sat'enik (II.50), the abduction of Sat'enik (II.50), her marriage (II.50), the abduction of Artawazd (II.61), Sat'enik's desire (to be discussed in here) (I.30), the feast provided by Argawan (I.30), Artawazd building Marakert (I.30), Artawazd's grievance (II.61) and Artashēs' curse (II.61).

In line with the development of the Classical Armenian language, all these poems reflect grammatical and morphological changes, keeping in line with linguistic progress and acquisitions, such as derivatives, articles and augmentative suffixes. According to Adjaryan all the parts of the whole poem belong to the first half of the second century BC,[27] while their phonology and morphology, in step with the development of the language, have changed. In my opinion most of the phrases contained in this poem are, more or the less, in the Armenian that prevailed in the early second century BC, bereft of Pahlavi words. The diacritics belong to later times and it is also possible that the second *a* of *zartakhur*, a conjunctive article attaching two roots together in the creation of a compound, belongs to later times; the other two suffixes of *s* of *tench'ans* and *n* of *barts'its'n* and the conjunction *ev* are the result of regular language evolution. I would make an exception to Adjaryan's theory over the phonology, which has not changed since the days this poem was created,[28] as evident in the phrase '*zartakhur khawart ew ztits' khawartsi*'.

Scholarship has understood the first four words of this poem but the rest, I believe, has not been understood correctly by even the ancient writers, hence its survival in its original state which may represent the last stages of evolution between the Proto-Armenian and the Classical language. To this effect I would point out that Khorenats'i, who is

---

27.   Adjaryan, *History of the Armenian Language*, see vol. II, p71.

28.   The Proto-Armenian inscriptions from the country of Aram shed light on phonological changes; these are discernible between inscriptions of the tenth-ninth centuries compared to those of the eighth-seventh centuries BC. See *Pre-History Volume III*, pp 59-90.

usually happy to explain the ambiguous and the allegorical, in this particular instance is silent.

Adjaryan's *Dictionary of Armenian Root Words* has two separate entries for the word *artakhoyr*: it lists all the opinions and explanations scholars have come up with. None of these explanations, or even the interpretations, are correct, an opinion that Adjaryan must have shared, since he classes his second entry as 'an uncertain word'. However, he explains the first entry of the word as 'crown' which, in my opinion, is erroneous even though it is close enough to the actual meaning of the word, and it may well be the case that a few of the older writers have used the word in that sense.

Malkhazyants' in his translation of the history from Classical to Modern Armenian adds his note 90 (Thomson in his own translation quotes this incorrectly as note 60) for these two lines. He admits the obscurity of the poem, and therefore he does not attempt a translation. But he quotes the opinion of Khalat'yants', taken up by K'. Patkanyan.[29] The former's explanation is based on ancient practices and the superstition of placing aromatic herbs under the cushion of a person, and then transferring the same herbs to one's own cushion in order to make the other fall in love with him/her. There may have been such superstitions but they certainly do not apply to the poem under discussion.

Of the most recent two translators, Mahé and Thomson, the first admits the difficulties involved and adopts Dowsett's translation,[30] which explains the four words as *'La tiare de verdure et le bandeau de fleurs'* and adds as the continuation *'Du coussin brodé d'Argavan'*, a nonsensical translation. Thomson also accepts the obscurity of the poem, translating it as: 'But Queen Sat'inik had great desire for the vegetable *artakhur* and the shoot *tits* from the table of Argavan.' This is another nonsensical explanation, for if the queen had indeed desired a variety of greens or embroidered and floral cushions, or had desired to eat salad, I am certain she would have found the choicest in the palace.

On the other hand, A. Bahat'rean[31] ascribes entirely wrong meanings to the words and yet somehow achieves a near enough convincing explanation that 'Sat'enik expected to become pregnant in the bed of Argawan and give birth to a child'.

Let us now examine the poem, explain the obscure words and

29. Malkhazyants', see note 90 (p336) to his translation of Khorenats'i's History.
30. Dowsett, 1986; quoted in Mahé's translation of Khorenats'i, p340.
31. A. Bahat'rean, in *Hoviv*, 19018, pp 415-6. Quoted by Adjaryan in *Dictionary of Armenian Root Words*, Erevan 1971—see the word *artakoyr* in vol. 1, pp 339-42.

understand its exact meaning. I reproduce the two lines, again, for convenience.

Tench'a Sat'enik tikin tench'ans, zartakhur khawart
ew ztits' khawartsi i bardzits'n Argawana

The first line *'Tench'a Sat'enik tikin tench'ans'* means 'Queen Sat'enik had a great desire' and, since this has been universally understood, there is no need for further explanation.

Zartakhur: This word is the compound of *z* prefix + *art* + *khur.*

Z is a preposition used for the accusative, comprehensive, historical (the ancients called this *patmakan,* which sense is covered by the present ablative)[32] and for emphasis. In this present position *z* is a *patmakan* prefix.

Art is a root word and the meaning is 'out, outside and away'. I have not come across this word in my translations of Proto-Armenian literature in hieroglyphic script.

Khur or *khoyr* are the same word spelt differently. The meaning is 'mitre, tiara, diadem and crown'. This is a loanword, most probably from a branch of the Semitic languages (Aramaean?), since the Proto-Armenians did not know it and used, like the Greek *tiara,* the word *'diar'.*

Therefore the word *zartakhur* means 'out of Crown' and has also the senses of 'away from the responsibilities of the Crown' and 'away from the attention of the Crown'. These last two are the meanings used in the poem. However, in time *artakhur* has also been used in its literal meaning of 'out of Crown', which indicated the two ribbons descending from the back of the crown to the nape of the neck (lappets). This is the reason for the sense of 'Crown' given by Adjaryan.

Khawart: Another compound, composed of *khaw* and *art.*

Khaw is a root word and means 'complicated, difficult'. It has also acquired the later meanings of 'slice, sliver', etc. This is another word that I have not detected in the Proto-Armenian inscriptions.

As for *art,* its meanings and details can be seen above.

Therefore, the compound *khawart* means 'out of complications' and 'away from difficulties'. The actual sense of the compound in the poem is, I believe, 'away from complications'.

---

32.   Adjaryan, *Dictionary of Armenian Root Words,* vol. II, p75.

Ztits': This is the accusative plural of the word *ti*, which means 'day, year, age, the height of a person, century, duration or time-span', etc. One notices that all these meanings are connected and have to do with the span of time. It is a fact that in the ancient manuscripts *ti* is found only once in the compound of *'erkti'* meaning two days. Therefore, it was not possible to know the various cases or the declension of the noun. It was thought that the accusative plural of the word might be *ztis* (singular = *zti)*, of which the *s* ending was the Classical Armenian accusative plural suffix. However our example from the poem indicates that the more ancient plural suffix was *ts'* as in the *ztits'* of the poem, which means that the word had not gone through the process of replacing the *ts'* suffix with an *s*, since by the Classical Armenian era it was seldom used, as supported by its rarity.

This word is confirmed in the Proto-Armenian language in various inscriptions over and over again. For example, we have *'ti wa ti'* (Carchemish A11c:2), which means 'day come day' equated with the Modern Armenian *ōr əst ōrē* ('day by day'). Other examples are: *'i-ti wa'* ('come this day') and *'ti na ti-i'* ('day after days' or 'for days'). One of the most interesting examples is found in inscription Sultan Han, line 10: *'za pawa ara maza kha sa-a zara i-ti ti-i'* meaning 'gave to or did to (*ara*) this (*za*) fraudulent (*kha = khardakh*) person (*pawa → haga*) a beating (*maza*) made him (*sa-à*) this day (*i-ti*) servant (*zara*) forever (*ti-i*). Note that the final *i* of *ti-i* is the most ancient plural suffix, whereas the initial *i* in *i-ti* is the same preposition as found in the accusative and ablative cases of Classical Armenian. *Pawa*, meaning a person, transcribes as *haga*, which means a breath representing a person. The word *khardakh* is one of the augmentations of the *'kha'* of the inscriptions, which also happens to be the most difficult to translate, while *zara* transcribes as *tsara* meaning 'slave, servant'.

Khawartsi: This is the compound of *khawar* and *tsi*.

Khawar means 'dark, darkness' and is also lacking in the Proto-Armenian inscriptions. However, its form suggests that it is indigenous, which makes the claim that it is a loan from the Iranian untenable— besides the Persian word had the meaning of 'west'.

Tsi is the root of the later words *tsitsal* and *tsalr,* meaning 'to laugh, laughter, to play happy games, to cheer, joke, sneer, gossip, to mock', etc. It is claimed that *tsalr* is the stem of both words,[33] which cannot be

---

33. Ibid., vol. 11, p439.

sustained—in reality, the Proto-Armenian shows the stem was *tsi*. We have two good examples of the use of this word in the hieroglyphic inscriptions.[34] In Carchemish A2:3 of Katuwa (Kaypak) we have '*waza da-a mi-ia-za si zi za*', which translates 'they (*da-a*) ran (*waza*) and joined (*mi-ia-za*) the wonderful (*si* → *hi*) games (*zi za*)'. The second example, again, comes from Carchemish Aıïb:4 of Katuwa: '*zana da waza-a u-paha zi a-ta*' = '(he) run (*waza*) to his acquaintance (*zana da*) and hid (*u paha*) and gossiped (*zi a-ta*)'. Note that the *si* of the first example transcribes as *hi*, which is the stem of the modern word *hianal* ('to admire, wonder', etc). The word *ziza* of the first example and the *zana* and *zi* of the second transcribe as *tsitsa*, *tsana* and *tsi*. The final word of the second example is *a-ta*, which has the meanings of 'to give' and 'to strike' (the Modern Armanian verb is *tal* = 'to give, to strike', etc).

The conclusion is that *khawartsi* means 'games after darkness'.

Bardzits'n: This is the last word to be examined, since the next one is a personal name, that of Argawan. *Bardz* is a familiar word that means 'cushion' and therefore *bardzits'n* means 'the cushions of'. In Modern Armenian the cushions referred to in the poem are called *ankołin* (a bed), which is a later composition and is made up from *ank* + *koł* (*ank* 'go down' + *koł* 'side, flank'; in the composite *ank-koł* one of the *ks* has dropped) or *mahchakal* (augmentation of *mahich* meaning 'bed' or 'coffin'). The ancients slept on stuffed sacks (the poor filled them with dried grass and the rich with wool), which they called 'cushions' in the same manner as it appears in the poem. Though the word has acquired other meanings such as one's position in court or a seat, none of these additional senses apply to our present poem.

In conclusion it must be said that history acknowledges that Queen Sat'enik had fallen in love with Argawan, which I find reassuring, since the poem says: 'Queen Sat'enik had great desire *to be out of responsibilities of the Crown, away from complications and when the days darken revel in Argawan's bed.*'

Chapter 31

This chapter is about Tigan's prowess and his descendants. Khorenats'i writes about the three individuals who are most dear to him: Hayk, Aram and Tigran. The case of Hayk is understandable as after all he was the

---

34. Soultanian, *Pre-History Volume II: Inscriptions from Aram*, pp 51-55, 65-67.

first Proto-Armenian who won a battle against the Assyrians and in the process killed their king, Sargon II. But Aram and Tigran cannot be treated in the same manner, since the first was the name of the land the Hays inhabited and the deeds ascribed to him were those of other persons. As for Tigran, his qualities and deeds are those of Tigran the Great (known as the Second), which has been wrongly ascribed to Tigran Sakawakeats', the prefect of the Medes. We do not know much about this Tigran, except for the wrong ascription of Khorenats'i and what appears in Xenophon's *Cyropaedia*. Besides, if this Tigran was a king, then Tigran the Great would have been known as the Third.

The names of the descendants of Tigran may derive from Mar Abas Katina, but the equation of these names with various houses within Armenia derive from oral traditions. Mar Abas Katina has no knowledge of the affairs of Armenia Major, which is the reason Khorenats'i telescopes various reigns and confuses the Arsacids and Artaxiads due to the traditional tales he has gathered and believes. This supposition is confirmed by Khorenats'i himself when he admits that after Vahē, who was killed by the forces of Alexander of Macedon, he has nothing to add to his history. This means that the local traditions and stories do not cover the period until Vałarshak's reign in Nisibis of Atropatene, which, again, Khorenats'i erroneously transfers to Armenia.

Chapter 32

Khorenats'i must have been under great pressure to write his History, which we can see from this chapter and what he says. The lengthy first paragraph needs no explanation save to mention that from what Khorenats'i says it is inferred that he is sending to his patron each chapter as soon as he writes it.

The last paragraph of Book 1.32 is in connection with the Trojan War and the Proto-Armenian participation. Khorenats'i mentions Homer but he could not have read the Iliad. My reason for saying so is due to the fact that he does not know who Tewtamus, Pelasgians, Paeonians or Pyraechmes were. If he had read the Iliad he would perhaps have known that Tewtamus was the patriarch of Larisa, the Pelasgian chief and father of Lethus.[35] I doubt too if he would have guessed that Pyraechmes was his Zarmayr, the leader of the Paeonians or the Proto-Armenians (Iliad, Book 11.840-850). The information about the Trojan War and Zarmayr derives from indigenous demotic tales, since it was an interesting story it

---

35.   Homer, *The Iliad*, Loeb Classical Library, 2001 in two volumes; see vol. 11, p.123.

would have endured through the ages, repeated from generation to generation. However Mosēs sees a different version of the story in Eusebius, whose source was Diodorus Siculus (Book 11.21.22) who cites Ctesias. Therefore Mosēs accepts what Eusebius writes, but keeps the name of Zarmayr, since the Memnon of Eusebius does not belong to the Armenian language, and thus would not make sense. Mosēs had a better perception than Awgerean (Pazmavēp 1946-47) who equates Zarmayr with Eusebius' Memnon. The Assyrians had no role in the Trojan War nor could they have sent an army to help Priam, since after Tukulti-Ninurta I (1244-1208 BC) Assyria was in decline and the renewal of its powers do not start until Tiglath-Pileser I (1115-1077 BC). If Mosēs had stuck to his original source, the demotic tales, perhaps his account of Zarmayr and the Trojan War would have been better than that of Eusebius and Diodorus.

For me the most surprising part of Mosēs' action is his keeping the name of Zarmayr, irrespective of what Eusebius writes. According to Diodorus, repeated in Eusebius, Tewtamus, the Assyrian king, placed an Ethiopian army under the command of Memnon, son of Tithonus.[36] But in the Iliad there is no mention of Memnon and Tithonus or the Assyrians and Ethiopians (although the latter are recorded twice in different contexts). There are however Pelasgians and Paeonians. Pyraechmes comes from the banks of the river Axius from the city of Amydon (the later Amid in Armenia commemorates the name) in Paeonia and is the commander of the Paeonian contigent. Mosēs could not have known these facts of Homer's writing and he also could not have known that the names Pyraechmes and Zarmayr have identical meanings, i.e. the Greeks transcribed the name of Zarmayr as Pyraechmes. Pyraechmes means 'Flame Tip' (from the ends of tongue-like flames) and comprises *pyr* 'fire, flame' + *aechmes* 'sharp end of needle, tip of arrow or spear'— some have translated this as 'spear'). Zarmayr means 'Flame Tip', the same as Pyraechmes, and comprises *z* emphatic prefix + *arm* 'end, point, tip' + *ayr* 'fire, flame'. (The *arm* has been explained as *armat* 'root', which is incorrect since *armat* is the compound of *arm* + *at* 'capable tip/end' = 'root'. Both *arm* and *at* stems can be seen in the Proto-Armenian inscriptions of Aram in *Pre-History Volume II*).

Khorenats'i's last sentence says: 'Zarmayr was wounded by the valiant Hellenes and died. But I would have wished (he was killed) by Achilles and not by an ordinary soldier.' This part of the story too, derives from

36. Quintus Smyrnaeus, *The Fall of Troy*, Loeb, 2000. The Memnon who is the son of Tithonus in Book 11 does not exist in Homer's *Iliad*.

the indigenous demotic tales that mentioned Achilles. It seems Khorenats'i's wish was partly answered. Yes, Zarmayr (Pyraechmes) was not killed by Achilles but by his intimate, Patroclus (Iliad, Book XVI, 284-294). Nevertheless, the next commander of the Paeonians was Asteropaeus who, according to Homer (*Iliad*, Book XXI 136-209), was definitely killed by Achilles. The first book of the history ends at this point. There is an addendum concerning the Fables of the Persians which is outside the scope of this study.

Chapter II.7

I have discussed the Ostan organization and the entry of the Proto-Armenians into Urartu in detail in *Pre-History Volume I* (pages 170-192). Here I shall treat the case of Ostan in a concise manner for those who have not seen my first volume.

Khorenats'i, writing in chapter 1.30 about Tigran Sakawakeats', says that 'Tigran sent his sister to live in Tigranocerta and that they say that the nobility of that region called Ostan had descended from her as a royal line'. However, in chapter 11.7 Khorenats'i returns to the subject of Ostan and adds 'the actual Ostan consisted of the descendents of the ancient kings of Haykid (progeny of Hayk) origin, and their descendents used to inherit villages and estates . . . but more recently, at the time of the Persian kings, I understand, other sections have been brought into being who call themselves Ostan. I do not know whether this is due to the diminishing numbers of the older generation'. And a sentence later, Khorenats'i insists that 'the first Ostan definitely consisted of the descendents of the ancient Hay kings'.

I have already written about Ostan while discussing chapter 1.12 of Part III, (pages 113-14) and Toumanoff's misguided opinion on pp.38-9. Here I shall add that the Armenian people were aware that the Arsacid kings were of Parthian origin and their own 'Fathers', the Manawazeans, were their true leaders, which means that the house of Manawazeans were treated with higher respect than an Arsacid king. It is easy for a governing class to conspire and devise conditions for certain 'houses' creating disorders for its own benefit, particularly an ingenious Hayr Mardpet of the middle Arsacid era. Khosrov Kotak and Hayr Mardpet were successful in exterminating the 'Fathers' (Manawazeans) and the 'Sons' (Bznunik') hoping that the Arsacids would become both the kings and the 'Fathers' of the nation; but it appears the Hay people were not so easily won over, which we note from the new distorted meaning of the usurped word Ostan, starting with the times of Khosrov Kotak and onwards. Considering that the new meaning of Ostan had become 'main city', 'court' or 'royal residence' other 'houses' too started using and distorting further the word. These are the reasons P'awstos, Eɫishē and Łazar use Ostan in the sense that was prevalent at their time, since their histories were of periods after the time of Khosrov Kotak.

Ostan is an indigenous word and means 'The Branches (of Hay kingdoms)' of Aram country, who unified attacked the Medo-Scythian army, that had destroyed most of Urartu, and after winning the battle dispersed to predetermined lands in the periphery of the highlands. The members of the Ostan organization represented the first Hays who established themselves as patriarchal houses in the new Armenia; they were the Manawazeans, Bznunik', Khorkhorunik', Geɫark'unik', Sisakeans, Kadmeans, Angeɫats' Tun and Shahunis. There was not a house to watch the northern borders, which was soon remedied by the appearance of the Gusharids, a branch of the Shahunis, which is the reason Khorenats'i sends Shara to the north and derives his name from Shirak. It is only Khorenats'i that knows and explains what the true Ostan means.

Chapter II.10

In the first paragraph of this chapter there is a short sentence which appears spoiled by later scribes. As it stands it does not make good grammatical sense although the meaning can be clarified from the last sentence of the chapter, where it is said 'the war of Vaɫarshak with Pontus and with Phrygia, and his victory'.

The sentence in question says: *'Sa, əndardzakeal i veray sahmanats' iwrots'.'* Three amazing translations are provided—Malkhazyants': 'He independently reigned over his frontiers', Thomson: 'He extended his authority over his territories', Mahé: 'étendit son autorité sur tout son empire'. These translations are worse than the corrupted sentence and remarkably bear no relationship to the sense of what is written in the chapter. Mosēs is referring to his previous Book 1 (1.8) where he writes: 'For the frontiers of the brave are their weapons; as much as they cut, that much they hold.' This chapter's sentence is therefore bound to contain a similar sense: 'He extended the frontiers adding to what he had.' In other words Vaɫarshak, after his victory over Pontus and Phrygia (which should be Cappadocia), extended his borders and enlarged his territory. The primary meaning of the expression *'i veray'* is 'on top of' which I have translated as 'added'.

Khorenats'i's chapter II.10

We shall begin our narrative for you from the fifth book of Africanus the Chronographer, to which Josephus and Hippolytus and many other Greeks lend (corroborative) witness. For he transcribed everything from the charters of the archives of Edessa, that is Urha, which concerned the history of our kings. These books had been transported there from Nisibis (Mtsbin), and from the temple histories of Sinope of Pontus. Let no one doubt this, for we have seen that archive with our own eyes. And as a closer witness the 'Ecclesiastical' (History) of Eusebius of Caesarea is a guarantee...

The above is a good translation by Thomson, being as near to Khorenats'i's text as possible. There are a few additional points requiring explanation. Khorenats'i makes it clear that it was only the Nisibis archives that contained material relating to our kings. The archives from Sinope that were transferred to Edessa by the Romans we now know to have contained the temple histories and their register of taxes (II.38).

What Khorenats'i says about the transport of the archives makes sense because, according to him, the king, Abgar, transferred his palace from Nisibis to his new capital city Edessa (II.27). Without doubt this move would have included the archives. Nisibis was the capital where the first Parthians reigned, such as Vałarshak and his son Arshak, in addition to being the hometown of Mar Abas Katina.

On page 13 of his introduction to the History of Khorenats'i Thomson writes that 'one's confidence in Mosēs' "archives" is even more shaken by the patently false claim in II.10 that Eusebius in his Church History (1.13) bears witness to the existence in Edessa of archives dealing with Armenia, for Eusebius merely says that in the Edessan archives he had found correspondence between Abgar of Edessa and Jesus Christ.'

Thomson's comment on what the archives in Edessa record is misleading. Careful examination reveals that Mosēs does not say 'archives dealing with Armenia' but 'which concerned the history of our kings'—and 'our kings' have not always been of Armenia, as discussed under chapters 12, 19 and 22. Besides, when one thinks of the first Parthian kings of Nisibis, such as Vałarshak and his son Arshak and the country comprising mainly of Hay population, one is convinced of the veracity of what Mosēs writes. However, the full quotation in 1.13 of the Ecclesiastical History of Eusebius says (my italics): 'There is also documentary evidence of these things taken from the archives of Edessa, which was at that time a capital city. At least, in the public documents there, which contain *the things done in antiquity* and at the time of Abgar.'[37] Furthermore, on page xxxix of the introduction to Eusebius' Ecclesiastical History the translator remarks (again my italics): 'According to H. E. i. 12. 3 ff. Eusebius made use of material in the Archives of Edessa. These appear to have consisted of two divisions. There was an *ancient royal archive* and a later ecclesiastical one which was probably not instituted until the beginning of the fourth century.' And he adds: 'It is not certain whether Eusebius had himself seen this archive or made use of it only at second-hand through the writings of Julius Africanus.' The inference from these remarks is that Julius Africanus had benefited from the archives in the case of the 'things done in antiquity' since, as it is claimed by the translator, the ecclesiastical section of the archives was instituted beginning with the fourth century, which will be after Africanus.

Another point to be made concerns Abgar, the king of Edessa. His full name was Abgar Uchama. The Uchama part Khorenats'i transcribes into Armenian as Arshama, which is the genitive form of Arsham. Arsham being an Armenian name, Khorenats'i concludes that Abgar was an Armenian king (Abgar born to Arsham) of Edessa. It was only nearer to our own times that Uchama was interpreted as an epithet meaning 'dark-skinned'. Khorenats'i did not know that. The conclusion, therefore, is that the archives of an Armenian king, i.e. Abgar, relating to antiquity must concern the old kings reigning over the Hays outside of Armenia. Because we do not know exactly what was written in these archives, the subject is academic. But it is a fact and it must be pointed out that during the times Mosēs refers to in this chapter, both Urfa and Nisibis with their districts had the largest population of Hays.

A final point worthwhile mentioning is the fact that Khorenats'i in this chapter has cited Eusebius and his work, the Ecclesiastical History. He informs his patron Sahak Bagratuni that 'if he searches in Gełark'uni in the province of Siwnik' he could find this book'. Thomson in his note 9 for this chapter makes the comment: 'Why Mosēs associates Gełark'uni with a copy of the Ecclesiastical History is obscure.' Obviously, Thomson has not given much thought to the matter, since there is nothing obscure in what Mosēs says. The Armenian capital cities Armavir, Artashat, Vałarshapat and Tuin were situated in the Gełark'uni

---

37. Eusebius, *Ecclesiastical History*, Loeb Classical Library, 1992; see vol. 1, p87 (1.xiii.5).

region of Siwnik'. Thus Mosēs is saying that this book will be found in one of the ancient capital cities, and in particular Vałarshapat (present-day Etchmiadzin), which also happens to be the seat of the catholicos of Armenia. Because Mosēs does not know in which of these cities the said book will be found, he quotes the name of the district as Gełark'uni and narrows it down to a region within Siwnik'.

Khorenats'i's chapters II.11-14

For the names of the very ancient kings of the Hays (Armenians) of the country of Aram, which Mosēs presents as the kings of Armenia, and the first Arsacid kingdom of Atropatene to the south of Armenia, Mosēs had the work of Mar Abas Katina. This book had provided him with the correct history of ancient times, which he did not understand fully. All the same, he faithfully records the names and a few known anecdotes concerning these kings under the guise of an individual named Aram, and, in some cases, he also indicates the later abode of the descendants of these kings in Armenia from after *c.* 588 BC.

However, for the continuation of his narrative he does not have a reliable and connecting history available to him. He believes that the Parthian kings of Atropatene were the first Arsacids and therefore kings of Armenia, and relying on snippets of information gleaned from various sources in addition to demotic stories, he concludes that Artashēs I was the son of Arshak of Atropatene, whereas Artashēs is in reality the older king. Nevertheless in this way he is able to give us a continuous narrative by creating a monolithic dynasty of Arsacids, which includes Vałarshak and his son Arshak of Atropatene, the Artaxiads and the real Arsacids of Armenia. The true Arsacid dynasty starts with Trdat I of AD 53-100, crowned king in Rome by Nero in AD 66. His chronology and the description of events in these chapters is hopeless, but that is only to be expected considering that, irrespective of his knowedge of the real facts—such as 'between our Artashēs (190-159 BC) and Nectanebo (360-343 BC) of Egypt there is a gap of 200 years and between the latter and Croesus (560-546 BC) there is another gap of over 200 years'—Khorenats'i decides to follow unproven sources. Reading these chapters one cannot help feeling that they have been interfered with.

Mosēs has been persuaded by his sources (Polycrates, Evagoras, Scamadros and Phlegonios) that it was Artashēs who took Croesus of Lydia prisoner. He knows however that other sources indicate it was Cyrus who had taken Croesus prisoner (II.13) and had also waged war against the Massagetae; that Darius had fought the Scythians and fled;

that Cambyses had warred against the Ethiopians; that Xerxes had marched against Hellas and in great difficulties abandoned all his treasures and pavilions and fled to save his skin; the Pythian oracle, which Croesus had consulted;[38] the war in Bactria where Artaxerxes emerged victorious after a battle in sandstorm and the agreeable story connected with Croesus calling out the name of Solon when he was placed on the pyre.[39] So why is it that Moses offers us such a confused and completely wrong history?

As I mentioned above, I think that chapters 12, 13 & 14 of Book II of the History have been interfered with some time after the seventh century by an editor or a copying scribe, who confused king Artashes of the Armenians with the Achaemenid king Artaxerxes (465-424 BC) of Persia since the name Artaxerxes is also Artashes in Armenian. There are a few indicators to support my view and so we should best examine the said three chapters.

Chapter 12 is all about King Artaxerxes of Persia, which becomes obvious when we read that 'Artashes ordered an army to be raised from the east and north'. Since Armavir, the capital city where the seat of the government of Armenia was based at the time, was in the northeast of the country there were no eastern or northern parts for raising an army. All the same, there are two phrases in this chapter which, depending on their translation, could render the entire chapter suspect: 'tay berel i hays', and 'tay berel yashkharhs mer'. The final parts of the phrases ('i hays' and 'yashkharhs mer') mean 'to Armenia' and 'to our world', both meaning Armenia, so the important part of both is 'tay berel'. Tal means 'to give', hence tay is the third person singular of the verb, meaning 'gives', while the verb perel means 'to bring', hence the two together (tay berel) mean 'gives to bring'. Both Malkhazyants' and Thomson's translations are not exact and liable to misinterpretation, the former offering 'having brought' and the latter 'had them brought'. The correct translation would have been 'he grants to be taken (to Armenia)', which clears any misunderstanding and confirms that this chapter concerns Artaxerxes alone. To support this view, I should add that the Persians were adherents of Zoroastrianism and had no use for the idols which Artaxerxes is granting to the Armenians as reward for their participation in his war.

Chapter 13, too, is all about Artaxerxes, king of Persia, but there are four odd entries—in my opinion interpolations—which need explanation. In the second paragraph the sentence says: 'many who say

38. Herodotus, *The Histories*, Penguin Classics, London, 2003; see Book 1.53.
39. Ibid., Book 1.22 & 86.

that our Artashēs took Croesus prisoner.' In this sentence the 'our' is added by an unknown scribe. The other oddity, repeated three times, identifies Artashēs as Parthian. If this Artashēs was an Armenian he should have been identified as Arsacid. It appears that the scribe who wrote the words Parthian Artashēs did not know the Achaemenids, or else it is possible that the Greek historians Polycrates, Scamandros, Evagoras and Phlegonios did not differentiate the Achaemenids from the Parthians since we could not ascribe this mistake to Khorenats'i. Because of all the different ethnic names he would make 'our Artashēs' an Arsacid, as we have seen above while discussing Toumanoff's objection in Part 1. Besides, the Armenian Artashēs I (189 BC) never ruled Thebes (Egypt) or Babylon.

Chapter 14 is about Artashēs's son Tigran, who is said to have ruled in the 49th year of the Parthian king Arshakan of Persia. However, even in this chapter there is an interpolation: 'They had taken it upon themselves to set up on their private lands the statue of Heracles'—to which the scribe has added 'sent by his own father'. In conclusion we note that chapters 12-14 have been distorted by a scribe or an editor. Therefore, chapters 12 and 13 concern only the Artaxerxes I of Persia, and chapter 14 Tigran the Great (95-55 BC) of the Armenians.

But Mosēs is supposed to be writing the history of the Armenians and not that of the Persians. Why then does he involve himself with Persian history? In my opinion, his digression is intended to legitimise the import of the various idols into Armenia with a sound explanation, which also establishes the fact that the Persians of Artaxerxes' time, who followed Zoroastrianism, a monotheistic religion to start with, had no use for these idols.

Thomson says that 'Mosēs introduces quotations describing the Armenian king from numerous obscure or unknown Greek writers', but he agrees that of these Greeks Phlegonios is mentioned by Eusebius (Introduction, p15). Malkhazyants' in his note 142 claims that all these four are real persons but that their works have not survived save for bits of manuscripts. If we ignore what Malkhazyants' says, we should at least try to understand Mosēs's predicament. He knows the accepted history connected with Cyrus and Croesus, as outlined above, yet too many sources have different views, of which he gives us the names of Polycrates, Evagoras, Scamadros and Phlegonios, and from each he quotes a summary of six to twelve lines. Mosēs adds that he was persuaded by the sheer number of the writers he follows. Therefore Mosēs is absolutely truthful, except that he has been unlucky to have made the wrong choice. The non-survival of the manuscripts of these Greek historians appears to be due to the fact that they too were unlucky in their choice. This line of reasoning makes me also consider Mosēs not knowing Greek. I wonder then in which language he read the Greek manuscripts that did not survive? And, I might add, the non-survival of a manuscript is not proof of its non-existence in the olden days.

However, I am sure these historians did not mention the Armenian king Artashēs. Mosēs mentions him as 'the Parthian Artashēs', a transcription into Armenian of the name Artaxerxes. The story in these chapters in its present state is confusing and appears to be interpolated. Therefore, Thomson and Mahé are correct in pinpointing them. Why do these ancient historians consulted by Khorenats'i make Artaxerxes the greatest warrior and ascribe to him such valour? I suspect the subject has its origins in Herodotus[40] where the etymologies of the names of Darius, Xerxes and Artaxerxes are given as 'Worker', 'Warrior' and 'Great Warrior' (in the same order). This myth of the 'Great Warrior' has continued, as we see in Cornelius Nepos (c. 100-25 BC) who refers to Artaxerxes' 'incredible military valour' and adds that 'King Artaxerxes was dissuaded from going in person on the Egyptian expedition'.[41]

Finally, the place name Ashtishat, where the statue of Aphrodite was erected, has been explained as 'the place for multiple sacrifices' and derived from Pahlavi by all scholars up to the present. It is obvious that Pahlavi, too, had such a word, but each time the same word with similar phonetics is found in Pahlavi it does not necessarily mean that the Armenians have borrowed it. *Asht* is a word indigenous to Armenian and its basic meaning is 'not to be trodden' (as the Greek city name Astibēs), in other words a 'holy place', and Ashtishat was so named in perpetuation of the city name Astibus (present-day Shtip in the Republic of Macedonia), the holy city and capital of the Hays in the Balkans. Similarly the entire district to the west of Lake Van was named Tarawn, between 180 to 150 BC, after the name of the royal family of Terrones (the god of healing was also called Tarron) of the Balkans (compare this with Gel → Gełark'unik'). In connection with *asht* (> *ashtishat*), I quote here the related word *yaz*, which has also been ascribed to the Iranian! *Yaz* has been in use since the tenth century BC, therefore it should be considered an indigenous word. The Proto-Armenians wrote it as *lazi* (*l* > *y* = *yaz*) and *iazi* (*ia* > *y* = *yaz*), meaning 'sacrifice'.

40. Ibid., Book vi.99.
41. Cornelius Nepos, Loeb Classical Library, 2005; see Book xxi.1.4, p249.

Chapter II.66

In this chapter, Mosēs writes about Bardesanes as the source for a short period of his History, covering five chapters (II.61-65). It appears that Mosēs has benefited from Eusebius' Ecclesiastical History and another unknown historical work, which may be that of Bardesanes (AD 154-222). Eusebius does not mention that Bardesanes was from Edessa (Urfa) but Mosēs does, and the fact that Bardesanes was not a Hay adds weight to Mosēs' claim. Caracalla started a persecution of the Christians, after the capture of Urfa (AD 216), when Mani took flight to the east of Persia and Bardesanes to the north, to the fortress of Ani in Armenia.[42] Mahé, in his note 3 for this chapter, writes that Bardesanes after his excommunication, according to the *Philosophoumena* of Hippolitus, went to Armenia around AD 216, which agrees with what Mosēs writes. But Thomson, according to his commentary (pp 16, 35, and note 1) is not convinced and for him 'Bardesanes going to Armenia and entering the temple at Ani are all further fancies of Mosēs' own inventions'. As for the temple archives and the history composed by Olympius the priest, which Bardesanes completed and translated into Syriac, Thomson tells us that such a 'temple history is one of Mosēs' imaginary written sources'. On the same subject, Toumanoff in his *Studies* (p105, note 100) tells us that 'it is worth remembering that temples, and in fact temple-states, were actually found in Armenia; that some of them had archives and written records, presents nothing unexpected'.

As further support for the existence of Temple archives in Armenia, which Thomson ascribes to Mosēs's imagination, my most recent work, Volume III in the *Pre-History of the Armenians* series, concerning the Anatolian hieroglyphic inscriptions of the Proto-Armenians, reveals some aspects which even I found surprising. The five Kululu Lead Strips are translated with commentaries in the volume (pp 93-123), all of which are temple records from the eighth century BC, containing information about the gusans and drummers of the same period ('Kululu Lead Strip No. 1', reverse 1.41-42) and much more to captivate one's attention.

Chapter II.75

I had made some fleeting remarks about this chapter in Part 1 (p54) of the history. In my opinion this is one of the most enigmatic chapters. The compilers of the Middle Ages, I think, have made a real muddle of it by either deleting certain parts, or by placing a series of unconnected themes

---

42. H. J. W. Drijvers, *Bardaisan of Edessa*, Van Gorcum, Assen, 1966, translated by G. E. van Baaren-Pape.

and sources in order to give the impression of a genuine chapter, in addition to which it is so tightly written that Malkhazyants', Thomson, Mahé and the previous editors of the history have not understood exactly what Mosēs is saying. However, any scholar with an interest in the History of Mosēs knows that in the first paragraph of this chapter Mosēs replicates Eusebius. For the accusations of 'complete fake' and 'replete with extraordinary anachronisms' of Thomson, the misgivings of Mahé and the misunderstanding of Malkhazyants', Mosēs cannot be held responsible. My conviction that the compilers of the Middle Ages are responsible for the misunderstandings derives from the very last sentence of this chapter, where it says (my italics): 'So having accurately gained our information, about the reign of Trdat and after him, in such matters from the reports of *wise men and antiquarians*, we have given you a faithful account.' We know Mosēs is sending each completed chapter to his patron and, we also know that he has not yet written anything about Trdat, never mind 'what happened after him', and so the claim of 'accurate information (about Trdat)' and so on containing the name of Trdat do not fit in here, but in fact may be the true continuation of the first paragraph of chapter 87, which is practically the end of the information concerning Trdat. And yet the 'wise men and antiquarians' without the name of Trdat, will make sense and could be identified with 'this same man says' of chapter 76, and the start of chapter 79 which Malkhazyants' mistakenly attributes to Firmilian.

Chapter II.74 at the present finishes with the sentence 'Agat'angełos informs you of the rest'. In my opinion, to this chapter should be added the first part of the second paragraph of chapter 75, which says: 'But as for his account of events after the death of Khosrov down to the reign of Trdat in the period of anarchy, considering this to be accurate we shall repeat it for you briefly.'

After such hypothetical changes, the present chapter 75 will contain only one paragraph (the present first) which, again, is the combination of two different subjects requiring more detailed discussion.

Of the translators of the history, Malkhazyants' does not offer any explanation as to why Firmilian has been attributed with the contents of this chapter. Thomson, in his introduction (p16) says: 'Mosēs claims the authority of Firmilian of Cappadocian Caesarea (died soon after 268) for the history of Armenia down to the reign of Trdat'. On page 35 he adds: 'Mosēs invents a "history"; this time he attributes it to Firmilian, of whom he knew from Eusebius' *Ecclesiastical History*, etc', which is repeated on pages 42 and 221.

Jean-Pierre Mahé mentions the case of Firmilian on pages 36, 45, 71 and in his notes, numbers 4-6, for this chapter. He is of the opinion that Mosēs follows Eusebius, except in the matter of the martyrdom of Peter of Alexandria in 311, since Firmilian died in 268. He also states that Mosēs ascribes events of the period of two separate reigns (Khosrov the Great and his son Trdat) to Firmilian.

Of the more recent commentators, Aram T'op'chyan[43] mentions the views of Gagik Sargsyan that 'at the present it is difficult to explain events relating to Firmilian'. T'op'chyan, himself, does not offer any persuasive conclusion, though he has devoted some twenty pages to the matter.

The criticism of this chapter starts in the nineteenth century, perhaps with Gutschmid, but that is not a problem to be dealt with at the present. All one can say is that the scholars mentioned are highly respected, erudite and good armenologists (except for Gutschmid, who had to rely on the Latin version of the Whiston Brothers and the French of Langlois), which is no guarantee against misunderstanding, particularly when one has to evaluate Mosēs's history.

Below are extracts from both Mosēs and Eusebius which help to explain how one is to understand this chapter. After much thought I have come to the conclusion that there is nothing intentionally falsified in the first paragraph of this chapter, and for the accusations of 'complete fake' and 'replete with extraordinary anachronisms' of Thomson, the misgivings of Mahé and the misunderstanding of Malkhazyants', Mosēs again cannot be held responsible.

The heading of the chapter says '*Yałags P'ermelianay episkoposi Kesaru Kapadovkats'wots' ev patmut'ean norin*', which can be understood in two different senses, since the Armenian word *patmutiwn* means both 'story' and 'history'. The two alternative senses are: 'Concerning the story (relating to the person) of Bishop Firmilian of Cappadocian Caesarea', or 'Concerning the history (written by) Bishop Firmilian of Cappadocian Caesarea'. Scholarship has understood the second sense whereas Mosēs is in fact writing about the former, i.e. the story relating to the person of Firmilian. This should have been simple enough to understand if scholarship had taken note of the last third person pronoun of *norin*. In Armenian we have *nora* (derived from *na*) and *norin* (from *noyn*) as third person genitive singular pronouns, both of which are translated into English as 'his'. However there is a subtle difference

---

43. Aram T'op'chyan, *Movses Khorenats'u Yunakan Ałbyurneri Khndirə*, Matenadaran, Yerevan, 2001.

between the two. For example, the Armenians address their catholicos as *'norin srbutiwn'* ('his holiness'), meaning the holiness of the person of the catholicos; but if the catholicos had written a history, then the phrase would be *'patmutiwn nora'* ('his history'). A second example to reinforce this subtle but important difference between the two possessives is the fact that when praying one asks God for 'his blessings benevolently to bestow on mankind'—*zołormutiwnd norin hacheats' dzonel nots'in*—here in this sentence one cannot use *'nora'* since the 'blessings' are uniquely part of God's singularity.

Knowing that in this chapter Mosēs replicates the *Ecclesiastical History* (Loeb, vol. II, p79, and partly repeated on p211), scholars should have taken care to understand the heading correctly, which would have also facilitated understanding the rest of the chapter. The entire story concerning Firmilian runs from the heading of the chapter II.75 plus the first two and a half lines; the continuation of 'he composed many treatises' refers to Eusebius.

I cite below the parallel extracts from Mosēs and Eusebius' *Ecclesiastical History* (vol. II, Book VI.XXVII), and follow these with my explanations:

A: *Mosēs:* Firmilian, bishop of Caesarea in Cappadocia, was a marvellous scholar who in his youth had gone to study with Origen.

A: *Eusebius:* Now, at this time Firmilian, bishop of Caesarea in Cappadocia, was distinguished; he displayed such esteem for Origen, that at one time he would summon him to his own parts for the benefit of the churches; at another, journey himself to Judaea, and spend some time with him for his own betterment in divine things.

These two quotations have identical senses thus they require no remark save that Mosēs' writing is more compact than that of Eusebius. The heading plus the first sentence of the chapter is the total sum of the story relating to Firmilian. The folowing sentence from Mosēs has no connection with Firmilian, and is the second aspect of scholarly misunderstanding (the first was the heading):

B: *Mosēs:* He [meaning Eusebius] composed many treatises, among them a history of the persecutions of the Church, which arose first in the days of Maximian [should be Maximin 235-238] and Decius and last of all in the reign of Diocletian; <u>he also included in it the deeds of the kings</u>.

B: *Eusebius:* The parallel to Mosēs' sentence, except for its under-lined parts, we find in the *Ecclesiastical History* in three different sections. First the persecutions of Maximin in Book vi.xxvii, which says: 'Maximin Caesar through ill-will towards the house of Alexander, raised a persecution, ordering the leaders of the Church alone to be put to death.' Next we have in Book vi.xxxix: 'Decius, on account of his enmity towards Philip, raised a persecution against the church.' And finally in Book vii.xxx we read: 'Diocletian and those who were brought in after him ... accomplished the persecution of our day and the destruction of the churches.'

The 'he' at the beginning of Mosēs' sentence in B (underlined) has been wrongly ascribed to Firmilian—Eusebius does not tell us of any treatises or books by this author. Some might think that this could refer to Origen, since in Book vi.xxviii Eusebius mentions his works on *Martyrdom* (not 'Martyrs' as Mahé has it) related to 'Maximin's persecutions' and 'the 22nd Expositions of the Gospel according to John'. The latter, the exposition, appears to have had a limited scope as it mainly involved the explanation of the Gospel according to John, besides the improbability that Mosēs might have possessed such a document.

After reading Mosēs' history over and over one becomes familiar with his style. Usually, Mosēs refers to an author as 'he says', 'in this book', 'he writes' or just 'he', and it is up to the reader to discover what these uncertain terms stand for: a reference to what he had written in one of the previous chapters or to a person or book he had mentioned or will be mentioning.

I do not agree with Thomson's translation of Mosēs' last sentence highlighted by underline in B above (this is another misunderstanding). The phrase 'included in it' gives a wrong impression since the Armenian wording of this sentence is *'sharayareal i na ev zgorts's t'agaworats'n'*, which should be understood as 'in line with it he (also) wrote books about the deeds of the kings' (*sharayareal* = 'in line added': *shar* 'row, in line, order', *yar* 'attach, join, add', *i na* 'with it/to it'), i.e. which makes it clear that after writing the *Ecclesiastical History* Eusebius also wrote, and added to it, his *Chronicle*. This also finds confirmation in the fact that

Moses had extracted from the *Ecclesiastical History* when and under which king the persecutions took place; the other deeds of the kings in chronological order were written later in a separate work known as the *Chronicles*.

> *C: Moses:* In this (book) he says that Peter, the sixteenth bishop of Alexandria, was martyred in the ninth year of the persecution.

'In this (book) he says' applies, again, to Eusebius and his *Ecclesiastical History*. It is in the singular, unlike the plural form of the previous reference of 'he composed many treatises'. The excerpt from Eusebius, quoted below, however, does not mention that Peter was 'the sixteenth bishop'. The number sixteen has been taken by Moses from the *Chronicle* (Part II, p302), the only source where this information exists. (This is further confirmation of the sense of *sharayareal*, and reasserts that the *na* ('he') explained above, the third person singular pronoun of 'he composed many treatises', refers to Eusebius.) The actual quotation from the *Ecclesiastical History* (VII.xxxii, repeated in VIII.xiii) says:

> *C: Eusebius:* Peter succeeded to the episcopate of the Alexandrians ... he was beheaded in the ninth year of the persecutions [AD 311].

As a final note, I must add that I find it difficult to understand why Moses would write about Bishop Firmilian of Caesarea, a subject completely unconnected with the history of the Armenians. Indeed the inclusion of such a theme makes me wonder whether the original manuscript contained far more information than what has reached us.

Chapter II.76
Moses begins this chapter with the words 'The same man says...'. Thomson is certain this refers to Firmilian and expresses his disagreement, which we see in his note 1 for this chapter. Mahé is not so sure: he mentions Firmilian but adds that this is rather problematic. We see here the continuation of the misunderstanding of the previous chapter, where the translators ascribed everything to Firmilian. In fact the words 'the same man says' can only apply to the 'wise men and the antiquarians' mentioned at the end of the previous chapter.

Chapter II.81
I explain the arrival of the Mamikoneans in Armenia in my study *The*

History of Bishop Sebēos (pp 98-102). I shall repeat here a few of the known facts and what a number of scholars write in this connection.

Here another of Toumanoff's unending speculations favour a Georgian origins for this family (*Studies*, pp 209-211) and he makes Mancaeus, Tigran the Great's general in charge of the defence of Tigranocerta against the Romans in 69 BC, the eponymous designate of the later Mamikonean family. It is peculiar that for the next four hundred years, after Mancaeus, we hear nothing about the Mamikoneans and that none of the ancient historians mention the name until the time of Khosrov Kotak (AD 336-343).

The opinions of both Mahé and Thomson suffer from preconception, both believing as they do that Moses' history was not a product of the fifth century, meaning that they then have to seek periods in the future to which they can ascribe the work. This sort of artificiality is bound to mislead one and will sooner rather than later end up in contradiction.

Mahé, on page 33 of his commentary says: 'The information given by Moses on the origin of the Mamikoneans, the great rivals of his masters Bagratunis, is manifestly designed to downgrade, even to discredit this illustrious family of Mamikoneans.' He has not given sufficient thought to the implications if Moses had written his history in the fifth century, in a cave in Siwnik' years before becoming bishop of the Bagratunis. How could Moses write anything in his Books I and II about the family or any individual Mamikonean if they had not arrived in Armenia until after AD 225, as we shall see below?

Thomson, in his commentary and notes, has a few remarks in connection with this matter of the Bagratunis versus the Mamikoneans. On page 31 he writes: 'The Mamikonean family, whom the Bagratids had replaced as the dominant force in Armenia and whose role Moses consistently negates'—wrong since it is precisely the opposite of what happened three or four generations after the arrival of the Mamikoneans. On page 58 he states that 'Moses puts his erudition to a definite purpose—boosting the repudation of the Bagratid family', but at the time Moses was writing his history he had no connections with the Bagratids except for young Sahak, who had comissioned the history. On the following page the claim is made that 'more important is Moses' attitude towards the Bagratids and his bias against the Mamikoneans', also wrong considering that the Mamikoneans appear in history at the time of Khosrov Kotak, which is after AD 330, and so belong to the third book of the history.

Remarkably, after the date of 330, I find the Mamikoneans recorded two to three times more frequently than the Bagratids. Thomson adds that 'Mosēs' History reflects the period when the Bagratids were gaining the upper hand over their Mamikonean rivals', and (p60) that 'However, Mosēs' History fits most appropriately into the first decade of Abbasid control over Armenia'. These two sentences illustrate Thomson's preconceptions and my remarks about Mahé apply equally to his position. Furthermore Thomson appears to ignore chronology and certain aspects of history such as in the History of Agat'angełos, which he translated and published in 1976, in section 121 we read: 'Tachat, son-in-law of Artavan the High Constable.' This same Tachat is mentioned by Mosēs in chapter 11.78 as 'Tachad... abducted a beautiful maiden from among Artavazd's sisters...', which confirms that Tachat was a brother-in-law of Artavazd and that the latter was the son of the high constable Artavan! Does this not confirm that the position of high constable passed from the father, Artavan, to his son Artavazd *Mandakuni*. However, most scholars make this Artavazd a Mamikonean (I can find no valid reason for such an act), which may have some bearing on Thomson's opinion.

Thomson is correct in his note 10 under 11.76, that 'the position of high constable or *sparapet* was hereditary in the Mamikonean family in the fifth century', but the part of the history discussing the Mandakunis belongs to the second part of the third century when the Mamikonean family had not yet become prominent, and they are not mentioned in any work. The name Artavazd is not the exclusivity of the Mamikoneans as some would have us believe, since there had already been seven kings bearing this name in Armenia before the Mamikoneans besides other personalities.

We must now look into the story of the Mamikonean family and their arrival into Armenia. Our main source is Mosēs and his history. Sebēos repeats the story in his own style, adding a few pieces to it, which can be seen in my study of the work. Besides Mosēs, we know a little more about the migrations of the Parthians and the Tocharians into the eastern lands of Persia and of the events of AD 224-226 which saw Artashir, the Sassanian, on the throne of Persia. Agat'angełos does not mention the Mamikoneans and P'awstos starts his history from the time of Khosrov Kotak, when this family had started to gain prominence. Another source is Koryun, who mentions Hmayak Mamikonean without recording his position in the governance of the country. Other sources, including Sebēos, come after Mosēs finishes his history in AD 440 and so are not original, but are based mainly on Mosēs.

Towards the end of the second century BC a people living to the northwest of the Chinese, and known to them as the Yueh Chi, migrated south to the east and northeast of Persia, settling exactly where their tribal relatives, the Parthians, had settled before them (the southwestern and eastern regions around the Caspian Sea). During the reign of the Parthian king Vologases I, around the 50s, disorder and local insurrection rose up in the country, since the Yueh Chi, known also as the later Tokharians, sought to rid themselves from servitude to the Parthians and run their own affairs. Around the same time, the Roman general Gnaeus Domitius Corbulo was creating havoc in Armenia, where the Yueh Chi sent an embassy in AD 58, probably for the purpose of asking the Romans to pressurise western Parthia, which might give them a free hand to achieve their objectives of creating an independent kingdom for themselves in the east. As it happened in AD 60 the Yueh Chi/Tokharians (known in Armenian history as the T'etalians) achieved their objective and declared a new kingdom in Bahl and the surrounding lands, which became known as the kingdom of the K'ushans. This lasted until AD 225.

In AD 224 Artashir Papakan won his decisive battle against the Parthian king of Persia, Artavan V, and in 226 established the new Sassanian dynasty of Persia. However, in 225 Artashir had already destroyed the kingdom of the K'ushans to the east, and he had moved some of the asistocracy to Persia. The eponymous ancestors of the Mamikonean family, one of the noble families of the Tocharians, were exiled to Armenia either by Artashir himself or by his son and the next king Shabuh. The dispersion of the Tocharian noble families was an important part of the exercise to ensure security for the conqueror and the peaceful domination of the conquered land. Agat'angełos knows of these facts, which is obvious from his statement in section 26, where Artashir promises to Anak the reward of 'to return to them their native Parthian rule, and their own Pahlavi dominations', which is also repeated by Mosēs in II.67 (also in II.74) as: 'I shall return to you your own native honourable Pahlav again and reward you with a crown.' P'awstos, too, knows this fact, since he writes in Book IV.32 that 'Dehkan, patriarch of his people, was entrusted by Shabuh with a large army in order to invade Armenia, and this Dehkan was racially related to the Mamikoneans'.

The conclusion of this short history is that the ancestors of the Mamikoneans could not have arrived in Armenia before AD 225. It appears they arrived in Armenia at the time of the reign of Trdat II (AD 217-252). From the date of arrival of the ancestors of the Mamikoneans it would take three to four generations for them to prove themselves and earn prominence. In fact Mosēs has a short extract in this connection in chapter 81, where in the last paragraph (no. 5) reveals the following statement: 'Trdat received him (Mamgon) but did not take him with him in his war against Persia. However he gave his entourage a place and a stipend for food; he changed their residence from place to place for many years.'

*

Part IV
The Enigma of Mar Abas Katina

The case of Mar Abas Katina has preoccupied me for a while and I think I have now examined it from every possible angle. There are some scholars, particularly in Armenia, who blindly believe that such an erudite person existed and that his work is the first written history of the Armenian nation. My research allows me to agree with them, but still one is obliged to substantiate such a claim at the very least with a modicum of circumstantial evidence, particularly when the matter has acquired such prominence that most of those working in Armenian studies have, sometime or other, had to tackle it in the course of their carreers.

In this chapter I shall not discuss any of the numerous opinions, since such an effort will be of no benefit to the reader. It is only recently that the results of my research into the pre-history of the Armenians have become available, and without the wide historical background I have uncovered it would have been impossible for any researcher to comprehend precisely what Khorenats'i wrote and in which period of time he completed his history. My second reason for not discussing the works of other scholars, such as Patkanyan, Khalat'yants', Carrière, Adontz and Manandyan, is due to the fact that their endeavours and consequently their conclusions suffer from their preconceptions, specifically concerning the date of Khorenats'i's history, which greatly restricts any perspective on their side.

However, prior to discussing Mar Abas, it is of utmost importance to examine his work according to Mosēs Khorenats'i, which will involve the examination of all the names appearing in Book 1, chapters 12, 19 and 22 of the History of the Armenians, and the four decisive battles the Hays fought between the eighth to sixth centuries BC. Khorenats'i claims to have derived these names and the battles from Mar Abas, which cannot be doubted; because Khorenats'i does not even have an understanding of some of them, and whenever he tries to explain certain aspects of the names or the persons bearing these names, he is usually wrong. Additionally, the names he records are not those appearing in the Assyro-Babylonian or hieroglyphic inscriptions of the Hay kings, because the ancient names had been recomposed in the course of the Classical Armenian era for the understanding of the people of the time. Khorenats'i knows none of the ancient names and most of the recomposed names are beyond his understanding, as the case has been with scholarship in general for the past 1,500 years or so. As for the four battles, Khorenats'i presents these in his own style which, although historically ascertainable events, present great difficulties not only for the reader but also for the historian and armenologist in general.

THE GENERATION DESCENDED FROM HAYK (CHAPTER I.12)

The following names represent the generation of Hayk according to Khorenats'i. However, here the name Hayk represents the Hay people and not an individual person, irrespective of the story Khorenats'i has intertwined.

FIRST GENERATION:	*Aramaneak	*Manawaz	*Khor	
SECOND:	*Kadmos	*Aramayis	*Baz	
THIRD:	*Amasia	*Shara		
FOURTH:	Gełam	P'arokh	Ts'olak	*Erast
FIFTH:	Harma	Sisak		
SIXTH:	*Aram	Garnik		
SEVENTH:	*Ara the Fair	'Tork' Angeł'		

a) Names with asterisks do not appear in the known Assyro-Babylonian inscriptions.

b) Names in italics do not represent persons. Aramaneak means the 'Circuit of Aram' (Aram + Maneak, and note that in syllabic script two consonants cannot follow each other), Aram represents the 'Country of Aram' and Kadmos is Kadmukhi.

c) Erast and Ara the Fair (in bold) represent the same person.

d) Tork' Angeł is listed in inverted commas because it in fact appears in chapters 1.23 and 11.8 of the history, translated by Malkhazyants'.

The names and remarks

Hayk was made the primogenitor of the Armenian people, yet he belongs to the late eighth century BC; the Proto-Armenians had kingdoms and kings in Carchemish and Gurgum (Marash) some 280 years before him. He has also been attached to the building of the biblical 'unruly tower', when the division of languages was supposed to have taken place, and he was the sole giant to oppose Bēl. He certainly deserves all honours bestowed upon him since in the whole of Proto-Armenian history he was the only person to oppose the Assyrians and prevail. His Proto-Armenian name, recorded by the Assyrians was Ēshpai the Kulumean.[1] The name Ēshpai means 'Ass Hay', where *ēsh* ('ass') is an epithet and stands for 'brave, huge, manly, strong'. The Kulumean part of the name is a cognomen deriving from the city name of Kuluman, in southeastern Assyria, where he was exiled and lived for a while[2] (most probably the exile of the people of Zapkaka, Hayk's habitation place, took place in 708 BC when Sargon was building fortifications in five cities, one of which was Kiaka),[3] until the time he ran away to his own abode. In the Classical Armenian era his name was recomposed as Hayk, the meaning of which is unknown (I am inclined to think that the *-k* ending of the name is a suffix); but in literature and history it usually stands for both a person and for the Hay nation. The constellation of Orion was named after him, but he never acquired divinity, irrespective of the wishful and imaginative writings of certain scholars. I shall return later to the subject of Hayk when I deal with the battle of Hayk and Bēl.

Aramaneak was, according to the legendary narrative of Khorenats'i, Hayk's firstborn in Babylon. The name at the time it was created had the exclusive meaning of the land of the 'Circuit of Aram' (*Aram* the country + *maneak* = 'circuit, circler, necklace, bracelet'). Aramaneak has been presented as a person and assigned a son named Kadmos, which is another country name. Aramaneak as a name does not appear in any inscriptions be it hieroglyphics or Assyro-Babylonian. Nowadays it is a popular name, though many confuse it with Armenak'.

1.   J. D. Hawkins, 'The Neo-Hittite States in Syria and Anatolia', in *Cambridge Ancient History*, vol. III, part 1, 1982, p422.
2.   L. Waterman, *Royal Correspondence of the Assyrian Empire*, Ann Arbor, 1930-36. vol. 1, letter no. 129.
3.   D. D. Luckenbill, *Ancient Records of Assyria*, Chicago 1926-27, see 'Sargon II: The Annals', §27.

Manawaz means 'Fiery Magus' (*man* 'magus' = *mog* + *aw* 'being' + *az* 'fire'). The patriarchal house of Manawazean derives from him. He was the second king of Gurgum (Marash) and his Proto-Armenian name was Muwazisa,[4] meaning 'The Fiery Magus' (*muw* → *mog/mow* + *az* 'fire' + *isa* 'this one'). This name does not appear in the Assyrian inscriptions.

Khor is not a personal name but represents the Hurrian population of the country of Carchemish and the patriarchal house name of Khorkhorunik' derives from it. The name does not appear in the Assyrian inscriptions, which is understandable, since there was no such person.

Kadmos is the name of the country of Kadmukhi in the south of the Armenian Highlands. The patriarchal house of Kadmeans derives from this country name. Kadmos was the only Hay king of Kadmukhi in the city of Hubushkia. As there was no continuation of this Hay kingdom, in Khorenats'i's history he has been made a son of Aramaneak, which means a branch of the Hays of Aram country and has been assigned no progeny. In history the real name of this king was Dati of the time of Shamshi-Adad V (823-810 BC) the husband of Semiramis; see Shamshi-Adad's third campaign in the Assyrian inscriptions.[5]

Before the middle of the second century BC, with the arrival from the Balkans of the Mygdonians, Doberes, Laioi and so on who augmented the Gordyina population already settled in Gordyene in the south of Armenia some two hundred years earlier, the Kadmean lands with its capital city of Nisibis (Mtsbin) contained the largest concentration of Hays in the whole of Armenia.

Baz or **Bazuk** are two forms of the same name: in chapter 12 it is Baz but reoccurs in chapter 19 as Bazuk. Both mean 'arm', hence 'minister, chargé d'affaires, deputy'. His Proto-Armenian name was Sastura, which means 'Grand Admonisher' (*sast* = 'to reprimand, scold' + *ura* = 'augmented, grand' = 'Grand Admonisher'). In ancient days such a person was either the king himself or his prime minister. Baz/Bazuk was the son of Arayan Ara (Yarairaisa) of Carchemish, the prime minister of King Astiruwa (Erast or Ara the Fair) and inherited the position on the death of his father (754 BC), becoming the prime minister of Kamana (Havanak),[6] and

4. G. Soultanian, *The Pre-History of the Armenians, Volume II*, 2004; pp 120-23, 'The Marash Lion Inscription'.
5. Luckenbill, *Shamshi-Adad V*, 'The Monolith Inscription', §718.
6. G. Soultanian, *Pre-History Volume II*, 'The Cekke Inscription of Kamana', p102.

on the death of the latter the prime minister of Pisiri (Husak),[7] the youngest son of Ara the Fair. The house of Bznunik' derives from this name. The Assyrian inscriptions make no mention the name of Sastura, Baz or Bazuk.

Aramayis means 'the Wind of Aram' (*Aram* the country + *ayis* → *ays* 'wind'). His Proto-Armenian name was Tuwatis meaning 'Wind like King/Kingdom' (*tuw* → *t'ag* 'king' or 'kingdom' + *atis* → *ayis* → *ays* 'wind' [intervocalic *t>y*]). He was the king of Tabal and was given the title of 'Great King' (in Proto-Armenian *apawa* → *awag* where *p>w*, *w>g*) in the inscription Kululu 1 of Ruwas.[8] He died at nearly the same time as Astiruwa in the plague that had started in Carchemish and spread to other districts. The Assyrians do not record his name but the Urartians do. This compound name confirms that it was composed in southern Armenia where Mar Abas lived; this is inferred from the fact that in the north and the northeast of Armenia the word for wind was *sik* or *siwk* (a loan from the Aramaean), whereas in the south, the newly arrived migrants from the Balkans used the indigenous word *ays*.[9]

Amasia was a contemporary of Muwazisa of Gurgum, though he was a king of Carchemish. Both of these kings belong to the first half of the tenth century BC. His name means 'Preacher of Amity' (*am* 'joint' [as in *am-us-in* 'husband'] + *as* 'to say'; the *am* shares the same root as English 'amity'). His Proto-Armenian name was Asatuwatimaza,[10] which has the same meaning (i.e. *as* = to say + *a-tu-wa* 'to become' + *ti* 'bodily' + *maza* 'coalesce' = 'Preacher of Amity'). The Assyrians do not record this name.

Gełam. He was the son of Khelaruata/Vstamkar and inherited the throne of Melid after his father's death. His name means 'Wholly Noble', but the *geł* part of the name, and those other names that contain *geł*, has been misunderstood. His Proto-Armenian name was Sulumal (*sul* → *ts'ol* 'radiance' + *um* 'who is' + *al* → *ał* 'salt'; salt was the ancient endearing diminutive, hence 'Radiance Who Is Affable'). The district and the patriarchal house in Armenia have both the same name of Gełark'unik', but none derives from the name Gełam, although Lake Lychnides was renamed after him as Lake Gełama, and the Vishap

7. Ibid., 'Inscription Carchemish A22b of Pisiri', pɪɪɪ.
8. Ibid., 'The Kululu 1 Inscription of Ruwas', pp 150-53.
9. Adjaryan, *Dictionary of Armenian Root Words*, vol. 1.
10. Soultanian, *Pre-History Volume II*, 'Inscription Carchemish A14b', p47.

Stones of the Geł Mountains derive from his slaying of the dragon Illuyanka. He is remembered in the inscriptions of Tiglath-Pileser III (745-727 BC) of Assyria.[11]

P' aṛokh—there were two kings of Gurgum (Marash) who had this name. I am of the opinion that Khorenats'i records the second P'aṛokh, since the first does not appear in Assyrian records. P'aṛokh is one of the more difficult names to explain, since the meaning of the second root *okh* has also the meanings of 'revenge, spiteful' and so on. He was a priest king and, according to his Proto-Armenian name, was a fanatic in religious matters, and therefore I have translated the name as 'Blessed Diligence' (*p'aṛ* + *okh*, with the sense of 'he was illiberal so far as worship of the god was concerned'). His Hay name was Larazamasa (*lar* → *yar* 'attached' + *az* 'fire' + *a-masa* 'to the God' → 'Attached to the Fire of the God'), but the Assyrians called him by his demotic name Palalam,[12] which has a similar meaning. The name Palalam is explained as *pal* → *hal* 'attached' + *alam* → *ałam* 'salt together' (see *am* in the name Amasia and *al* in the name Sulumal), which has an identical meaning to the Modern Armenian *ałakits'* 'to take salt together' = 'inseparable + devotion'.

Ts'olak was the eunuch of Tiglath-Pileser III, who gave him the governorship of Kunalua of Patinu in Unqi on the Orontes river.[13] His Proto-Armenian name was Kulani, which means 'Inane Radiance', having the sense of 'Radiance with No Say' in matters of state (*kul* → *ts'ol* = 'radiance' + *ani* = 'devoid, empty, worthless'), which has changed to Ts'olak (*ts'ol* = *kul* 'radiance' + *ak* 'source') in later composition (an obvious euphemism has taken place by changing the *ani* ['empty, worthless'] to *ak* ['source']). Khorenats'i presents him as a son of Amasia, but in reality there is an interval of two hundred years between the two.

Shara is supposed to derive from the district name of Shirak (at his time there was no such district) but in reality it is an imitation of the word *shariat*, which means 'usury, interest'. In ancient history the name of this person is recorded by the Urartians as Shakhu ('Usurer') and in one case

11. Luckenbill, §801.
12. J. D. Hawkins, 'Assyrians and Hittites', in *Iraq* 36, 1974, pp 733-75.
13. Hawkins, 'The Neo-Hittite States in Syria and Anatolia', *CAH*, vol. III, part 1, 1982, p410.
14. Diakonoff, *Pre-History of the Armenian People*, p199, note 119.

King Menua calls him Shadawale[14] ('Extremely Stingy'—over time an obvious euphemism has occurred by changing *shakh* ['usurer'] to *shah* ['legitimate profit']). The patriarchal house (later dukedom) deriving from him took the name of Shahunis, where the *shah* means 'legitimate profit'. The Assyrian inscriptions do not mention this king of Melid.

Harma was a great king of Tabal whose Proto-Armenian name is Wasusaramimasa,[15] which means 'Throne of God Sarami'. The Assyrians acknowledge him but write his name as Uassurme, which present scholarship writes as Wassusarma. Both of the latter two forms have the meaning of 'throne Sarma', which is the same as the ancient name. The translator of the Assyrian rendering of Uassurme has simply taken the *sarma* part and transcribed it as *harma* ($s \rightarrow h$). Harma was a usurper although he did manage to earn for himself, in the hieroglyphic inscriptions, the title of 'Great King', while in the History of Khorenats'i he became 'Father of Aram', meaning the leading king of Aram. His battle with Bar-ga'ya (Payapis K'aałea) of KTK (Kaskans) is described in the Topada inscription,[16] but in Khorenats'i's history this battle is ascribed to the non-existent patriarch Aram (representing the country of Aram).

Sisak is the transcription of the Proto-Armenian Kikki. Both Sisak and Kikki cannot be explained in the Armenian language. I am of the opinion that Kikki belongs to the Hay colonizers from the Balkans who started to arrive together with the Phrygians around the end of the ninth century BC and settled to the east of the Phrygians in the extensive lands of Tabal. Kikki is recognized by Shalmaneser III of Assyria[17] in the years 837 and 836 BC, which more or less validates my conjecture concerning the time of their arrival in Tabal. I think the name derives from the Greek *kikus* or *gigas*, the first meaning 'strength, vigour' and the second 'giant'. The city of Sissu (Sis) in northern Cilicia was named after him, the same as the district of Sisakan in Armenia.

Erast. The river 'Eraskh' Khorenats'i says in chapter 1.12 was named after Erast, which is impossible, as the two names do not correlate (Erast, like Astir, means 'Mighty Thinker/Just', whereas Eraskh means 'Foremost Worthy/Wonder'). The name represents Astir, king of

---

15.   Luckenbill, §772.
16.   Soultanian, *Pre-History Volume II*, pp 154-162.
17.   Luckenbill, §772

Carchemish, who died young and much later the myth of Ara the Fair was woven in exultation of his person. The syllables of Astir have been transposed at some time in the past, i.e. Ast-ir → Ir-ast. In the inscription of his son Kamana (Havanak) Astir is also called Ira,[18] which has become Ara. All the same, Astir or Ara was not a contemporary of Semiramis, the wife of Shamshi-Adad V of Assyria, nor has he any connection with the Er of Plato's *Republic* as has been suggested by others.

Aram as a country has been known to us since the days of Naram-Sin of Agade as the ancient name of southeastern Anatolia. However the old Armenian writers have continued to use the name in this respect and they have also believed that Aram included the extensive lands of Tabal and Melid kingdoms, since Tegarama or Togarmah (T'orgoma Tun), their Biblical home, was on the border of Melid and Tabal. Furthermore, the three battles described by Khorenats'i in 1.13 and 14 are ascribed to Aram as a person, creating the non-existent patriarch Aram. I think these ascriptions were due to the fact that the actual names of the kings involved were not known. The two simultaneous wars of the middle of the eighth century were by Harma, in the north, against Payapis K'aałea the Parzutean, and by Kamana against Mati-ilu of Arpat in the south. The third war, in *c.* 588 BC against the Medo-Scythian army under the generalship of Mades was by the Ostan organization (Branches of the Hays) under the leadership of Haykak 'the Other', the Manawazean of Gurgum (Marash), hence their land was called Hark' (Fathers = Leaders) and the township Haykashēn was founded in his name.

Gaṛnik—it is amazing how a name like Sangara, meaning 'Nurturer Lamb', with the sense of 'Caretaker of his People' has become merely Gaṛn-ik, meaning 'Lamb' in the diminutive and endearing form. Gaṛnik was king of Carchemish at the time of Shalmaneser III, and his name appears many times in the Assyrian inscriptions.[19] It is most likely that he was also the great-grandfather of Astir (Erast/Ara the Fair)—this is the impression given by the inscription of Körkün[20] (see *Pre-History Volume II*, pp 90-94, for the translation of this inscription).

---

18. G. Soultanian, *Pre-History Volume III: The Anatolian Hieroglyphic Inscriptions of the Proto-Armenians*, 'Inscription Carchemish A5a.2'.
19. Luckenbill, §599.
20. Soultanian, *Pre-History Volume II*, 'The Körkün Inscription', pp 90-94.

Ara the Fair is discussed under Erast above. Due to the myths around the person of Astir (Erast), the compiler of the list thought he was dealing with two distinct persons.

Tork' Angeł is a name that does not appear in the same chapter (1.12) as all the others discussed above. But he is an integral part of the design of the chapter. Khorenats'i mentions him as an afterthought in chapters 1.23 and 11.8. The name Tork' Angeł means 'Thunder the Ignoble'; his Proto-Armenian name was Tarkunazi (*tark* 'thunder' + *un* 'devoid' + *az* 'fire' = 'Thunder Devoid of Fire'). This name has been misunderstood. Scholars explain the name as 'Tork' the Ugly', which would have been correct and in line with the intentions of the original translation provided that they attributed the ugliness to his character and not his physical appearance. He was promoted to kingship by Sargon II of Assyria, perhaps in 718 BC, but a while later, in 712 BC, a displeased Sargon sent his army in order to apprehend him.[21] Tarkunazi left his city of Melid and the population to the mercy of the Assyrian army and fled to Til-Garimmu (Togarmah) in order to save his skin, which was one of the reasons he was called Thunder-Devoid-of-Fire (Tarkunazi). The people of Togarmah, in fear of the Assyrian army, handed him over, when he was taken to Nineveh in chains.

The names Manawaz, Khor, Baz, Aramayis, Amasia, Shara and Erast/Ara the Fair do not appear in the Assyrian inscriptions and are therefore taken from the place names existing in Armenia. The name Sisak/Kikki appears in the records of Shalmaneser III together with his father Tuatte, but in the lists there is no such name as Tuatte (→ Tagat 'Capable King/Kingdom'), which tells us that Sisak, too, may have been taken from the place name Sisakan, The remaining names of Gełam, P'arokh, Ts'olak, Harma, Gaṛnik and Tork' Angeł are recorded by the Assyrians, but they could have been easily derived from place names of Gełark'uni, P'aṛakhot, Ts'olakert, Gaṛni and Angeł Tun. However, it is noteworthy that these names from the Assyrian inscriptions, do not appear in the second comprehensive list of chapter 1.19, which creates some doubt as to whether the entire list was composed from the place names existing in Armenia after the second half of the second century BC, or the work of Mar Abas was supplemented and had undergone editing as we shall see.

21. A. G. Lie, *The Inscriptions of Sargon II, King of Assyria: Part 1, The Annals*, Librairie Orientaliste Paul Geuthner, Paris, 1929, §§ 206-213, p35.

The composition of the name of Aramayis tells us that the list was prepared in the south of Armenia and points to the late second century BC when the newcomers from the Balkans settled. I believe Mar Abas could not have composed this name, since being a Syriac he would have used instead of *ays* the word *siwk*, which was in circulation in the northern parts of Armenia. There is no doubt that Mar Abas has taken all the names (except a few, which I shall discuss) appearing in the second and third name-lists, those of 'the Genesis of our Grandees, correlated with Hebrews and the Chaldaeans' (1.19) and 'the Order of our Kings' (1.22), from the Assyrian and Babylonian sources.

List one, enumerated above, gives us the deployment of the various ancient Hay patriarchal houses in the highlands. It also hints at a political arrangement between the ancient Ostan houses with the centralized three most important as arbitrators, nipped in the bud by the Medes soon after their settlement. One can easily determine the eight houses and the reason why they selected their various locations of settlement by sorting out the place names of the list from those of later known dukedoms.

In my opinion, this first name list (Book 1.12) of Khorenats'i's History is a masterpiece of ancient historiography, since its analysis gives us the history of the Hays' entry into Urartu and the dispersion of the Indo-European language speaking newcomers throughout the highlands. Therefore it is important that we have a deeper understanding of what is written. The names of the list represent the progeny of Hayk, but Hayk in this capacity stands for the Hay people. When we look at all the three name-lists (Book 1.12, 19, 22) we note that each starts in a most peculiar manner. The first begins with the son of Hayk, Aramaneak, the second with the son of Aram the Patriarch, and the third with Paroyr, as the first person to whom kingship was granted by Cyaxares. Is it not remarkable that these individuls never existed but that all three names represent place names: Aramaneak is the circuit of Aram, Aram is the country so called from times immemorial, and Paroyr is the city Par (= Missis, the later Mamestia) in Cilicia Campestris where reigned a few kings of the Hays. The other peculiarity is that the first list after starting with the place name Aramaneak, ascribes to it (i.e. to a place name!) a son named Kadmos, which is another place name.

My explanation of this strange but extremely clever manner of writing ancient history is that the Hay people, in the guise of Hayk, had their kingdoms in the country of Aramaneak (circuit of Aram) and one single branch in Kadmukhi, which starts and ends with Kadmos (Dati), making the branch of Kadmukhi an offspring of Aram. After making this part clear the list starts to enumerate the names of the other sons (kings) of the Hay people. When we discard all the names represented by place names in Armenia, we end up with eight ex-royal houses, who entered Urartu under the banner of the Ostan organization and settled on the periphery of the highlands, except for the three most important who settled to the north and northwest of Lake Van, i.e. Khorkhorunik', Bznunik', and bordering them both to the north the Manawazeans, incorporating the district of Hark'—these three houses were centrally situated in the Highland of Armenia. The remaining five houses settled on the periphery of the highlands were: Gełark'unik' (northeast), Sisakeans (east), Kadmeans (south), Angeł Tun (southwest) and Shahunis (west).

The patriarchal houses comprising the Ostan

It is important that we have a good knowledge of the background of all the eight houses, since they were the first leaders of the nation, which later, in the times of Vałarsh I during the first half of the second century AD, were reduced to the rank of dukedoms.

Gełark'unik': Urartian kings Menua, Argishti and Sarduri II had penetrated Malatya, plundered the country and relocated great numbers of Hays in the northeast of the highlands in order to create a buffer zone between the barbarians and their own country.[22] The country where the Hay slaves were relocated, at the time of Sarduri II, under the leadership of the relocated royal hostages, became known as Uelikuni = Gełark'unik' (*geł* = 'noble' + *ark'unik'* = 'royal family'; hence 'Royal Family of Nobles'), the royal family of Gełs. These slaves were responsible for the building of the settlement named Erebuni (later Erevan) in the time of Argishti in 782 BC. It is thus obvious that the followers of the royal house of Gełs (Khelaruata/Vstamkar and Sulumal/Gełam) of Malatya would want to settle in the northeast, where

---

22. The Urartian kings Menua, Argishti I and Sarduri II brought from Melid and Tabal, in the course of their attacks on these countries, huge numbers of slaves. In the case of Argishti it is known that the number was nearly 30,000 plus 6,600 soldiers. It may well be that the total number of these relocated people exceeded 120,000, in view of voluntary migrations, such as the family of a soldier, father, mother and brothers of a slave, or even friends and distant relations. This hypothesis makes it plain that Erebuni was built by the original relocated Hays and by the time of Sarduri the Hay population was large enough to call the district by the name of the Melitinean royal hostages' become the leaders of the colony as Gełark'unik', the 'Royal House of the Nobles'.

they perhaps had relatives or, at least had some of their own people already settled. When Artashēs I became king of Armenia with his capital city in the northeast, this house became extinct.

Sisakeans: Originally the people of Tabal, who had close links with Malatya, since the last kings, Mugallu (Mshak) and his son ...ussi (Anushavan) were kings in both Tabal and Malatya. It was therefore advantageous that they keep their neighbourly connections functioning by settling to the south of Gełark'unik', which is the reason Khorenats'i makes Sisak a son of Gełam with the extensive lands of Sisakan (later Siwnik').

Kadmeans: This was the second oldest family settled in the south of the highlands, around Nisibis (Mtsbin), since the time of Shamshi-Adad v of Assyria. The name of the king was Dati. They never moved away from their lands and in the course of the second century BC the ex-royal family of Dati became the most powerful, since their territory had the highest concentration of Hay people, newly arrived from the Balkans and bearing the names of the Mygdonians, Gordyene, Laioi, Doberes,[23] etc. When Vałarshak the Parthian was appointed the viceroy of the lands north of Mesopotamia, this house became extinct.

Angełats' Tun: The epithet Angeł ('ignoble') is a creation from between the second century BC and the second century AD. It is the replacement in Classical Armenian of the Proto-Armenian compound *unaz*, meaning 'fireless'. The whole name has been misunderstood. Scholars studying the History have understood the name of Tark/Tork' as that of the god of thunder of southeastern Anatolia. In reality Tark means 'thunder' only, unless it is preceded by the sign for god (no. 360), and only in such a case does the reading become 'God Tark' (for further details see 'The Real Tork' Angeł' in Part IV). Therefore, the Tork' of the Armenians should have been understood as 'thunder' and the remaining *angeł* as 'ignoble', hence 'Ignoble Thunder' = 'Thunder Devoid of Fire', as explained above. This is the oldest house settled in the southwest of the highlands and they may be the remnants of the Hays of the Mushki conglomerate.[24] At the time of the relocation in the highlands of the population of Malatya and surrounds, obviously the followers of the house of Angełs would settle in their ancestral lands.

---

23. Soultanian, *Pre-History Volume I*, pp 32, 37.
24. A. K. Grayson, *Assyrian Royal Inscriptions*, Wiesbaden, 1972-76: vol. II, 'Tiglath-Pileser I', §12, p6.

Shahunis: This name derives from that of Shakhu, king of Malatya and father of Khelaruata (Vstamkar). One notices a euphemism in the later composition of the name as Shah, which means 'legitimate profit', whereas Shakh means 'usury'. Khorenats'i equates his name of Shara with the district of Shirak, whereas it derives from the word *shariat*;[25] at the time there was no place known as Shirak (this is a reference to the Gusharids of the north, a branch of the Shahunis, who were not members of the Ostan). I think it was this Shakhu's efforts to extend his domain to the other side of the Euphrates river—where his people, i.e. the followers of the house of Shakhu, settled, with the district becoming known as Little Sophene—that gave reason enough for Menua to attack Malatya and even penetrate Tabal. Khorenats'i also tells us that the Gusharids, a later house to the north of the highlands, formed a branch of the Shahunis. But the Gusharids were never a member of the Ostan organization and their name does not appear in the first name-list (Book 1.12) nor any other list.

Khorkhorunis: This is a duplication of the root *Khor*, which means Hurrian. These were the armenicised Hurrians of the country of Carchemish, which is the reason why in the first list (Book 1.12) Khor has no progeny. They were important since most of the Hurrian people of southeastern Anatolia looked up to them as their leaders. The northern shores of Lake Van were the ancient settlement areas of both the Hurrians and the Manda people. This may be the reason why this new wave settled in the centre of the highlands and the district they named Khorkhorunik'.

Bznunik' (also Bznunis or Bznuneans) is the name of a house deriving from Baz/Bazuk (Sastura), the prime minister of both Kamana and Pisiri. In 718 BC Sargon II of Assyria put an end to the kingdom of Carchemish. The king, Pisiri, and his entire family together with his retinue were taken to Nineveh,[26] which means there was no royalty left behind. By this time, it appears, Baz/Bazuk had already died and his family escaped exile. Therefore, in the absence of a royal family, the house of Baz/Bazuk became the leading family of the Hays of Carchemish. When these Hays participated in the Ostan organization and entered Urartu, this was carried out under the flag of the house of Baz/Bazuk (Sastura). This family and its followers settled to the northwest of Lake Van and the district became known as Bznunik', who

---

25. Adjaryan, *Dictionary of Armenian Root Words*; see the word *shariad*.
26. A. G. Lie, *The Inscriptions of Sargon II, King of Assyria: Part I, The Annals*, Librairie Orientaliste Paul Geuthner, Paris, 1929, lines 72-74.

were actually the descendants of Arayan Ara (Yarairaisa), the father of Baz/Bazuk.

Manawazeans: This derives from Muwazisa or Manawaz, the second king of Gurgum (Marash).[27] The ex-royal family of the Manawazeans of Marash were the most important and perhaps the oldest of all the kingdoms while the Hays lived in the land of Aram. It was their patriarch Haykak who lead the Ostan army of Hays into Urartu and conducted the battle against the Medo-Scythian forces. For this reason the Manawazeans became known as the 'Fathers', which means Leaders and Seniors of the Nation, and their lands bordering both the Khorkhorunis and Bznunis, to the north of Lake Van, became known as Hark'. In other words this was the place where the 'Fathers' of the nation lived. A township was either built or renamed Haykashēn, after the name of Haykak, the patriarch of the ex-royal family.

All the patriarchal houses settled in places where they already had either a following population or an interest, with the exception of the Manawazeans and the Bznunis. These two settled centrally since they were the leading families and were two of the three centrally placed houses (the third being the Khorkhorunik'), who appear to have possessed the jurisdiction to solve problems arising between all the houses established in the new country. Surprisingly, Urartu never took part in the organizations of the Hays, irrespective of the fact that the remnants of the Urartian army may have also joined in the fight against the Medo-Scythians, since their kingdom had already been annihilated and the country was being burned and destroyed under the Median army led by Mades.

Now that we know a little of the personalities and the patriarchal houses deriving from them, we should now examine the case of Ara the Fair, also known as Astir or Erast. The Mesopotamians, Assyria and Babylonia, do not know this name nor the person bearing the name. The compiler of the name-list, Mar Abas Katina or another person of later times, would have known of the minstrels (gusans) who sang the praises of Ara the just and benevolent king of the Hays. My own research has revealed that the Hay people had classes of minstrels as early as the eighth century BC that we know of,[28] which means that from the time of Ara up to the time of Mar

---

27. See note 4 above. Halparutiya III records the genealogy of the kings of Marash, his ancestors, totalling seven names including his own.
28. See note 18 above. The Kululu Lead Strip No.1, line 41 records *tasa kusana* and line 42 *tasa tapaia*, which means the class of minstrels and class of drummers.

Abas the various songs or praises of this king were being sung. Of course, in time such perpetuations start to mutate and modify in line with the minstrel's taste and creativity and a parabolic language which may be essential in order to keep an audience spellbound and may be the first steps of such mutations. Mar Abas was versed in Greek and the Chaldaean languages and in Mesopotamia his research would have included the histories of Ctesias, particularly the parts involving Semiramis (connected with the building of the city of Van and its canals) and Memnon of Trojan fame (these have been preserved in the histories of Diodorus Siculus). The conclusion must be that either the minstrels had heard of what Ctesias had written prior to Mar Abas' journey to Mesopotamia, or else it would have to be the latter himself who had spun such fantastic stories around the person of Ara the Fair, who actually died in the plague of *c.* 770 BC. But there remains a third possibility, which I shall discuss in the concluding part of this analysis. Khorenats'i was aware that the information in part derives from the songs of the gusans, since in Chapter 1.8, concerning Shamiram, he says that the legends of our country confirm what Mar Abas writes. However, he did not suspect that the latter's book had been subject to editing and that its editor based his additions on stories that he had gathered from the songs of the minstrels and written down, while himself remaining an unknown and unimportant person.[29]

Another facet of this first name-list is that in the History of Moses, in chapter 12, we have no names of the contemporaries of the Proto-Armenian kings either from the Assyro-Babylonians or Hebrews, such as the names of the Hebrew patriarchs and the Chaldaean kings of list 2 (ch. 19) and the names of the Median kings in list three (ch. 22). The nonexistence of foreign names in chapter 12 is intentional, since the author, Mar Abas, does not want to divert attention from the entry of the Hays into Urartu.[30]

Finally, my opinion is that most of this first name-list has nothing to do with the Assyro-Babylonian records. It is instead based on the political conditions prevailing in the highlands in the sixth century BC onwards, and is compiled in such a clever manner that it divulges the

---

29. Moses Khorenats'i, *The History of the Armenians*, Book 1.14.
30. Abelyan, contemplating chapter 12, states that it represents the move of the Proto-Armenians into Urartu ('Erker', vol. 1, *Academia*, 1966, pp 39-40). However, his discussion of Hayk, Aram, Ara the Fair, Tork' Angeł and so on are light years away from the truth. It appears erudite scholars never credit 'ordinary people' with creative powers, even when they are aware that such creativity is the source of the livelihood of the ordinary storyteller (and who were the first storytellers, scholars?). Abelyan may have been a great linguist and philologist, but never a deep thinker, since the damage he has done to the Armenian language is only now being realised.

Hays' entry into Urartu. This thinking points to the real reason for compiling three distinct name-lists which, though different from each other, contain names alien to the Assyro-Babylonian records. In other words, Mar Abas could have written this name list without having to go to Mesopotamia for research. But the question is, had Mar Abas actually written this first name list and the various battles of the Hays?

THE AGREEMENT OF THE GENEALOGY OF THE HAY NATION WITH THOSE OF THE HEBREWS AND CHALDAEANS

The start of the second name list in Book 1.19 is disorderly, since in chapter 14 Khorenats'i records the name of Mshak, which is not included in this name list. Besides, he also starts with the names of Arayan Ara and his son Anushavan. Therefore it is important to sort out these three names prior to examining the remainder of the list, which is mainly taken from the Assyro-Babylonian records.

Mshak: The meaning is that of 'husbandman, tiller of the land' (Greek 'Geōrgos'), but here it has the sense of 'cultivator', since in chapter 1.14 Mshak was made a caretaker of the extreme west around Caesarea and was instructed by Aram to teach the people the Armenian language. His name in the Assyrian records was Mugallu, a contemporary of both Esarhaddon and Ashurbanipal.[31] Mugallu means 'Progressed Affable Person' (*mug* > *moz* 'progressed, mighty, augmented' + *allu* > *alu* = 'affable, benevolent, kind'), which does not have the same meaning as the 'Mshak (Cultivator) of Moses'. Mugallu was the king of Togarmah and Malatya but after the mysterious disappearance of Ishkallu of Tabal, his rule also extended to cover Tabal. He was the father of Anushavan. The meanings of Hay Mshak and Assyrian Mugallu do not correlate. It is only through the history of the times that we know that both names represent the same person. Mar Abas could not have found Mshak in the Assyrian sources. Remarkably, Mosēs too mentions the name outside of the second comprehensive name-list of chapter 19 which, again, shows that the name derives from the local Hay legends.

Arayan Ara: At the end of chapter 15 of his history, Khorenats'i refers to Arayan Ara as Kardos, which is truly remarkable, since the name means

---

31. Luckenbill, *Ashurbanipal*, third campaign, §781.

'Sharp Speaker'. It appears the songs of the minstrels have perpetuated the fame of Yarairaisa, who in his inscriptions of Carchemish A6 and A15b tells us of the many languages he spoke. The name Arayan Ara means 'Ara Belonging to Ara', which illustrates how in time oral traditions mutate facts. Yarairaisa means 'Attached (*yara*) to Ira (*ira-i*) This One (*sa*)'. Ira is the diminutive of Astir, and this is how Kamana, Astir's son, calls him. The name Ira in time has become Ara, and the *y* of Yara has dropped (perhaps they thought it was an ablative prefix from Classical Armenian) to yield another Ara, and so the end result was 'Ara of Ara' or 'Arayan Ara', who was the first minister of Astir and Kamana. This is another name missing from the records of Assyria and which, as we have seen with Mshak above, derives from local legends, although Kamana (Havanak) in his inscription Carchemish A24.2.6 remarks that Yarairaisa died in Nineveh and that the Assyrian king Ashur-nirari V (754-745 BC) made the funerary oration.[32] In chapter 19 he is made the father of Anushavan, which is wrong. Arayan Ara's son was Baz/Bazuk.

Anushavan: This is a name that has been completely misunderstood ever since its composition. For a correct explanation one has to know the history of the times as well as other contemporary details. Adontz and Adjaryan explain the name as 'Anaoshō-urvān', a loan from the Zend-Avesta (in the seventh century BC?), meaning 'Immortal Soul', while others have explained it as 'Lovely/Sweet Village'. The actual meaning of the name of Anushavan is 'Without (*an*) Memory (*ush*) and Resting Place (*avan*)', since he died in a palace fire and no trace of him was found, which Ashurbanipal considered as divine retribution,[33] in view of the prevailing animosity between the two rulers. Ashurbanipal had the name of Anushavan wiped from the inscriptions, except for the last syllable of 'ussi' (hence his name '...ussi'), which reconstructed may have been Apananus-si ('Without Memory and Resting Place': *apan* > *avan* = 'resting place/house' + *an* = negative suffix [English *un-*] + *ussi* > *ush* = 'memory'). In view of this erasure of the name one has to agree that Mar Abas could not have obtained it from the Assyrian sources, but again had to rely on local data.

We have now seen the first three names and the improbability of their

32. G. Soultanian, *Pre-History Volume II*, 'Kamana's Inscription Carchemish A24', line 2.6 where it is recorded that the Assyrian king Ashur-nirari V (754-745 BC) gave the funeral oration when Yarairaisa (Arayan Ara) died in Nineveh in 754 BC.
33. Hawkins, 'The Neo-Hittite States in Syria and Anatolia', p432.

derivation from the Assyrian sources, except for Mugallu. We can therefore start examining the names which Mar Abas has gleaned from the Assyro-Babylonian or written Greek sources available in those days in Mesopotamia. But first it must be emphasised that parallel to these names Khorenats'i also gives us the alleged names of their Chaldaean and Hebrew contemporaries, which have all been taken from the Chronicle of Eusebius by Khorenats'i himself and not Mar Abas.

Parēt: This name is also written as Paret, which in my opinion is the correct spelling. Also, I do not think it belongs to this name-list and I shall revert to it while discussing the third list.

Arbak: This is Urballa of the Assyrian inscriptions, a contemporary of both Tiglath-Pileser III and Sargon II. Iranian origin is claimed for the name of Arbak, which is incorrect. In fact the name could not have been any more indigenous, comprising as it does of: *arb* 'satellite' (*arbaneak*) + *ak* (endearing diminutive suffix), hence 'Lovable Little Satellite (i.e. Vassal)'. The demotic name recorded by the Assyrians (Urballa) comprises *urb* 'satellite' + *al* (endearing diminutive), resulting in the same meaning, since he was the vassal of Harma (Wasusaramimasa). His real name in his own hieroglyphic inscriptions was Warpalawa, 'He Who Conducts Good Conversation', which Mosēs does not know since his list derives from the Assyrian sources, who record only his demotic name.

Zawan: The name of Zawan, if there was such a person, I am unable to confirm.

P'arnak: The name means 'Source of Pomp' and his Proto-Armenian name was Ambaris, which means 'Complete Splendour'. Adjaryan's explanation and derivation is wrong.

Sur: This means 'sword' and 'sharp'. The Assyrian way of writing the same name was Surri.[34] He was not a contemporary of Hesu (Joshua) as mentioned in the history of Khorenats'i, but of Heu (Jehu) of Israel.

Havanak: This is the eldest son of Ara the Fair and his name means 'Consenter'. His Proto-Armenian name was Kamana, meaning 'Devoid of Will'.[35]

---

34. Luckenbill, §585—Shalmaneser III, year 28.
35. Soultanian, *Pre-History Volume II*, Inscriptions Carchemish A6, A15b, A24 and Cekke.

Vashtak: This means 'Source of Battalions' and his Proto-Armenian name was Kundashpi, meaning 'Groups of Cavalry'.[36]

Haykak (Arnak): This name has been duplicated and it appears for the second time as Arnak. The first name Haykak can only be explained as 'Little Hayk' but Arnak means 'Source of Bravery'. The Proto-Armenian name was Sanduarri,[37] which means 'Fiery Brave Person'. He should be in list three. The Assyrians do not record the Haykak version of the name.

Ampak: The name means 'Source (*ak*) of Lightning (*amp*)'. His Proto-Armenian name was Qatazilu[38] which means 'There Are (*qat* → *kay*) Fire/Sparks (*az*) Overflowing (*ilu*)'.

Shavarsh: This name is borrowed from the Iranian and means 'He Who Has Black Stallions'. The Proto-Armenian name was Kushtashpi,[39] meaning 'Flanks Full of Cavalry'.

Norayr: The name means 'New Fire', which by extension could mean 'New Man' (Greek 'Neandros'). His Proto-Armenian name was Azatiwata, meaning 'Capable Burning Dawn'. He also called himself Asizatiwara,[40] which means 'The Chosen Fire'. This name belongs to the Cilician kings in list three. The Assyrians do not know this name.

Vstamkar: The name means 'Wholly Noble and Capable'. The Proto-Armenian name was Khelaruata, meaning 'Capable Noble Male' ('male' = 'brave'). His name is not acknowledged by the Assyrians, but the Urartians mention him as king of Melid, a son of Shakhu and father of Gełam (Sulumal).[41]

Gorak: This is the rebellious Gurti of Til-Garimmu of the time of Sennacherim of Assyria.[42] Gurti means 'Time of Upheavals/Rebellion' and Gorak means 'Source of Upheavals/Rebellion'.

---

36. Luckenbill, §610—Shalmaneser III, year 6.
37. Idem., §§ 513, 528—Esarhaddon.
38. Idem., §599—Shalmaneser III, year 1.
39. Idem., §769—Tiglath-Pileser III, year 3.
40. Soultanian, *Pre-History Volume II*, 'The Karatepe Bilingual Inscription of Azatiwata, also named Asizatiwara (Norayr)', pp 133-149.
41. Diakonoff, *Pre-History of the Armenian People*, p199, note 119.
42. Luckenbill, §§ 290-92, Sennacherim's campaign against Til-Garimmu of 695 BC. In this inscription the name has been read as Hidi, which was later corrected as Gurdi. See also Soultanian, *Pre-History Volume II*, Karahöyük-Elbistan inscription, pp 195-201.

Hrant: There have been three kings of Marash with this name. It is most likely that the name recorded by Khorenats'i belongs to the last, Hrant III.[43] The Proto-Armenian name was Khalparutiya as acknowledged by the Assyrians and confirmed in his own inscription, which means 'Battering Ram of the God Runtiya'. From this name Mar Abas has taken only the 'Runt' part, the name of the god which the Hays wrote as 'Rutiya'. Since there are no indigenous Armenian words starting with the *r* phoneme, he has added an initial emphatic *h* and made the name 'H-runt' > 'Hrant' (compare how Ruth becomes Hrut'), which could not be explained without knowing this history of the name.

Əndzak: This name means 'Little Leopard', which is a euphemism considering that his Proto-Armenian name was Gunzinanu[44] (*zəndzinanu*, split into its basic elements gives us z + *əndz* + *inanu*), which means 'Arrogant/Meritless Leopard'. Khorenats'i writes it as Əndzak.

Głak: The name means 'Source of Extreme Desire'; *geł* in Modern Armenian has become *giełdz* 'extreme desire' + *ak* 'source', which explains the person well. His Proto-Armenian name was Kiakia, also its shortened version Kiaki,[45] which means 'Life, Life'—in other words, the bearer of the name had the extreme desire and hunger to live life to the full.

Hōro: The spelling of the name is wrong, since at the time of Khorenats'i the Armenians did not have *ō*. Its meaning remains unknown as does the person.

Zarmayr: This name does not belong in this list—in fact it does not belong to any of the lists. It is the oldest Hay name recorded in history which I shall discuss at the end of this section.

Perj: The name has the meanings of 'elegant, magnificent, superb' and so on. The parallel name would have been Urimme,[46] but I remain unsure of its spelling. This is the Assyrian version, which Hawkins writes as U(i)rimme. The person to whom this name could have applied probably is this U(i)rimme, provided the reading is *u(i)r* + *ime* (*u[i]r* —> *ger* 'uppermost, loftiness' + *ime* 'what a'), which gives 'What a

---

43. Soultanian, *Pre-History Volume II*; see note 4 on p174 above.
44. Luckenbill, §26.
45. Ibid., §7.
46. Ibid., §772.

Loftiness'. He was a contemporary of Tiglath-Pileser III of Assyria.

Arbun: The name consists of two roots, *arb* and *un*, and means 'Devoid of Intoxication', which may be interpreted as 'He Who Talks and Behaves Like a Drunkard and Yet Is Not Intoxicated'. His real name was Muwazali,[47] which means 'Acerbic Fiery Priest'. Khalparutiya III in his inscription adds that 'his speech was full of fire'.[48] The Assyrian name for the same king was Mutali, which means 'Bitter Devoid of Intoxication'. The Armenian word *arbunk'* (plural form) derives from *arbun* and means the age of puberty. Mar Abas has taken the Assyrian name Mutali and translated it into Armenian as 'Arbun', since neither he nor Khorenats'i knew the original name of Muwazali.

Bazuk: We have seen this name in the first list as Baz, that of the progeny of Hayk.

Hoy: The Assyrians write the name as Khully,[49] which means a 'ram' or 'battering ram'. Hoy, also written as Khoy, means the same thing.

Yusak: This is pronounced as Husak and means 'Dear Little Last One', which is to be understood as the last and youngest of the sons of Astiruwa (Erast/Ara the Fair). His Proto-Armenian name was Pisiri,[50] which transcribes as Hisiri = *his* + *ir-i*, meaning 'Memory Left Behind (= *his*) + by Ira (*ir-i*)'.

Kaypak: This consists of two roots, *kay* and *pak*, and means 'Fearsomely (*pak*) Solid Presence (*kay*)'. His Proto-Armenian name was Katuwa,[51] which means 'Being (*uwa* → *oga*) of Solid Presence (*kat* → *kay*, *t>y*)'.

Skayordi: The Assyrians do not know of Skayordi since his reign starts after the destruction of Assyria. By rights his name should be in the third list, since he reigned in Cilicia Campestris in the city of Par (Missis). The Assyrians knew his father as Ishkallu[52] or 'Affable Giant' and Skayordi means 'Son of the Giant'.

47.   Ibid., §599.
48.   G. Soultanian, *Pre-History Volume II*; and see note 4 above.
49.   Luckinbill, §802; see also A. G. Lie, lines 194-97.
50.   A. G. Lie, lines 72-75.
51.   *Pre-History Volume II*, see inscriptions Carchemish A2, A3, A11a, A11b, A11c, and A23, pp 51-75.
52.   Hawkins, 'The Neo-Hittite States of Syria and Anatolia', in *Cambridge Ancient History*, vol. iii, part i, 1982, p428.

With Skayordi the second list of chapter 19 finishes. In this list we have seen names which are not known from the Proto-Armenian hieroglyphic inscriptions, these are the demotic names as used by the Assyrians: Arbak/Urballa, Arbun/Mutalli and P'aṛokh/Palalam of the previous list. These confirm that a Mar Abas existed, that he was sent to Mesopotamia in order to find out who the Hays around Nisibis were and that Khorenats'i, as he acknowledges, is indebted to him for the pre-history of the Armenians. Khorenats'i hmelf in chapter 21 adds: 'we know the names of the ancestors through the records of the Chaldaeans, Assyrians and Persians, because these same ancestors have been the vassals, satraps and agents of those countries, hence their names were incorporated in their archives.' We should also not overlook the fact that if the Proto-Armenian names of the various kings were not available through the medium of Mesopotamian records then we would have none of these recomposed names in the Classical Armenian language. Khorenats'i knows nothing of the original names of the Proto-Armenian kings, which part of Anatolia they ruled (Khorenats'i believes they were kings in Armenia) nor the family connections of these kings. He does not even have a proper understanding of the meanings of some of the Classical Armenian compositions of the names.

The only name that creates difficulties for us is that of Vstamkar/Khelaruata, since, as mentioned above, the Assyrians do not know of him. In my opinion, Khelaruata was obtained from word-of-mouth information circulating in the district of Gełark'unik' (Uelikuni), since this district was thus named at his time and derives from the name of the royal house of the Gełs ('Nobles'). This district was for the first time named Uelikuni in the time of Sarduri II, which was due to the fact that great numbers of Hay slaves had been relocated from the country of Malatya by Menua, Argishti and Sarduri II, and, it appears that within the number of the slaves there were also hostages of royal descent who obviously became the authority the Hay population looked up to and after whom the district was called, the 'Royal Family of the Nobles', i.e. Gełark'unik'/Uelikuni. This conjecture also supports the fact that the designation of the district as Gełark'unik'/Uelikuni happened at the time of Khelaruata/Vstamkar and had no connection with the name of Gełam, after whom Lake Lychnides (so named in memory of their Lake Lychnides in the Balkans, the present Ohrid) was renamed Gełama (present-day Lake Sevan) and the mountains Geł. Furthermore, the Vishap Stones spread around the Geł Mountains were mainly in commemoration of the myth of Gełam's (Sulumal) feat of slaying the dragon Illuyanka with the help of his son (see image on page 8).

Before we start on the third name-list of chapter 22, we first need to deal with Zarmayr, who was the first to be sent to Troy and was killed there by Patroclus (Homer, *Iliad*, 16.287). Zarmayr means 'Tip of Fire' (< *z* [prefix] + *arm* 'end, tip, terminal point' + *ayr* 'fire, flame') is the Pyraechmes ('Tip of Fire' < *pyr* 'fire, flame' + *aechmes* 'tip, end') of Homer's *Iliad* and the leader of the first Paeonian ('Hay Beings' < *Pae* —> *Hay* + *on* 'being, creature') contingent.

Zarmayr had been almost forgotten by the second century BC save for his name and that he participated in the Trojan War and died there. This is hardly surprising considering that the second contingent sent by the Paeonians in the last days of the war under the leadership of the 'god-like' Asteropaeus ('Son of Stars', *Iliad*, 12.102 onwards) has been erased from the national memory of the Armenian people. What I find remarkable is the fact that what the collective memory lost, certain individuals, possibly the minstrels, have tried to make good by ascribing to Zarmayr the deeds of Memnon, king of Susa, who went to Troy with an army of Eastern Ethiopians (Quintus Smyrnaeus, 11.100) at the request of Tewtamus, king of Assyria. For Tewtamus as king of Assyria there is support in the writings of Ctesias of Cnidus (replicated in Diodorus Siculus, 11.22), whereas in Homer's *Iliad* Tewtamus is the father of Lethus and the patriarch of Larisa in Thessaly (*Iliad*, 2.843), and Zarmayr (Pyraechmes) being a Paeonian (Hay) went to Troy with an army of Paeonians. Therefore I think that Khorenats'i, following the various demotic stories, included the name of Zarmayr in the second list (chapter 19) and expanded the theme in his own manner, since he had seen the name Tewtamus in the Chaldaean contemporaries listed by Eusebius in his Chronicle (Part 1, p97; 11, p134). Such support from Eusebius was sufficient to convince Khorenats'i of the truth of the matter.

'THE ORDER OF OUR KINGS AND THEIR NUMBER'

Chapter 22 contains the names of Cilician kings starting with Paroyr which, as stated above, is not a personal name but the name of the city of Par (Missis/Mamestia) and where, after the collapse of all the previous kingdoms of Aram and Tabal, a new reign was created with the consent of Cyaxares the Median, around the end of the seventh century BC. Similar to the previous two name-lists (the first started with Aramaneak, the second was the progeny of Aram), this one too starts with the place name Par where the monarchy was established. However, the name has been misunderstood ever since its creation, and accepted as that of a person, the first king and that in Armenia. The names of the list, as with the previous name-lists, are not chronologically recorded but a blend of five which, in reality, should have numbered at least eight, if not more.

Khorenats'i writes that for helping Cyaxares to annihilate the kingdom of Assyria, Paroyr was granted kingship. He does not specify where the new dynasty ruled, and it is accepted that he was a king in Armenia. It is important to know the meaning of the name of Paroyr in order to establish his base which would also tell us where to find the names of the Proto-Armenian kings congruent with those recorded in this list. In my opinion, the person who helped Cyaxares and was granted kingship as a vassal was Skayordi. Remarkably one writer of the seventh century AD, Mosēs Kałankatuats'i in Book 1.15 agrees with this view even though after his statement he includes Paroyr in his list with the other names. Therefore we must now turn to the names of these Cilician kings, starting at the end of the seventh century BC with Skayordi.

Skayordi: The name means 'Son of the Giant'. There has been only one ruler in Tabal district with the name of 'Benevolent/Affable Giant' known as Ishkallu, and as it happens the time difference between this Ishkallu and Khorenats'i's Skayordi points to a father and son connection. I therefore think it is safe to conjecture that Skayordi was the son of Ishkallu; the latter disappeared in mysterious circumstances from Tabal and his domain was taken over by his contemporary Mugallu (Mshak) of Melid. Skayordi would have been in advanced years at the time he became a king and may have died soon after his succession, which may be the reason he is overlooked in history as the father of Syennesis (Pachoych). The name Paroyr means 'Par (city) to Which (Kingdom Returned)'. Once we know this meaning it then becomes easier to conclude that the kingship was granted to Skayordi of the city of Par. As for the city of Par, this is the same place as Azatiwata's (Norayr) Pahar, which is recorded in his inscription of Karatepe: 'I stored barley in Pahar city in case of difficulties' (sentence VII).[53]

Parēt: I had mentioned above that I would return to the name of Parēt in this third name-list. I do not think that in this case we have the correct

53. *Pre-History Volume II*, The Karatepe Bilingual, pp 133-49.

spelling nor is it the name of a person. Adjaryan explains it as 'Overseer and Guardian' and tells us that the name is also written as Paret. Unfortunately he is unable to give us the etymology of the word and the few opinions he quotes are unconvincing. In my opinion Paret means 'Back to Par' and is synonymous with Paroyr. In other words the arcane message that the kingdom returned to the city of Par is duplicated in Paret and Paroyr. Therefore we may conclude that there was no person with the name of Paroyr nor was there a person with the name of Paret. Mosēs has misunderstood the intention and the manner of recording these names by Mar Abas.

Hrach'eay: This name means 'Fiery Eyes' (*hr* → *hur* = 'fire' + *ach'eay* = 'eyes'). He was the king of Khilakku (later Cilicia) and his Proto-Armenian name was Sandasarme,[54] which translated gives us the names of two gods: Santas ('god of fire, lightning'), and Armas ('god Moon'). The translation of the name does not yield a correlation with the Classical Armenian and thus in this case we have to interpret the ancient name and use the attributes of the two gods mentioned in order to attain a perfect correlation. This procedure is necessary since we know that at the time of this king the mention of eyes was taboo,[55] which we also note in the inscription Carchemish AⅠⅠc.3 of Katuwa (Kaypak) from the late tenth/early ninth century BC in which he curses his enemy saying: '*nara sa kura wa*' (*nara sa* = 'his eyes' + *kura wa* = 'become blind'). In fact the word *nara* does not mean 'eye(s)', but 'holes, openings, slits.; We also see the word in inscription Cekke C of Kamana (Havanak), meaning 'omphalos', and in Topada A6.32 of Wasusaramimasa (Harma) meaning 'to split'. To conclude, we have fire (*santa*) and an eye in the sky (the Moon) which together give us 'Fiery Eyes', a perfect correlation. Note that the Armenian word *shant* ('lightning') derives from the name of the god Santa. Mosēs, in chapter 1.22 says that this king requested from Nabuchadnezzar (604-562 BC) a certain Jewish prisoner named Shambat, the primogenitor of the Bagratids. But Sandasarme was a contemporary of Ashurbanipal (668-627 BC) and not of Nabuchadnezzar of Babylon.

P'aṛnawaz: This name belongs to the ninth century BC Pikhirim of Khilakku,[56] meaning 'Insurgent for Which He Is Admired', whereas

---

54. Luckenbill, §782—Ashurbanipal, third campaign.
55. Adjaryan, *Dictionary of Armenian Root Words*. Under the word *ak* ('eye') Adjaryan quotes A. Meillet's statement.
56. Hawkins, see note 52 on p191 above.

P'arnawaz means 'Famous for His Fiery Nature'. There are other explanations of the name, which in my opinion are not correct.

Pachoych: This is Syennesis of Cilicia,[57] son of Skayordi, a contemporary of Nabuchadnezzar of Babylon. He enlarged and embellished the country, hence his name Syennesis (*shen* 'to build, enlarge' + *nes* → *nish* 'to adorn, embellish, decorate'). Pachoych means 'to embellish, decorate'. After the first Syennesis the later kings of the dynasty continued to use the same name but neither Khorenats'i nor Mar Abas know this fact.

Kornak: Adjaryan hesitatingly says that this means 'Lion's Whelp'. In my opinion, the explanation is not a sound one. The Proto-Armenian name of this king was Kurati[58] meaning 'The Time of the Eunuch' (*kowr-a* 'castrated person' + *ti* 'time'). The name Kurti (written Kura+ti) can also be explained as 'The Time of the Shameful' (*kur-n* 'bent neck with shame' + *ti* 'time'), which would be consistent with Kornak meaning 'Source of Shame'.

Baos: This name has been corrupted in the manuscripts; some have it as P'aros or P'arwos and others as P'awos. The spelling of the name should be Baos, which automatically will be pronounced as Bawos. The only name which makes sense is Baos and it means 'Idle/Ineffectual (*os*) Speaker (*ba*)'. This correction has been deduced from the Proto-Armenian name of this person, which the Babylonians wrote as Appuashu.[59] The Proto-Armenian version of the name would have been Apuwasu (Ap-uw-as-u), which would yield *ap* → *ah* 'dread' + *uw* 'being' + *as* 'speak', therefore 'a person of dreadful speech', which I have translated as 'Person of Idle/Ineffectual Speech'.

With Baos the names of the Cilician kings come to an end, but the list continues with names which have no connection with Cilicia. The additional entries are Haykak 'the Other', Eruand and his son Tigran. These three have been added by the Editor of Mar Abas' manuscript, since none are to be found in the Mesopotamian sources as they all belong to later Armenia.

---

57. Herodotus, *Histories*, Book 1.74.
58. Lie, *The Inscriptions of Sargon II*, lines 70-71. The name is written as Matti of Atuna, which has been corrected to Kurti. See also Soultanian, *Pre-History Volume II*, pp 186-190.
59. A. K. Grayson, *Assyrian and Babylonian Chronicles*, New York, 1975, Chronicle 6.

Haykak is the commander of the Proto-Armenian forces that entered Urartu and battled with the Medo-Scythian forces of Mades. He is the patriarch of the house of Manawazeans and after him a township was either established or renamed Haykashēn.

Eruand and **Tigran** were Median satraps of Armenia, as discussed by Xenophon in the *Cyropaedia*, and it appears that around the twilight of the Median kingdom Tigran managed to build up a strong kingdom for himself. However, most of the actions ascribed to him by Khorenats'i belong to Tigran the Great of the last century before our era.

The two names of Haykak/Aṛnak and Norayr placed in the second name-list should by rights be in this third list of the Cilician kings, considering that Haykak/Aṛnak was king of Sis and Kundu and Norayr was the prime minister of Adana, who for a time acted as a king because the real king of Adana, Awarakus, had died and his heir to the throne, Urikki, was only an infant.

THE FOUR BATTLES OF THE PROTO-ARMENIANS

The other important events in the first book of the History of the Armenians are the four battles of the Hays and the reforms of Vałarshak of Book II.7-8, which Khorenats'i ascribes to the authority of Mar Abas. The former's narrative and presentation of the wars are wrong on chronological grounds, but that is not a problem since we know exactly when these battles took place as well as the people involved.

The chronological order and titles Khorenats'i assigns to the four battles of the Hays are:

1) the battle of Hayk and Bēl
2) the battle against the Medo-Scythians
3) the battle against Barsham
4) the battle against Payapis-K'aałea.

Of these battles, numbers 3 and 4 were fought simultaneously in the middle of the eighth century BC. The battle of Hayk and Bēl was fought at the end of the eighth century BC, and the battle with the Medo-Scythians under the leadership of Mades, was fought around 588 BC. I shall therefore treat the order of these battles according to these facts which means that the Khorenats'i's chronology will be ignored.

Khorenats'i presents the last two wars as being fought by patriarch Aram, in the name of the country of Aram, since he does not know the names of the Hay kings. Fortunately however he gives us the names of Payapis-K'aałea and Barsham, which enables us to relate them to historical events. Of the two wars, the one against Payapis-K'aałea was fought by Harma (Wasusaramimasa) of Tabal, in the north, and the one against Barsham was fought by Hawanak (Kamana) of Carchemish in the south. We know that there was a treaty between the northerner, Payapis-K'aałea, and the southern king Mati-ilu (Barsham) of Arpat, which has survived to our own times in Aramaic.[60] It appears the treaty between these two enemies of the Proto-Armenians had the intention of annihilating the kingdoms of the country of Aram, and to divide the lands between themselves, for otherwise the treaty cannot make sense considering the huge distance along with the existing Proto-Armenian kingdoms between them. The wars were to be conducted in a pincer movement from the north and the south. At the end the efforts of this alliance served only to achieve the destruction of their own kingdoms as we see in the hieroglyphic inscriptions of Harma (Topada inscription) and Hawanak (Cekke inscription) that have survived to our own times.[61]

The Northern War

When Aramayis (Tuwatis) of Tabal died in the plague of *c.* 770 BC, he had no son capable enough to take over the kingdom—this is according to the inscription of Ruwas (Kululu 1.3b-c), his adviser and prime minister. Harma (Wasu*sarami*masa) came with his army of braves and took over the kingdom; in other words Harma was a usurper, as he admits in his inscription.[62] In the Assyrian inscriptions of the time of Ashur-dan III (772-755 BC) there is an oblique reference to Parwata, who was growing powerful in the north and extending his realm. Usually scholarship equates this Parwata with Burutish, but Burutish is a place name whereas Parwata is not and transcribes as Bargaya, which is the Payapis-K'aałea found in Khorenats'i. Other scholars have equated Parwata with Paroyr, which is sheer speculation.

Harma, in his inscription of Topada, tells us that the king (he does not name him) of the city of Parzuta attacked, creating havoc, smashed the

---

60. Grayson, 'Assyria', in *Cambridge Ancient History*, vol. III, part 1, 1982; see p277, Ashur-nirari V.

61. Soultanian, *Pre-History Volume II*, pp 102-7, 256-62.

62. Ibid., The Topada Inscription of Wasusaramimasa (Harma), line A1.3.

royal stables and drove away with a great number of horses. Later the same king returned with chariots to engage in battle while his cavalry and soldiers seized the borders, and it appears there were three separate attacks on Harma's city, which created great anguish and fear in both the inhabitants and himself. The year ended in calm.

The following year Harma organized his army and, with twice the number of the enemy's men, he besieged and attacked the city of Parzuta. The inscription mentions the clashes, the sacrifices to gods, destruction of the borderlands and the burning of strong-walled Parzuta. Harma adds that everywhere in the city was charred and he was loaded with plunder and so was the beginnings of his fame. There is no other reference, either in the Assyrian inscriptions or in the Urartian or Aramaic, which means that Mar Abas could not have procured the story from Assyro-Babylonian sources. So how can one explain the fact that the story appears in the History of Khorenats'i disguised as one of Aram's valorous acts (see the concluding section below)?

The War in the South

In the south, around the same time as those in the north, there was war between Mati-ilu of Arpat, an Aramaean kingdom, and Kamana (Hawanak) of Carchemish,[63] at the time when Sastura (Baz), the son of Arayan Ara, was the adviser and prime minister of the Hay kingdom. Apparently Mati-ilu, the southern party of the treaty mentioned above, attacked and took over the city of Kamana, one of the cities belonging to Carchemish named after the king, and was plundering the countryside with the help of his sons.

Kamana says that he beat and killed the population, imposing higher taxes, confiscating the animals, effects and the idols of the temples and burning and destroying the city. Clearly it was a long drawn-out war which ends with Kamana's victory and the annihilation of the enemy. This war too is mentioned by Khorenats'i with slightly different details, which may be due to the fact that the spelling of Assyria/Assyrian and Aramaean are identical in Armenian, and many times it is difficult to distinguish the one from the other as we have seen above. The sole historical source we have for this war is that of Kamana's Cekke inscription which, again, shows that Mar Abas could not have procured it from the Assyro-Babylonian sources.

---

63. Ibid., The Cekke Inscription of Kamana (Havanak), line B.2.

The battle of Hayk and Bēl

This is the third battle, described in parabolic language by Khorenats'i in his first book (chapter 11). Khorenats'i tries to identify the genesis of the Hays with this Hayk as the primogenitor. Besides, he also tries to connect Hayk to the Biblical Bēl and the Tower of Babel, which creates difficulties for the reader and corrupts chronology. It is true that there was a person with the name of Ēshpai, which much later was changed to Hayk, who battled with Sargon II in 705 BC and prevailed. But the many details Khorenats'i provides cannot be found in any source and there is no connected inscription. The Assyrian sources say that 'Sargon on the seventeenth year of his reign went against Tabal and was killed by Ēshpai the Kulumean.' As the rest of the inscription is unreadable, the Babylonian Chronicles can only confirm that Sargon went against Tabal. Khorenats'i says that the story derives from Abydenus, which may be true, but even in this case, Abydenus (chapter 1.5) could not have written any more than the Assyro-Babylonian inscriptions. Further- more, the name of the source (Abydenus) quoted by Khorenats'i could have come only from Mar Abas; in other words Khorenats'i has not seen the works of Abydenus. In connection with Hayk living in Babylonia, prior to escaping to his own abode, Zapkaka (later Kiaka), we have a letter from Sargon's plenipotentiary which informs Sargon of the movements of the people of Zapkaka in exile. Apparently Sargon was worried and wanted to know every move made by these exiles.[64] Khorenats'i does not know of Zapkaka or where and why Hayk and his followers were living in exile, which implies that Mar Abas procured information only about Sargon's death and the name of Ēshpai (Hayk). The rest of the story derives from local oral sources.

Nevertheless, the battle of Hayk and Bēl is something to admire, provided one has sufficient knowledge of history in order to analyse the details and uncover the truth behind the downgraded manner of Khorenats'i's description of events and the organization of Hayk's army. What I find remarkable is that Khorenats'i believes in his account and in a few words makes it clear that Hayk's army was only a small contingent comprising his immediate relations. He writes:

Hayk gathers his sons and grandsons and other men, which, considering the forthcoming battle, are very few in number. He

---

64. Leroy Waterman, *The Royal Correspondence of the Assyrian Empire*, vol. 1, Letter 129 in Kouyounjik Collection, K5458.

places Aramaneak and his two brothers, Manawaz and Khor, on his right side. Kadmos, the grandson, with two more of his sons and others he places on his left. Hayk leads with the multitude behind him and the fight begins. It is a stalemate, since the whole of Bēl's army had not yet arrived, which is advantageous for Hayk, who manages to kill Bēl and the district since then is called Hayots' Dzor (Valley of the Hays) and the place Hayk. Where Bēl is killed becomes Gerezmank' (Cemeteries), but Hayk takes Bēl's corpse to Hark' and the country since then is called, in the name of Hayk, Hayastan.

What Khorenats'i writes, at first sight, appears to be simplistic to say the least, but when one considers the implications of the story in this form it is apparent that the battle was a full-blown war between the Assyrians and the inhabitants of the various kingdoms of Aram. This is the first time when all the Hay kingdoms of Aramaneak (Circuit of Aram) joined together with the addition of outside help; and this was the only time that there was a real organization for which Hayk was responsible.

My interpretation of this war uncovers a number of facts which have been veiled up to now. Manawaz and Khor, the two sons that Hayk placed on his right, are not persons as given in the narrative. Manawaz was king of Gurgum (Marash) at least 250 years before Hayk, and Khor represents the armenicised Hurrian people and the Hays of the country of Carchemish. What we in fact are being told is that the army of Gurgum and the army of Carchemish country were on Hayk's right-hand flank. The person representing Kadmos is Dati, who reigned at least a hundred years before Hayk, hence Kadmos represents the army of the Kadmeans of Kadmukhi.

Who then were the other sons of Hayk (Hayk = the Hay people in this context) who were on the left flank together with Kadmos? In my opinion these represent the armies of Tabal and Melid-Togarmah—we cannot consider Kummukh, since an important part of its population Sargon had already moved to the borders of Elam.[65] Another question is, who were the 'other men'? These would have to be the Phrygians and the people of Cilicia Aspera. The latter were of Hay origin, which we surmise from the fact that their kings had Hay names and are recorded by Khorenats'i. But the case of the Phrygians is conjectural since no source mentions them. My conclusion is based on the fact that in the great tumulus of Gordion (Gordium, the Phrygian capital) a bronze

---

65. Lie, *The Inscriptions of Sargon II*, lines 15-6.

situla or ceremonial bucket with a lion-head base was found along with a fluted bowl of colourless glass with moulded ornaments (see images on page 8).[66] The precise parallels of these articles can be seen in the palace relief of Sargon II. How do these articles find their way to Gordion, if not as part of the loot that was the share of the Phrygians?

As for Hayots' Dzor (Valley of the Hays), at the earliest this belongs to the second century AD, since prior to that Urartu was still an independent country. But Gerezmank' (Cemeteries) was known since ancient times as the place the princes of Kummukh were buried: the Nemrut Dağ in Kummukh, where the corpse of Sargon II of Assyria was laid to rest. There was no place called Hark' in Hayk's times—it would take at least another 125 years for the Hays to enter Urartu. In other words Hayk never set foot on the soil of Armenia.

Khorenats'i says that from Kadmukhi Hayk travelled northwest to Hark'. The direction is correct but the northwest of Kadmukhi is precisely the place Hayk lived in, namely Zapkaka (Hark' is directly north of Kadmukhi). The other point Khorenats'i recalls is the route Hayk took to meet Sargon's army. He says Hayk and his sons travelled and reached a salty lake with small fish in it, and here they organized the army. The lake referred to is the salty waters of Hazar, south of Elaziğ, which makes sense if one travels south from Zapkaka (Kiaka). It could not have been Lake Van since at the time it was part of a strong Urartu. Hayk was stationed on the right shore of the river whereas Bēl stood his army on the left. This river could only be the Euphrates (there are no such large rivers in Hayots' Dzor), which points to the battle taking place in Kummukh. None of these details are to be found in the Assyro-Babylonian or Mesopotamian Greek sources so how is it that Mar Abas can write about them?

The last war of the Hays

The last war of the Hays concerns their entry into Urartu. Nowhere can one find information relating to the conquest of Urartu or any other part of the highlands. In fact, none of the Armenian historians or writers had any knowledge of Urartu and, so far as the Armenian records are concerned, Urartu might never have existed. When St Gregory was evangelizing, he is not recorded as having visited any part of Urartu, consequently the capital Van and other parts of the country have no mention in the book of Agat'angełos. Even the king of Armenia,

66. Seton Lloyd, *Early Highland Peoples of Anatolia*, Thames & Hudson, London, 1967, p133 & illustrations.

Tridates III never interferes in Urartian affairs, as if Urartu or the central parts of Armenia never existed. Khorenats'i is the first to mention the citadel rock of Van and some cuneiform inscriptions, but he has no knowledge of Urartu or any details relating to the country and its people.

Nevertheless, Khorenats'i makes it clear that the Hays fought with the Median army who were under the leadership of Mades and prevailed. But Khorenats'i, as well as a number of recent scholars, believes that the Hays were already in Armenia when they fought with the Medians. This has no historical basis whatsoever: the facts are that most of Urartu was conquered by the Medo-Scythian forces, and according to archaeological evidence, the cities of Armavir, Bastam, Karmir Blur, Chavushtepe, Kef-Kalesi and Toprak Kale were burned and destroyed.[67] It was only after this battle with the Medo-Scythians that the ethnic name Armenian and country name Armenia were created by non-Armenians. The adoption of Armavir as their capital city, in the northeast of the country was due to the fact that there was an existing slave colony of Hays in and around Armavir, and the district was already known as Uelikuni/Gełark'unik'. Furthermore, since those days the capital cities of the Armenians have always been sited in the northeast; the centrally placed Van was the main city of the Urartians, which was out of bounds for the Armenians. The supposed Hay entry into Urartu has no historical backing since there are no sources in this respect. However, within reason, one can interpret what was most likely to have taken place and how. In my opinion a few of the noble houses of the Urartians that had survived the destruction of their country and the end of the monarchy approached the Hays, their western neighbours, for help. An agreement was struck, according to which the Hays would take over the lands on the periphery of the country (see the map on pages 262-3 showing the settlements of the Hays in the highlands, which supports this hypothesis), but Urartu to the east, south and west of Lake Van with its capital city of Van were to remain an independent enclave surrounded by the newly settled Hays.

A second agreement was concluded between the Hay noble houses, the descendants of the past royal houses, as explained above in the settlement places of the noble houses of the Hays. This agreement became known as the Ostan of the Hays (later on this Ostan designation was usurped by the Arsacids at the time of Khosrov Kotak and took on a

67. R. D. Barnett, 'Urartu', in *Cambridge Ancient History*, vol. iii, part i, 1982; see p364.

completely different meaning). The leadership of the Hay army was entrusted to Haykak Manawazean, the patriarch of Gurgum (Marash), which automatically made the house of the Manawazeans the 'fathers' or leaders of the Hay nation, and after their settlement their lands became known as Hark' (Land of the Fathers) and the district Manawazean; there a township was founded and named Haykashēn after Haykak, the leader of the invading army.

I also consider that remnants of the Urartian army joined with the Hays for the battle against the Medo-Scythians. The battle is described by Khorenats'i, and as battles go it is no different from most. At the end the Hays prevailed and Mades was nailed to the wall of Armavir. A few years after this event, the Medians overran the country and a certain Eruand (Orontes the Short-Lived) was placed as a satrap who, taking advantage of the weakness of the Median monarchy, ruled like a king. Xenophon has a few remarks about Armenia and Urartu of this period, of which most interesting is his statement (Anabasis, Book IV, chapter III.4) that 'they say Urartu is an independent country'. When Darius the Great was dividing the subdued territories into various satrapies, Urartu was separated from the Armenians and was placed under the eighteenth satrapy, whereas the Armenians, again as an entity separate from the Urartians, were placed under the thirteenth based in Malatya (Herod. Book III.93-4). This fact alone tells us much about Urartu and the interloper Hays, most of who were still living in the country of Aram.

THE FUSION OF THE PEOPLE OF THE HIGHLAND

The reforms of Valarsh
In the History of Khorenats'i the reforms of Valarsh appear in Book II (chapters 7 & 8). However, there is confusion and telescoping in the narrative. Up to the end of the second century AD there were three Valarshes: Valarshak the Parthian, who was made ruler in Mtsbin (Nisibis) by Arshak the Great; Valarsh I, who reigned between AD 117 and 144; and Valarsh II of AD 186-198. The reforms Khorenats'i refers to cannot be ascribed to Valarshak the Parthian of Nisibis (Mtsbin), as he was never king over Armenia, irrespective of what Mosēs says.

These reforms, if one may call a continuous process as such, must have taken place during the time of the first Valarsh of AD 117-144, which means that Mar Abas could not have known of them. The appointment of many noble houses as dukedoms or in some other bureaucratic role could have taken place continuously since the start of the monarchy. But the reforms referred to by Khorenats'i are something special, and which could not have taken place before the second century. This means that these reforms started in the time of Vałarsh I and continued throughout the period of the Arsacids and the foreign powers, who from time to time were the masters of the country. The subject of reforms is rather uncorroborated and controversial, let us therefore progress step by step.

Vałarshak of Mygdonia, Gordyene, Adiabene and Atropatene

In the time of Mithradates I (170-138 BC) the Parthians had already conquered northern Mesopotamia up to Armenia and the Euphrates in the west.[68] They had also clashed with King Artavazd of the Artaxiad kingdom of Armenia. This means that Gordyene, Mygdonia and the country of the Medes were in their hands, through which they could attack Armenia. Such a large country south of Armenia had to be entrusted to a governor, a viceroy or a satrap; otherwise these gains would have no meaning. The name of Vałarshak is not all that important—the important thing is to have someone governing the country on behalf of the Parthian kingdom. Khorenats'i says that Arshak the Great (in this case Arshak represents Phraates II, 138-124 BC) appointed his younger brother as king over the 'world of the Armenians' in Mtsbin (Nisibis). At the time these southern parts had the largest Hay population since the arrival of the Gordyina, Mygdonia, Laioi and Doberes Hays from the Balkans, expelled by Philip V of Macedonia in 182 BC,[69] and I do not see any difficulty in accepting that Vałarshak was appointed their viceroy, particularly when Khorenats'i telescopes the deeds of the later King Vałarsh.

It was Vałarshak of Nisibis who sent Mar Abas south to Assyro-Babylonia in order to find out what kind of people were the Hays, who were living all over the region. Mar Abas completed his research and returned with a long list of the names of the ancient Hay kings.

The Reforms of Vałarsh

The manner in which Khorenats'i introduces these 'reforms', gives the impression that for the first time Armenia had an administrative system. Wherever there is a monarchy or a governing centre, reform is a

---

68. H. Manandyan, *Critical Edition of the History of the Armenians*, Yerevan, 1941, vol. 1, p134.

69. John Willkes, *The Illyrians*, Blackwells, Oxford, 1992; see p151 for the deportations of the Paeonians. See also N. G. L. Hammond, *Macedonia*, Sidgwick & Jackson, London, 1991, p183 for the deportation of the people of Bylazora, and p22 for the royal family Terrones of Astibus, the capital city.

continuous process due to deaths and preferential treatment, therefore new appointments are a never ending exercise. We have evidence from the hieroglyphic inscriptions (Sultanhan, lines 4 & 6), which describes how by accumulating wealth and public acknowledgement one gains advancement as adviser to the ruler, which appear to have been honorary positions. Armenia, as a country under the rule of a monarchy, or, in the beginning under the suzerainty of the independent Ostan houses, could not have been any different. However, I think, these reforms highlight a unique period in the history of the Armenians.

We never hear of Urartu, the Urartians, their culture, ruling class, religion and so on. What is most surprising is that even the foreign powers who invade Armenia never touch the Urartian territories. The Romans and the Parthians while attacking Armenia never come into conflict with the Urartians, at least until the time of Shabuh II of Persia, who in AD 368-69 destroyed their capital city of Van. And, internally, the Armenians and their rulers can fight with their neighbouring countries and amongst themselves, and St Gregory can go around evangelizing in fourth-century Armenia, but Tushpa or Van in the enclave of the Urartians still remains untouchable. Furthermore, new waves of Hays arrive in the highlands from the Balkans right up to the middle of the second century BC, and after that the migrations into Armenia continue from the central and southern districts of Anatolia, but none of these impinge on the lands of the Urartians. In fact, the Armenians had no knowledge of any connection whatsoever with Urartu and the Urartians until a bare century ago, when inscriptions were deciphered and archaeological excavations yielded artifacts alien to the Hay language and culture.[70] All these, and much more, were potent reasons to make this period of 'reforms' a unique time in the history of the Armenians. It appears that it had taken bilingualism with Armenian more than seven hundred years to erode the Urartian language—and at that not entirely— and to enable the two distinct national identities to fuse together,[71] the

70. .M. A. Israelyan, *The Story of the City of Erebuni*, Hayastan, Yerevan, 1971. See pp 104-117 in connection with cultural break of the *c*. sixth century BC based on archaeological investigations, particularly the very last paragraph where it is said that 'the Scythians and the Medians invaded, but the Hays became the masters of the country' (Armenia).

71. H. Manandyan, *History*, vol. 1, p42. Manandyan stresses the point that the peaceful co-existence of the Hays and the Urartians in time accomplished the homogeneous nation of the Armenians. He does not reflect on the case of the language, and why the Indo-European Hay language triumphed. The phenomenon was due to the fact that the Hays were arriving in waves to the new country and their language was being continuously renewed, whereas the isolated Urartian language was by and by being eroded.

consequences of which can be seen in the administration of the highlands as a single whole, which brings us to the period of reforms under discussion, since this is the first time that we hear of Urartian and Mardian noble houses sharing responsibilities for the whole country as dukedoms of the first or second grade as well as prestigious positions in the court. The reforms of Vałarsh were the first steps towards the full integration of the population of 'Greater Armenia', which makes it a unique event of utmost importance for the Armenian nation. And yet none of this may be gleaned from the book of Mar Abas.

The time of the reforms and the building of Vałarshapat

Much has been written about these two subjects and I agree with Manandyan that Vałarshapat was built at the time of Vałarsh I (AD 117-144), since Dio Cassius[72] refers to it (*c.* AD 164) as the New Town, which is before the time of Vałarsh II. As for the 'reforms', in my opinion these too took place during the reign of the same king, since he is missing from the history of Khorenats'i, and his reign and deeds are telescoped with and ascribed to Vałarshak the Parthian, who was never a king of Armenia, irrespective of what Mosēs says.

Initially I was of the opinion that these reforms belong to after the middle of the third century. My reasons were practical and easy to follow. The dukedoms of Rshtunik', Mokats'ik', Andzewats'ik', Akēats'ik', Artsrunik' and Mardpetakan start appearing in the works of Agat'angełos, P'awstos, Ełishē and Khorenats'i in the fifth century, but none of these writers make any retrospective remark about the origins or any other aspects of these dukedoms in their history of the various periods. Secondly, we note that nearer to the fourth century the Urartian enclave was still an unknown territory bang in the centre of Armenia. The dukedoms mentioned are mainly Urartians (I do not agree with Toumanoff's speculations in connection with the dukedoms of Armenia), with the exception of the last which, as is evident from its name, represents the Mardian people. It is obvious that Mar Abas could not have known any of these factors since his time belongs more than three centuries before all these events took place.

Who translated the names into Classical Armenian and when?

This is the last remaining hurdle and a knotty problem which, unfortunately, can only be answered hypothetically based on purely

---

72.   Dio Cassius, *Roman History*, Book LXXI, Loeb edition, vol. 9, p78.

circumstantial evidence and reasoning. This may or may not yield the correct answers, as the logic of today might not apply to the affairs of the second half of the second century BC. Nevertheless, we should make every effort in this respect.

We know that the ancient names compared with those appearing in the History of Khorenats'i are not the same but that they do have, if not identical, similar meanings. We may conclude that the names were recomposed in the course of the Classical Armenian era for the understanding of the people of those days (most of the Classical Armenian names that Mosēs lists in chapters 1.12, 19 and 22 have not been understood by modern scholars but are explained in *Pre-History Volume I*). The names recorded by Khorenats'i contain some which comprise roots of Iranian provenance, such as Vstamkar (Khelaruata), or a few wholly of Iranian provenance, such as Shavarsh, Eruand and Tigran. At the time of Mar Abas, *c.* 130 BC, the majority of the population of Mtsbin (Nisibis) and districts were new migrant Hays from the Balkans, such as the Mygdonians, Doberes, Laioi and so on. These people would not have had the time to acquire Pahlavi loanwords—the accepted period for the adoption of Pahlavi borrowings is the second century AD onwards. Furthermore, my translation of the three-line poem transmitted by Khorenats'i, apparently from the second century BC according to the experts, shows that at those times the Armenian language was still a mixture of the ancient simple root system and newly inflected compounds. Mar Abas therefore could not have recomposed the names but would have brought with him the actual ancient names taken from the various Assyro-Babylonian sources.

Additionally, some of the names examined above, such as Arayan Ara and Erast, do not appear to have been recorded in the Assyro-Babylonian sources, therefore Mar Abas could not have listed them, which emphasizes the existence of an editor from the end of the second century AD. He is the one who, besides adding much to the book of Mar Abas, translated the ancient names into Classical Armenian. He has no name and there is no proof of his existence, but after considering all the information available, one has to agree that there had to be such a scholar with a deep understanding and knowledge of Greek and Armenian in equal part.

TO CONCLUDE...

The composition of the first name-list of chapter 12 is the work of an editor, since the Assyro-Babylonian records do not mention a Shakhu and at the time of Mar Abas the patriarchal house of Shahunis, as also Angeł Tun, were not part of Armenia, which makes it clear that Mar Abas could not have known of them. Tsop'k', the district wherein the Shahunis and Angeł Tun of Ingilene had settled, was part of the kingdom of Sophene until 94 BC when Tigran the Great attacked the last king Artanes and attached these lands to Armenia.[73] The Editor has taken the six names recorded by the Assyrians (Gełam, P'arokh, Ts'olak, Harma, Garnik, Tork' Angeł) from the list of Mar Abas, since these names are missing from the comprehensive list 2 of chapter 1.19. The Editor has also taken seven names (Manawaz, Khor, Aramayis, Baz, Amasia, Shara and Erast) from the existing names of the patriarchal houses and places in Armenia. There remains one doubtful entry, the name of Sisak, which could have derived either from the place name Sisakan or from the Assyrian inscriptions of Shalmaneser III.

The three place names of Aramaneak, Aram and Kadmos derive from the epic songs of the gusans and are the additions of the Editor. Mar Abas could not have written these since he was an Aramaean (Syriac) and he would have recognised all of them as place names; indeed, the Assyrians neither had nor knew such names. The intention of the Editor can only be explained as a purposeful composition of a list intended to show where these ancient kings derive from and at the same time inform future generations of their history, albeit in an allegorical manner.

The names Arayan Ara, Anushavan and Mshak of chapters 12 to 19 have been taken from the songs of the gusans, since each one of these contains a tale connected with them (the Assyrians mention only names). Again, this is the work of the Editor, as Mar Abas would not have known the details. But the name of Zarmayr was added to the list of chapter 1.19 by Khorenats'i himself; this is obvious since he had the works of Eusebius as his prime source in connection with non-Armenian subjects, and the name of Tewtamus is taken from this source.

The second name-list of chapter 1.19, however, derives wholly from Mar Abas with the exception of Arayan Ara, Anushavan, Paret and Zarmayr, as indicated above.

---

73.   Strabo, *Geography*, Book XI, 14.15.

With Skayordi's son Paroyr starts the third name-list of chapter 1.22. These are the Cilician kings of which Hrach'eay, P'aṟnawaz and Koṟnak are derived from the Assyrian records and Pachoych and Baos from the Babylonian. These five names derive from the work of Mar Abas, but the classification and the addition of 'Paroyr son of Skayordi, Haykak Ervand and Tigran' belong to the Editor. The Assyrian inscriptions could not have mentioned all the names in this third list, considering that the names, with the exception of Hrach'eay, P'aṟnawaz and Koṟnak, appear in history after the fall of Nineveh.

The two battles of the Hays, the one in the north against Payapis-K'aałea and the one in the south against Barsham derive from the epic songs of the gusans.[74] It is remarkable that the names of the Hay kings involved in these wars have been forgotten and yet the names of their opponents are mentioned, albeit ambiguously. None of these battles are recorded in the Mesopotamian sources; if they were then Mar Abas would have also known the names of the Hay kings, which tells us that it is not the work of Mar Abas, unless he went around the Hay districts in order to listen to the gusans in addition to his journey to Mesopotamia. Besides, Mar Abas being a Syriac would have known that there was no Hay person by the name of Aram, a name that comes from the gusans, which the Editor has used in addition to the various aspects of the battles. Furthermore, after the end of the northern battle, Mshak according to Mosēs (chapter 1.14) is made a governor of Caesarea by Aram (Book 1.14). Mar Abas does not know the name Mshak, since the Assyrians record only a Mugallu as discussed above. In the case of the southern war, Mar Abas would not have used the name of the Aramaean god Barsham for an individual, knowing full well that Barsham was worshipped in the Aramaean kingdoms of north Syria (the worship of Barsham in Armenia is a later development). He would not have transferred him to the north of Assyria, where he was allegedly killed.

Khorenats'i's history of ancient Hay events is based mainly on folklore rather than on written historical sources (since there were no such sources except for Mar Abas). Khorenats'i agrees in the last paragraph of chapter 1.14 with this statement, and confirms that the activities of Aram were collected from unknown and unimportant individuals, which reinforces

---

74. Khorenats'i's Payapis K'aałea is known as Bar-ga'ya of KTK in history. Diakonoff says that 'KTK' is Katak in Aramaean, which represents the Kaska people of north Anatolia. The Topada inscription and what Khorenats'i says support his claim.

my belief that the description and the addition of the two battles to Mar Abas' manuscript are the work of the Editor.

The battle of Hayk and Bēl, and what follows it, creates some difficulties because there is a degree of telescoping in the tale, for which Khorenats'i is responsible; he is not aware that an editor has added material to Mar Abas' manuscript and accepts the whole as the work of the latter. Of course, this is all done unwittingly but the result is that it creates a number of doubtful points and spoils the extensive war between the Hays and the Assyrians of Sargon II, which, in his history, has been so diminished that one gains the impression of a domestic quarrel between two families. Of course this abatement of the war serves an unexpected purpose: it glorifies Hayk and his standing as the primogenitor of the Hay people, which could only take place in an epic song of a gusan. The story mentions that the place where Bēl (Sargon II) was killed together with his braves was named Gerezmank', but Hayk took the corpse of Bēl to Hark'. This is again from the epic songs: at the time of Hayk there was no Hark' district and the two Hayks, primogenitor Hayk and the Manawazean head of the last war with the Medo-Scythians, Haykak the Other, have been merged. The contents of chapter 1.12, the division of the lands, likewise are merged since this happened at the time of Haykak. The telescoping again is done by Khorenats'i—he has seen the two similar names and, due to the scarcity of source material, has not realized that he is dealing with two different persons.

The last battle of Aram was in connection with the Hays' entry into Urartu. The entire story derives from the epic songs of the gusans, which the Editor has collected and presented as the first battle of Aram. It is remarkable that the name of the leader of the enemy, Niwk'ar Mades, has been preserved whereas the name of Haykak Manawazean is not known in connection with this battle, and the affair is credited to Aram country as a person. In list 3 Haykak is correctly mentioned as a contemporary of Cyaxares but that is all, nothing else is known of him since his deeds were partly merged with Hayk the primogenitor and partly ascribed to patriarch Aram.

Khorenats'i does not know Vałarsh I (the Arsacid). Everything that is connected with this king is credited to Vałarshak the Parthian, the viceroy at Mtsbin (Nisibis). It is obvious that the Editor mentions Vałarsh I and the building of the walls of Vałarshapat but that the two names and two separate deeds are fused into one. The reforms of Vałarsh I have also been credited to the Parthian Vałarshak. There is not much written about Vałarsh II, except that he became king in the thirty-second year of his namesake Vologasis III (AD 148-191) of Parthia, and had a soldier's death in battle against the northerners.

Mar Abas existed and gave us the names of the most ancient kings of the Hays. His manuscript has been rewritten with much material added, material unknown to Mar Abas since it derive either from the epic songs of the gusans, which are impossible to date, or had taken place after his time. Khorenats'i found the book of Mar Abas, as he admits in chapter 1.3: 'Is there a book in my possession ... or written history in connection with your ancestors, through which I could quote your correct family tree...' But he does not know that the book in his possession had been modified, accepting everything written as the work of a single author, and so he tries to apply an order to the narrative of the history—this must be the principal reason for the telescoping. Seeing the same names in different places, connected with different events and his lack of sources, compels Khorenats'i to merge them. Perhaps he even considered Mar Abas an untidy writer, one who does not follow chronology and writes about the activities of one person in many parts of the book. He tells us when Mar Abas lived but fails to make the connection that there is much material that could not have been written by him since these relate either to unverifiable or future times. If the Editor had marked the parts he had added, I am sure the first book of Khorenats'i's History would not have been such an enigmatic work, the subject of so much criticism, most of which appears to be unfounded.

Conclusions on Khorenats'i's source: Mar Abas Katina

Working on the case of Mar Abas and the history ascribed to him, I have come to the following conclusions which may serve as a guide when dealing with the subject. There was an individual (Khorenats'i calls him Mar Abas Katina) who compiled the name-list of the ancient Hay kings, deriving them from Mesopotamian sources. This claim is supported by the names appearing in chapters 1.12, 19 & 22. Some of these names represent the Assyro-Babylonian versions and differ from those found in the hieroglyphic inscriptions of the same kings.

From the time of Mar Abas no single manuscript could have lasted for 600 years (c. 130 BC to AD 474), in view of the prevailing conditions of the region, i.e. extreme cold of winter followed by the extreme heat of the summers, stored in humid premises or caves. Our experience of the manuscripts that have survived to our own times supports this view, considering their condition and the dates when they were reproduced.

Thus at some time within this period of 600 years Mar Abas' manuscript was edited and rewritten.

The reproduction of his manuscript has been subject to additions and editing by an individual who has left us no indication of his name or existence—the Editor—a fact of which Khorenats'i is unaware. The Editor must have had an interest in the history of the Armenians (perhaps he was one of the gusans) and had gathered a store of knowledge of historical subjects. It is difficult to place a date on the editing and rewriting since we know nothing about either the person or about such editing; all the same, I am inclined to place the event towards the end of the second century AD or the early third, for which there are a few hints and clues as discussed above.

Khorenats'i does not reproduce the whole of the history contained in the manuscript he has acquired. At the beginning of chapter 1.12 he observes: 'In the book of Mar Abas many things are narrated, but he will only write about those which are suitable to his compilation.' As a result of his selective extractions we have synopsis of events and merging of information pertaining to persons of similar names.

There is much in the history that derives from oral traditions, such as epic songs of the gusans, which are impossible to corroborate with any outside sources—in the majority of cases there are no such sources. This is not a unique condition, there are many aspects of history in general that we accept on reasoning and inferences. At least we know that the Hay people had classes of gusans throughout history, for which we have the earliest confirmation in the Kululu Lead Strip No. 1 from the eighth century BC.[75]

This study leaves many questions unanswered, such as in which language the edited manuscript of Mar Abas' work was written; why none before Moses had got hold of the manuscript or how Moses himself had acquired it; whether the reforms of Vałarsh were recorded by his chancellery and if so in what language; had there not been writers prior to Moses or various other works that were destroyed at the time the Armenians were adopting Christianity; and so on. For the present we cannot answer these questions but merely speculate on the truth.

Finally, in this article I have avoided reference to the Mar Abas of Bishop Sebēos. Instead I have dealt with this matter in *The History of Bishop Sebēos*,[76] where I have asserted that the short extracts composed by him are creations based on the text of Khorenats'i.

*

75. Soultanian, *Pre-History Volume III*; and see note 18 above.
76. Ibid., *The History of Bishop Sebēos*, 2007.

The Real Ara the Fair

One of the most captivating ancient mythological stories of the Armenians is that of Ara the Fair and Shamiram, which has been in circulation for at least the past 2,500 years. It is impossible to state with certainty when the story originated, but we can be sure that it could not have existed prior to 750 BC, i.e. more than 150 years before the Hay entry into Urartu (588 BC). In my opinion, one can roughly date the initial rudimentary beginnings of the story at its earliest to the era of the rule of Kamana in Carchemish, and it is similar to those poems and songs created by the travelling minstrels and bards of the second century BC.[1] The later development and refinement of the story appears to have taken place in Armenia. Our original source of the story is Khorenats'i's history (Book 1.15), written in the second half of the fifth century AD. Bishop Sebēos follows Mosēs and succinctly reproduces the same myth in the first chapter of his own history, in places verbatim,[2] in the second half of the seventh century. Apart from these two historians we have no other ancient writers who have dealt with the full story, although we have on record remarks by certain writers of the same period concerning the word *arlez* (also written as *aralez* and *yaralez)* and their own understanding of it, which is not an issue of central importance for this study, as we shall shortly see below.

There has been much scholarly discussion about this subject within the last 140 years and the various interpretations and descriptions that have reached us are, to put it mildly, confusing. Commentators have not always taken care to stick exactly to the original writings of the ancient

---

1. We now know that the Hays had had classes of gusans and drummers since the eighth century BC. See the Kululu Lead Strip inscriptions in *Pre-History of the Armenians Volume III*.

2. I quote here from Sebēos' History (Malkhazyants' edition) only the verbatim borrowings mentioned: 'Shamiram had heard of his beauty. She sent messengers to him with gifts and offerings. She took the host of her army and arrived in the plain of Ara. The armies clashed ... Ara [was killed] in battle. She ordered to place him in the upper chamber of her mansion. I have ordered my gods to lick his wounds and he shall be restored to life. But when his corpse became stinking she ordered it to be cast into a ditch and covered up. One of her paramours she had dressed up and gave out report that the gods licked Ara.'

historiographers. A few scholars claim an ancient Indo-European origin for the mythology, whereas others compare it with, or even ascribe to it, Egyptian, Babylonian, Persian, Indian and Greek sources. The desire to find a uniformity and interconnectedness for such mythologies ignores the issues of time, distance, possibilities of contact and language differences in the sparsely populated world of the ancients. For example, Alexander Matikian[3] tells us that 'the mythology in its original state derives from an Indo-European ancient source'; but he does not know what source, nor does he consider the possibility that the hero of the story might actually have been a king of the Hays (Proto-Armenians). In reailty, Matikian holds the opinion that the traditions relayed by Khorenats'i are the product of his imagination and so are not to be taken seriously.[4] Adontz is of the opinion that the story of Ara and Shamiram is indigenous but gives a confusing account of its beginnings when he introduces an Urartian inception continued by the Hays.[5] G. Łap'ants'yan[6] invents an unknown and unheard of religious order for the Armenians in the 'Worship of Ara' and is convinced that neither Ara nor the other patriarchs—such as Hayk, Aramenak (note that Łap'ants'yan, like Sebēos [chapter 2], in place of Aramaneak, which means 'Circuit of Aram', uses Aramenak, diminutive of the ethnic term 'Armenian'), Aramayis, Amasia, Gełam, Harma and Aram—are historical figures, summoning fanciful etymologies and equation of names in addition to quoting the Vishap stone monuments of Gełark'uni in support of his thesis. For him the divine Ara is a god of spring, vegetation, farming and produce, a dying and resurrecting god who also embodies a war-like nature. We may therefore be forgiven for thinking it remarkable that such an important god, in the name of Ara, was overlooked by our ancient writers, particularly by Agat'angełos and Khorenats'i. A. Petrosyan's thesis involves patriarch Aram,[7] whose essence he tries to ascribe to an unknown Indo-European source, also involving himself with the story of Ara. Chronology does not appear to be important for his endeavours and the explanation of some names and their alleged affiliations are designed

3. Alexander V. Matikian, *Ara the Fair* (in Armenian), Mkhit'arian Press, Vienna, 1930, p5.
4. Matikian, *Ananuna kam kełts Sebēos*, 1930, p70, he states that it is not possible to rely on the genealogy of the noble houses of Khorenats'i, since he had not seen the original Anonymous History, and in the course of the ninth century AD it was not possible to locate the true traditions.
5. N. Adonts', *Collection*, vol. 1, University of Yerevan, 2006.
6. G. Łap'anys'yan, *The Worship of Ara the Fair*, Academy of Sciences, Yerevan, 1944.
7. Armen Petrosyan, *The Myth of Aram in the Indo-European Context and the Case of Armenian Ethnogenesis*, Van Ardzan, Yerevan, 1997.

to suit his purpose. He has worked hard but the knowledge thus acquired is not always put to good use, such as the fact that there was no person named Aram and he is unable to connect BRGY of KTK (the name derives from an Aramaic inscription)[8] to Bar-Ga'ya of Katak or the Payapis K'aałea of Khorenats'i. Petrosyan mentions Gurti of Til-Garimmu from the inscription of the Assyrian king Sennacherim but again is unable to connect him with the Gorak of Khorenats'i.

It appears these scholars have no appreciation of the fact that since the creation of the Armenian alphabet to today, the only true pre-history of the Armenians written is that of Khorenats'i, irrespective of the fact that there is much that he has misunderstood or not understood at all. Therefore, when one exercises his imagination and creative abilities in the presentation of works diverting from the original writings of Khorenats'i or any of the ancient authors, he is guilty of trying to destroy, intentionally or otherwise, the only sources of the pre-history of the Hays available to the Armenians. I repeat my previous statement that *without Mosēs Khorenats'i there is no Hay pre-history.*

Continuing the discussion of Ara the Fair, it is a historical fact that he was a Hay king of Carchemish in the country of Aram, and lived perhaps near enough to two millennia after the Proto-Armenians had parted from the main Indo-European family. Most scholars interested in the mythology identify Ara the Fair with Er, the son of Armenius, of Plato's *Republic*.[9] To my mind this identification amounts to wishful thinking, imposing a non-existent unity on two distinct tales. The story of Plato's Er is as follows:

Er, the son of Armenius, a native of Pamphylia, was killed in battle. When the bodies of the slain were taken up ten days afterwards for burial in a state of decomposition, Er's body was found to be still fresh. He was carried home, and was on the point of being cremated, when, on the twelfth day after his death, as he lay on the funeral-pyre, he came to life again, and then proceeded to describe what he had seen in the 'other' world.

8. R. Rosenthal, 'Canaanite and Aramaic Inscriptions', in J. B. Pritchard (ed.), *The Ancient Near Eastern Texts Relating to the Old Testament*, Princeton, 1970. Also mentioned by I. M. Diakonoff in *The Pre-History of the Armenian People*, Caravan Books, Delmar, New York, 1984, p87. The same subject is also discussed by J. D. Hawkins in 'The Neo-Hittite States...', in *Cambridge Ancient History*, vol. III, part I, 1982, p407.

9. Plato, *The Republic*, translated by John Llewelyn Davies & David James Vaughan, Macmillan, London, 1929, p361.

In contrast, Ara the Fair's story in Khorenats'i (Book 1.15) is as follows:

A few years before the death of Ninos [Shamshi-Adad V—here the mythology appears to suggest that it might have been Shamshi-Adad I of the nineteenth to eighteenth centuries BC], Ara became the ruler of his fatherland. The dissolute and lascivious Shamiram having heard of his good looks, desired to see him, but did not dare to. However, after the death of her husband, Ninos, she openly sent messengers with gifts asking Ara to come to Nineveh and either become her husband and rule over all or simply gratify her desires and then go back. Ara, declining the offer, put a stop to the exchanges which made Shamiram very angry. Then with her multitudes she invaded Armenia, hoping to capture Ara alive and fulfil her desires by force. To this end she gave instructions to her generals. On her arrival at the plain of Ayrarat a battle duly took place and Ara fell and died. She sent despoilers to the battlefield to seek Ara, whose dead body was brought and placed in the upper chamber of her palace. She said to the people, 'I have ordered my gods to lick his wounds and restore him to life', hoping to revive the corpse by sorcery and magic. When the corpse started to decompose and stink she ordered it to be thrown into a pit and covered.

Now, looking to these two stories we find but a single common feature: both Er and Ara fell in battle. The name of Er, son of Armenius, is phonetically near enough to Ara, and Armenius can, perhaps, be equated with Armenian or Armenia. But it is stated that this Armenius was a Pamphylian, therefore Armenius in this case is the name of a person (there have been other Greeks with the name of Armenius, such as the Argonaut from Thessaly, allegedly the primogenitor of the Armenian people),[10] the father of Er, and not an indication of the bearer's ethnicity. Some have attempted to embellish the story of Ara by adding to it a reanimation, like that of Er, in order to suggest a connection between the two stories. But it should not be overlooked that whereas Er's body was fresh and came to life on the twelfth day, Ara's corpse started to decompose and stink and was thrown into a pit and covered up. There is no licker of Er's wounds and he was placed on a pyre, but in the case of Ara, Shamiram, who does not exist in the story of Er, placed his corpse

---

10.   Strabo, *Geography*, Book 11.4.8 & 11.14.12

in an upper chamber and promised to instruct her gods (not divine dogs) to lick his wounds and revive him, while she also resorted to sorcery and magic. Another point to be considered is the matter of a dog, which is absent from both Mosēs' and Sebēos' stories, as well as from the story of Er. However, because a dog usually licks its own wounds it has been postulated that the licker of Ara's wounds must be a dog and the conclusion is that Ara was a hunter and had a dog![11] But Shamiram says: 'she will instruct her gods to lick Ara's wounds'— it is only in such romantic stories that a human can instruct god or gods; there is no mention of a dog and the Assyro-Babylonian pantheon never had a dog god. When we look into the chronology of the two stories we find Plato's narrative is of an ancient story retold by him, early in the fourth century BC, in support of his moral and philosophical ideas, whereas Ara's story could not have been enriched and refined before Mar Abas' journey to Mesopotamia, where he may have learned through the writings of Ctesias about Shamiram's personality and enterprise. Plato and Ctesias being contemporaries, perhaps there was no possibility that the history written by Ctesias could have been known in Greece for a long while; therefore, Plato's story may not have connections with Ctesias. The indigenous story of Ara and Shamiram could not have spread within Armenia in its final form that has reached us, perhaps, as late as the second century BC, and of course the creators (ordinary people trying to make a living as minstrels) could not have known of Plato and his story.

For Armenius, Matikian tells us that: 'He is a historically attested person and his claim is supported by the names of Hayk's progeny, such as Aramaneak, Aramayis, Harma and Aram.'[12] This is so farfetched that one can only dismiss it as nonsense. Matikian does not know what these names mean, nor is there any effort on his part to learn their meaning. These names have nothing to do with Ara the Fair, Armenius or his son Er. As we already know, Aram was the country the Hays inhabited prior to their entry into Urartu, known also as Aramaneak, 'Circuit of Aram' (*Aram* + *manyak*). Aramayis was the great king of Tabal and his name means 'Storm of Aram', which in Proto-Armenian was Tuwatis (*tuw* → *t'ag* = 'crown, king, kingdom' + *atis* → *ayis* [Classical Armenian *ays*] 'wind, storm' = literally 'King/Kingdom Storm', meaning 'Storm-like King/Kingdom'). The last name of Harma is a little more involved,

---

11. Matikian, *Ara the Fair*, Mkhit'arian Press, 1930; see pp 314/5.
12. Ibid., p274.

representing as it does the Proto-Armenian king of Tabal, Wasusaramimasa (= 'Kingdom of the God Sarami'), which the Assyrians wrote as Uassurme,[13] and contemporary historians as Wasusarma.[14] *Wasu* transcribes as *gaho* (= 'throne' in the genitive), *Sarami* is the name of the Proto-Armenian god Sarma and *masa* means 'god, death, share/region'. The translator of the name of Uassurme has taken only the *Sarma* part and transcribed it correctly as Harma (*s* → *h*); perhaps he had not understood the initial *Uas* part of the name.

We must now consider the words *arlez*, *aralez* and *yaralez*. Unfortunately, there is no consensus as regards their meanings and here again each scholar has his own take on the words. I find Menevishian's explanation of *arlez* as 'licker of wounds' the most plausible.[15] But in this case one is told that the word is a compound of *ar* and *lez*, of which *ar* means 'wound' and is a remnant from the Aryan (no wonder we have not heard of this word and it cannot be found in any dictionary!) and *lez* is an indigenous word, the root of the verb *lizel*, 'to lick'. Some scholars explain *aralez* as 'licker of Ara', in other words *Ara* = the central figure Ara the Fair + *lez* = 'to lick'—but there are many philologists who disagree with the explanation. For *yaralez* we have the opinions of Durian and Matikian that it is a later medieval invention, while others explain the word as 'contiguous licker'. My opinion is that *arlez* is the original word, which has been augmented and become also *aralez* and *yaralez*. *Arlez* is the compound of *ar* and *lez* and has the meaning of 'primary licker', *ar* being an ancient and Classical Armenian prefix (a synonym of the word *era*, as in *erakhayrik'* '*first* fruit') with the meanings of 'towards, in front, at the time, opposite, comparative, instead of, primary and first', and of course, *lez* means 'to lick'. A similar composition can be seen in the ancient Armenian river name Arak'si, which means 'Original Value' → *ar* prefix (explained above) + *ak'si* 'value', a loan from the Greek, perpetuating the river name Axius of Paeonia. This river name was later completely armenicised as Eraskh of which *Era* means 'primary' and *skh* is the root of the word *skhrali*, which reinstates the meaning of Arak'si as 'Original Value'. Hence, the meaning of the compound *arlez* is 'Original Licker'. Mosēs Khorenats'i in his story does not mention *arlez*, but Sebēos says in his History that it was Shamiram who made the word *aralez* well-known![16]

From other writers of the fifth to the seventh centuries AD we have

13. Luckenbill, §802, Nimrûd Tablet.
14. Hawkins, 'The Neo-Hittite States of Syria and Anatolia', in *Cambridge Ancient History*, vol. III, part 1, 1982, pp 413-5.
15. Matikian, *Ara the Fair*, p10—Menevishian.
16. *History of Bishop Sebēos*, edition of S. Malkhazyants', Yerevan, 1939, p6.

references to the words *arlez* and *aralez*. We have Eznik Kołbats'i[17] and philosopher David Anhałt',[18] both of whom reject the existence of such entities. But Eznik goes further and tells us that '*aralez* originates from dog' since dogs exist and still lick their wounds—perhaps his remarks concern divine dogs. P'awstos Biwzandats'i has a rather interesting story about Musheł Mamikonean:[19] 'His corpse was placed on a tower, and since he was a brave man the *arlezes* might descend and revive him' (note that the *arlez* descends from heaven, so here too it is a divine being). Ełishē too has a reference in his *Questions*.

In support of his implausible theories Matikian quotes Josephus's *Antiquity of the Jews*, Book VII, chapter 5 (repeated by Łap'ants'yan) wherein it is related that: 'David [King of the Hebrews] marched to Sophene against king Adrazar, the son of Ara, and battled with him by the waters of the river Euphrates.' In other words, Ara of this extract is the Ara the Fair of the Armenians. The Bible, in both the English and Armenian versions has the same anecdote (English: II Samuel 8:3; Armenian: I Kings 8:3), where Adrazar's (also known as Hadadezer) father's name is given as Rehob and not 'Ara'. Also my copy of Josephus (Whiston's translation, 1960) gives the name as Rehob. But Matikian tells us that he is quoting from a Greek version of Josephus,[20] which says: '*Adrazaron tou Araou men nion.*' I would have thought the phrase had the sense of Adrazar/Hadadezer a son of Aram (country). Furthermore, it is possible that the '*Araou*' of the phrase is wrong due to a scribal oversight and should have been '*Aramou*'.

Who was Ara the Fair? No one has answered this question but that has not stopped scholarly speculations that Ara, like Hayk, was an ancient Armenian heathen god (this is truly amazing, since the Armenian pagan pantheon never mentions Hayk and Ara as gods, which exists only in the imagination of various scholars of the nineteenth and twentieth century), after whom was named a star, Ara—and, again, we find that nobody has been able to indicate which star, constellation or satellite. In fact later writers usurped the already existing name of the constellation of 'Altar'[21] (under the tail of Scorpio in the southern hemisphere), which was also known as Ara to the Greeks and Romans. (The constellation of Orion was named after Hayk for his slaying of Bēl [Sargon II], but that

17. Eznik Kołbats'i, *Ełts Ałandots'*, edition of A. Abrahamyan, Yerevan, 1970, pp 77-8.
18. Davit' Anhałt', *Erker*, edition of S. Arevshatyan, Yerevan, 1980, pp 35 & 63.
19. P'awstos Biwzand, *Patmut'yun Hayots'*, edition of S. Malkhazyants', Yerevan, 1968, p276
20. Matikian, *Ara the Fair*, pp 305-6.
21. Aratus, *Phaenomena*, Loeb Classical Library, Harvard, 1989, p201.

does not imply that he was deified. For more on Hayk, see *Pre-History Volume I.*)

The name Ara belongs to later times, when within Armenia the story started to circulate, and at the time the original story started his original name was Ira, an eighth century BC ruler of the kingdom of Carchemish, who died young in the plague of *c.* 770 BC. However, the name Ira is the diminutive of his full name Ast<u>IR</u>, also written as Ast<u>IR</u>uwa (the *uwa* > *oga* ending is an honorific used for rulers only, meaning 'soul/being'). Astir means 'mighty thinker/truthful/just' (*ast* 'strength, might' + *ir* 'think/truth'). In the early days of Classical Armenian and after the change of Ira to Ara, the two syllables of the name Ast-ir transposed, making the full name Irast (Ast-ir —> Ir-ast); it was only after this stage that the 'I' of Irast changed to 'E', disconnecting the name completely from Ara and creating two separate persons, Ara and Erast, as we see in the History of Mosēs. The name Erast does not make sense in the Armenian language; this phonetic change could not have taken place before the start of Classical Armenian, since the Armenians did not have any earlier the vowels *e, ē, ə* and *ō* (the three Proto-Armenian vowels were *A, I* and *U*).

In the eighth century BC inscriptions Ira was used as a diminutive of Ast<u>IR</u> (—> Erast), which can be seen in the inscription Carchemish Aṣa of Kamana (Havanak, see below). Ira on its own means 'thinker' or 'truthful' and, as shown above, in time it became Ara (a name that cannot be naturally explained in the Armenian language). The vowel changes of *a* to *e* or *i* to *a* do not present any difficulties—consider the Proto-Armenian substantive verb *a*, which has changed to *ē*, although some Armenian dialects still preserve *a*, or words that illustrate the phonetic change such as the ancient *kipu* —> Modern Armenian *k'aw* (intervocalic *p* —> *w*, 'atonement), and *kira* —> *ker* ('food, to eat').

All of our knowledge relating to Astir (Erast or Ara of the later mythology) and his historicity derive from the hieroglyphic inscriptions from Carchemish. There are no outside sources such as Assyrian or Babylonian inscriptions to help us. The reader can find all the relevant hieroglyphic inscriptions and their translations in *Pre-History Volume II*.

It is certain that the Editor of Mar Abas had gleaned the story of Ara and Arayan Ara (Yarairaisa) from existing ballads or stories circulating in various districts of Armenia. By the time of Khorenats'i the story of Ara may have been fully developed or else refined by him by adding various details taken from the existing ballads or stories. Mar Abas could not have written about Ara, since neither the Assyrian nor the Greek

Mesopotamian historians knew of Astir (Ara the Fair), the alleged king of Armenia. But in view of the fact that Shamiram was the wife of Ninos, Shamshi-Adad V (823-11 BC), who had invaded the southern Armenian highlands in his third campaign,[22] the Editor of Mar Abas could have followed Ctesias and written about the building, engineering achievements and the wars of Semiramis, without interweaving it with the person of Ara and creating such a romantic story.

A few words are necessary here in connection with Mar Abas' book, the first history of the Armenians to be written. Khorenats'i records the Proto-Armenian names in their Assyro-Babylonian versions, which were recomposed in the Classical Armenian era with more recent words keeping the same meanings (see Khorenats'i, Book 1, chapters 5, 12, 19 & 22, and their explanation in Part II of *Pre-History Volume I*). My assertion concerning Mar Abas Katina is supported by these names, which are not entirely the same as their corresponding versions in the Proto-Armenian inscriptions from the country of Aram. In other words the Assyrians had their own way of writing these names (as a rule, they opted for the demotic names of these kings) as seen above in the case of Wasusaramimasa which was written as Uassurme. We can add to this the name of the Proto-Armenian king Warpalawa written by the Assyrians as Urballa[23] (Arbak), Larazamasa as Palalam (P'aṛokh) or Suppiluliumas of Kumukh who is Ushpilulume (*spi* 'blemish' + *lul* > *loł* 'swim' + *ume* = 'Where Did This Blemish Swim From?') in the Assyrian records. The composition of these names indicates that the book of Mar Abas was edited some time in the late second or early third century AD and the names recomposed for the understanding of the people of that period.[24] This is also supported by the fact that Khorenats'i has no knowledge of the ancient names, he does not understand the meaning of some of the new ones and his explanations are wrong. The conclusion of this line of reasoning is that Mar Abas existed, that he wrote a history, which was edited and to which changes were made, such as Semiramis becoming Shamiram, wife of Ninos. The accounts of

22. Luckenbill, *Ancient Records of Assyria*, §718.
23. Ibid., §772.
24. We do not know exactly when Mar Abas' book was edited and by whom. My reasoned conjecture was based on the fact that no book in the prevailing conditions of those days would have lasted for six centuries; and secondly, the names Khorenats'i records are translations of the old ones. Khorenats'i does not know any of the old names and even the new recomposed ones are not all understood by him (it is a fact that most of the names in Khorenats'i's list are not understood by current scholarship). For further details, see the chapter 'The Enigma of Mar Abas Katina' in this volume.

her building works, canals and other accomplishments taken from Greek sources, particularly from Ctesias, whose writings we find in Diodorus Siculus,[25] were adapted for the Armenians, and were included in the building of Van (yet Armenians knew nothing of Van until the fifth century AD). At the same time Shamiram's lasciviousness was also interwoven with the story of Ara (Astir), who instead of being a 'noble person', much loved by his people and dying young in a by now forgotten plague, became the object of Shamiram's desire and died on a battlefield, which in commemoration of his name became known as Ayrarat! For further comments about Mar Abas see 'The Enigma of Mar Abas Katina' in this volume.

A few words must also be said about the history of Astir's period (Erast or Ara the Fair, Khorenats'i's name list is wrong in this case since it has two names for one person). There was an intermediate period after Sangara (Garnik) of Carchemish, who was last mentioned in the Assyrian records in 848 BC.[26] It appears the disturbances, which had marred the reigns of the first four Proto-Armenian kings, starting with Suhis I (Yoys) and continued during the reigns of Asatuwatimaza (Amasia), Suhis II and Katuwa (Kaypak) had erupted again after the death of Sangara. The conflict was between the Hurrians and the Hays for the control of the city-state of Carchemish.[27] According to the inscription of Ilapikasa (I+la+pi+kasa = 'Attacker and Smasher of States') of Körkün (near Carchemish), a cousin of Astir, his father had supplied soldiers in order to help him fight for the throne, his heritage from his great-grandfather. Ilapikasa adds that Astir was successful and after becoming king of Carchemish started a family, but died young. Ilapikasa's inscription also throws light on funerary customs, and the various roles of the deceased's family.[28]

We know from inscription Carchemish A7 of Yarairaisa (= Arayan Ara or Kardos = 'Sharp Speaker') that Astir had eight sons, the firstborn being Kamana (= Hawanak, the next king to Astir) and the youngest Pisiri (= Husak, the last king of Carchemish). However, Anushavan was not one of Ara's sons, irrespective of what Khorenats'i writes in his History. He was the son of Mshak (Mugallu) and his name, which the

25. Diodorus Siculus, 12 vols, trans. C. H. Oldfather, Loeb Classical Library, 1989, see Book 11, chapters 7 & 20.
26. J. D. Hawkins, 'Assyrians and Hittites', *Iraq*, 36, 1974.
27. Soultanian, *Pre-History Volume II*. For the inter-ethnic disturbances in the Proto-Armenian kingdom of Carchemish see inscriptions: A4b, A1b, A2, A3, A11a, A11c and the Körkün Inscription of Ilapikasa.
28. Ibid., see Körkün Inscription of Ilapikasa, pp 92-4.

four commentators mentioned above have derived it from the Iranian *anausho-urvan*, is indigenous Armenian (this is a subject for another article). Yarairaisa also records that 'Astir, the much loved king and noble man, died rather young in the plague' [of *circa* 770], which also claimed the life of the great king Tuwatis (Aramayis) of Tabal,[29] which means that the plague had spread.

Yarairaisa (Arayan Ara) was the first minister of the state (not the son of Ara (Astir) as Khorenats'i has it). In his inscription A6, after introducing himself, he says: *'the great gods are indifferent nowadays, since this great person* [Astir*] was struck down and died'*, and continues to describe the effect of the plague and the laments of the people. Again, in his A15b inscription, he repeats how the king died and adds that he built a shrine with fire for the glorification of his king.

Kamana (Hawanak) the firstborn of Astir and the next king of Carchemish dedicated his inscription A5a to his father, though this is rather badly damaged stele. The parts of the inscription that are legible say (I provide the complete translation because this inscription does not appear in *Pre-History Volume II*):

His (Astir's) many braves (soldiers) took him out from his house. I am his son. The God Sun gave me his throne. The assembled multitude and his many servants praised him; his royal children and his fighting men then honoured the Patriarch (Astir). He was delivered to his eternal tomb. It is true that Astir has expired and the throne and the weakened state of the deceased Ira (Ara) I shall shoulder ... grief stricken. I had to enshroud my own father and later deliver him to the gods, and offer a sacrifice for him. ... the journey had come to an end ... the expired king was to be abandoned to the god to enable him dispose of his anxieties. I succeeded to the throne of the state and I praise him. The suffering Queen of the deceased paid homage to god Sun (and thus) he was delivered to the powerful gods and thereby granted emancipation. A great number of people came to me ... Great person took care of the state conscientiously. He left the regions to the suffering Queen to rule and carry on ...

We must now consider the name of Yarairaisa, which is connected with Ara the Fair (Astir) and known to Khorenats'i as Arayan Ara. Khorenats'i

---

29.   Ibid., see Kululu I inscription of Ruwas of Tabal, pp 151-3.

says that he was a son of Ara the Fair. As mentioned above, Yarairaisa was the first minister of the state of Carchemish at the time of Ara the Fair (Astir or Erast) and continued in this role during, perhaps, the first fifteen years of Kamana's (Havanak) rule. He died in 754 BC in Nineveh, Assyria.

We note Yara-ira-i-sa has become Arayan Ara, which is easy to explain. The initial '*Y*' of the name has been dropped, perhaps, thinking that it is an ablative prefix, leaving Ara-ira-i-sa. Here we have the first Ara to which if we add the Ira in its changed form of Ara as explained above, we end up with Ara Ara. Add to this the 'i' genitive suffix appearing in the name of Yara-ira-*i*-sa, then we have Ara Ara-i sa., which means 'this is Ara belonging to Ara', or Arayan Ara.

Yarairaisa was also known as Kardos, since according to him he spoke twelve languages. We usually translate Kardos as 'erudite', but its actual meaning is slightly different. It comprises '*Kard*' and '*os*' roots. The Kard root means to shout, to name, to call, to proclaim, to talk in a loud voice, but above all 'to talk' and 'read' in a loud voice. The '*os*' root is not in use now and most people know nothing about it. This is the Classical Armenian verb *osh-anal*, which used to be written in the Proto-Armenian as *usa*, meaning to become sharp; therefore '*os*' as *osh*, on its own has the sense of sharp. Against Kardos we now have the explanation Sharp Talker (note that in Armenian *sharp* has also the sense of intelligent as in the word *sramit)*, which is exactly what Yarairaisa was known for.

Finally, I must give an account of the name of Nuard, Ara the Fair's wife. The name is usually explained as 'New Rose' (a loan from the Iranian), but the ancient name of this queen contradicts this. It appears that Nuard was a foreign bride (probably a Hurrian) of whom the Hays of the city did not approve; in other words, the much loved and respected king, Ara, married an outsider, whereas he could have picked any one of the daughters of other Hay kings. This was the reason they called her Tuwaraisa, which means 'King (*tuw*) Took (*ara*) This One for Himself (*isa*)' as his wife. In order to comply with the supposition that the ancient names have been recomposed for the understanding of the population of the Classical Armenian era but kept their original meanings, the new name given to Queen Tuwaraisa should have, if not identical, at least a similar or near enough meaning. The exercise involves a slight change in the Classical and Armenian orthography of the name in order to comply with this formula, such as if we change the last letter of Nuard from *d* to *t* then we have Nuart, providing the meaning of *nu* 'bride' + *art* 'outside' ('Bride from Outside'), which is identical in sense and a perfect correlation for the ancient name Tuwaraisa.

*

The Real Tork' Angeł

Most of the Armenian pre-history derives from traditional popular stories, particularly, from the songs of the gusans. Up to recent times this fact could not have been substantiated but with my translation of the Kululu Lead Strip No. 1, we now have confirmation that the Hays had gusans at the very latest starting with the eighth century BC.[1] Of course, each gusan had his own individual way of reciting or singing the various ancient events, which in time became subject to further mutations due to myriad interpretations, interpolations and changes or additional meanings acquired by some words, such as Angeł, which in the olden days meant ignoble, but by the fifth century we note it is explained as ugly, even though the *khel* (> *geł*) of Khelaruata has been translated as 'noble' (the first root *vest* of Vstamkar).

The stories of Ara the Fair and Semiramis, Tork' Angeł, Patriarch Aram and his three battles, Paroyr, Vałarshak the Parthian of Nisibis (Mtsbin) and others belong to this category. It is fortunate that in most cases we have historical evidence, such as the hieroglyphic inscriptions of various ancient Hay kings and the Assyro-Babylonian inscriptions, which help us to reconstruct the true events and compare them with what have come down to us through the history of Mosēs Khorenats'i, the only author to have reproduced in a well reasoned manner parts of such ancient stories.

The tale of Tork' Angeł is one of those deriving from the ancient gusans, but over time the story has mutated to such a degree that even the name of the hero has been misunderstood. This misunderstanding starts with Mosēs of the fifth century AD, who is our primary source.[2] It is true that Bishop Sebēos too has a few lines in his history of the seventh century,[3] apparently connected with the name of the same hero, but

---

1. Kululu Lead Strip no.1—sentence 1.41 says: 'Nunuya and Huliya from the class of gusans of the city (donated) 40 sheep.' Also sentence 1.42: 'Similarly Huliya and Nanamu from the class of drummers of the city (donated) 50.' The complete inscription and its translation can be seen in *Pre-History Volume III*.
2. *The History of the Armenians*, translated by S. Malkhazyants', 1940.
3. G. Soultanian, *The History of Bishop Sebēos*, a critical analysis of the first five chapters; see pp 75-7.

these are based on what Mosēs had written which scholars have explained in a distorted and imaginary manner creating more difficulties for the understanding of the true story.

In Book i, chapter 23, in the last paragraph Khorenats'i writes: 'The same historian (Mar Abas) says that the house of Angeł derives from a certain Pask'am, a grandson of Hayk' (not Haykak as some have it; Hayk and Haykak are two different persons). But in Book ii, chapter 8, he has a long paragraph describing Tork':

But Tork' was born to Pask'am from the line of Hayk. He was ugly, tall, physically grotesque, flatten nosed, with sunken eyes and harsh gaze, and because of these characteristics and particularly of his ugliness he was called Angełya. He was exceptionally tall and strong. He was appointed governor of the west and his tribe was named Angeł Tun (Khorenats'i understands this as the house of the Ugly), because of his ugly look. But, if you want, I can also tell you tasteless and unwarranted lies, similar to those stories told by the Persians about Rostom Sagdjik, as having had the strength of 120 elephants. Because he was a spirited and powerful person (Tork') they sang such stories, which are unseemly even for Samson, Heracles and Sagdjik. They used to say about him that he would strike cliffs of granite, which did not have any cracks, and according to his wish he would smash them to large and small pieces and shape them with his nails into flat tablets, whereupon with his nails he would draw eagles and similar things. When he encountered enemy ships on the beaches of the Black Sea, attacked them, but being unable to reach, since they were by now in deep waters about eight stadia away, lifted rocks the size of hills and hurled after them, sinking some of the ships and pushing others far away due to the huge waves created by the falling rocks. Oh, this is too much of a fiction, it is a tale of tales! But what can one do, since the man (Tork') was terribly strong and worthy of such stories.

Mosēs has taken the description of Tork' Angeł from the popular stories and he believes in them. But he rejects the absurd aspects of the stories connected with him, such as smashing granite and drawing pictures with his nails or throwing hill-sized rocks after the enemy. He does not know who Tork' Angeł was and never ascribes to him divinity—unlike recent scholars who under the cover of philology create new stories and yet they too do not know who the hero was, what his name means, but ascribe to him a non-existent divinity. They base their speculations on the popular stories Mosēs has outlined, even though they consider them to be flighty; in other words they do not share the healthy attitude which Khorenats'i adopts. Of course, they point to Bishop Sebēos's history, which unwittingly equates Angeł with godhood but does not mention Tork'. For Sebēos, Bagarat is Angeł which has no connection with the story Khorenats'i tells us. We should therefore best see what Sebēos says himself:

Chapter 1: (P'aṛnavaz) begat Bagarat, and Bagarat begat Biwrat, who begat Aspat. The sons of Bagarat inherited their legitimate legacy in the west, which was Angeł Tun, since Bagarat was also called Angeł, which in those days the barbarian nations called god. This P'aṛnavaz (father of Bagarat) submitted to Nabuchadnezzar, the king of Babylon...

Chapter 2: Bagarat P'aṛnavazian, a descendant of Aramenak and a great Nobleman went with his army to meet and offer (to Arshak) his services, etc. King Arshak made him *aspet* of the country of Armenia, which means a prince and commander of his entire kingdom...

Khorents'i in Book ii, chapter 3 says: 'but in the west of our country where the Armenian language is no more spoken, appointed (Bagarat) chief administrator...'; and in the same Book, chapter 7: 'He [Arshak] recompensed the Jew called Bagarat for his previously rendered services and his fidelity and valour by granting to his family the aforementioned rank of prince; he also gave him the authority to place the crown on the king's head and to be called coronant and *aspet*' (Thomson's translation). These two extracts from Khorenats'i are the sources of Bishop Sebēos's entire reference to Bagarat. But Sebēos, being an individualist, makes slight changes and introduces Nabuchadnezzar, which is an anachronism since P'aṛnavaz, the father of Bagarat, could not have known Nabuchadnezzar from more than four centuries earlier than his son Bagarat, a contemporary of Arshak (the name Sebēos uses for Vałarshak) the Parthian of Mtsbin (Nisibis). Sebēos has not given due attention to this fact, but his remarks about Bagarat being called Angeł is the result of logic since Angeł Tun is in the west of Armenia and Bagarat was appointed chief administrator of the west, so it follows that Bagarat was the Angeł whose name was perpetuated in the name of the family.

Adding the epithet of god to Angeł is due to the fact that Sebēos is groping in the dark and knows no more about the subject.

Khorenats'i and scholars after him have defined the adjective *angeł* as 'ugly' which, in my opinion, is an anachronism since in the Armenian language the word for ugly is *tgeł*. The true meaning of the word *angeł* has therefore remained elusive, hardly surprising considering that no one knew who Tork' was nor what had he done in order to deserve such an epithet. These reasons can more or the less justify scholarship's failing, but to accept Angeł as a heathen god, translating as 'Ugly God', is inexcusable. Because Sebēos blundered and created a god of his own making, does that mean that one has to accept his statement with no recourse to thought while at the same time conflating the words Tork' (Sebēos never mentions the word) and Angeł? The word *geł* means beautiful, but we never call a man beautiful; in the case of a man the epithet *geł* usually refers to his character, his affability, his concern and treatment of others, and the word *angeł* has been used in a similar sense, with the meaning of ignoble: *geł* 'noble', as in the name Gełark'unik' royal family of nobles, or Gełama 'wholly noble', or Geł mountains 'noble mountains'. Even the name of Khelaruata (this is the Urartian spelling) has the constituent roots *geł+aru+ad* = 'noble+brave+capable', which was translated into Classical Armenian as Vstamkar (*vst* —> *vest* = noble + *kar* 'capable') in bygone days. Adontz, A. Garagashyan, K'. Patkanyan and G. Khalat'yants'[4] (A. Khatchatryan's article on Tork' Angeł is not relevant since he repeats Adontz)[5] agree that the use of the word *angełya*, 'ugly', is an anachronism but they have not spotted that Angeł is only an adjective qualifying the real name of Tork'. If one is to ascribe godhood to any part of the full name of Tork' Angeł, then it is the initial Tork' alone that qualifies for this, and only then in certain instances, as we shall see below. It should be of interest here to look at a short article by M. Abełyan in Volume 1 of his *Hay Vipakan Banahiwsutiwn* (*Armenian Mythological Compositions*) as well as Adontz's extensive articles on the subject.

Abełyan admits that we know nothing about Tork' Angeł, but that does not stop him from equating the name Tork' with Turk' and speculating that the ancient name must have been written as Turk'. His supporting evidence derives from the fact that a cleric in the past was

---

4.   N. Adontz, *Collected Articles*, University of Yerevan, 2006; see vol. II, pp 79-85 for the 1911 article and pp 86-96 for the 1926 article.
5.   A. Khatchatryan, 'Tork' Angełya', in *Telekagir Gitut'yan ev Arvesti Instituti*, no. 5, Yerevan, 1931, pp 40-64.

named Turk', which means 'gift, grace and favour'. His claim that in Bishop Sebēos's history the genesis of Angeł Tun is mentioned is not one that can be accepted; as stated above Sebēos does not know of Tork' and he is only speculating about Bagarat in his own style which, though based on what Mosēs had written, is a poor and confused example of writing (see *The History of Bishop Sebēos*, p77).[6] As for Angeł being a god of the Armenians, which is repeated by other scholars such as Adontz, I wonder how this fact has become known and what are their sources. Mosēs is the only source for this story but where has he mentioned or claimed such godhood for Angeł or Tork' Angeł? The part where I agree with Abełyan is when he writes that 'the stories of Tork' Angeł do not correlate with Nergal's nature'. This is a reference to the translation of the Bible by Zohrapian of 1805 and Bałtatlian of 1895, wherein in IV Kings 17:30 the name of Nergal is translated as Angeł, which since has been corrected, reverting to the name Nergal (see *The History of Bishop Sebēos*, p45). As mentioned above, Abełyan rejects the claim that *angełya* means 'ugly' in Armenian, which is perfectly reasonable.

The two articles of Adontz, written in 1911 and 1926 respectively, are remarkable philological exercises that demonstrate how an erudite scholar is quite capable of creating a story from his imagination and cobbling together unconnected facts to shore up the validity of what he writes. Adontz's actual knowledge is limited to what Mosēs and Sebēos had written in the fifth and seventh centuries respectively but he is able to submit a wealth of collateral evidence which still fails to improve our knowledge of Tork' Angeł, even by an iota. Unfortunately his theories have been accepted without question. However, as I have pointed out above, it remains a remarkable exercise particularly since at the time when Adontz wrote his articles nothing was known of the hieroglyphic inscriptions of central Anatolia and very little of the history of the region. It was unknown that Tark or Tarku was the head of the pantheon of the Hays while they lived in central and southeastern Anatolia—the very same Hays whom Sebēos unwittingly calls barbarians since they worshipped Angeł!

Adontz attaches much importance to the eagles drawn in the story by Tork' Angeł with his nails, rejected by Khorenats'i as a fable. Adontz draws the conclusion that the story told by Mosēs is a reflection of the worship of god Tark or Tarku in Armenia in the shape of an eagle or vulture and he creates such birds of prey as part of the decoration of the

---

6.   Soultanian, *The History of Bishop Sebēos*, p77.

temple in Angeł Tun! Unsurprisingly, since the appearance of Adontz's articles, the name of the town and the castle in Ingilene have been changed by scholars to Angł ('Vulture'), a further distortion of the facts.

Adontz finds enough reason to also discuss the Armenian *Astuats* (God) and T'orgom (Togarmah). These are not subjects connected with Tork' Angeł, irrespective of the fact that Adontz tries to derive T'orgom from Tork'; there is no connection in the two names, as we shall see below. But in the case of *Astuats*, as he admits, he is following the erroneous etymology of Marr which has become the accepted explanation.[7] Despite the case that the subject seems unconnected with my present study, I feel obliged to write a few lines in order to correct the past mistakes of scholarship with the hope that my contribution may be a constructive and welcome addition.

While the Hays lived in the country of Aram, from which the Aramian and Armenian labels derive, they were the neighbours of the Phrygians. In the early seventh century BC Phrygia was no more and after the first decade of the sixth century BC the Hays entered Urartu, which became Armenia for non-Armenians and Hayastan for the Hays. This means that from the end of the ninth century BC to the beginning of the seventh century, a period of about 130 years, the Hays and the Phrygians as neighbours were in contact with each other. During the whole course of their stay in the country of Aram, Tabal, Cilicia, Kummukh and so on, the Hays called God Masa, and by changing the intervocalic *s* to *h* they also used Maha. The two terms were used side by side, which we have known since the tenth century BC through the hieroglyphic inscriptions of Aram, until the early days of Christianity by which time Masa had met a natural death and completely dropped out of the language, leaving only Maha. Maha now meant both 'God' and 'death', since in death the Hays believed that one joined the sun, i.e. ascending to heaven or joining the gods.

With the coming of Christianity, around the second to third centuries AD, it became imperative that a new word should be created, since *Maha* with the double sense of god and death was not considered appropriate. A new word of exceptional potency was created in the compound of *Astuats*, meaning 'Mighty Creator'. I am not the first to give this definition: our medieval writers had already expressed similar opinions, such as Vanakan, Vardan Patmich, Michael Asori, Tat'evats'i, Khosrov Andzevats'i, St Nerses Lambronets'i and, nearer to our time, Schröder.

7.   Adjaryan, *Dictionary of Armenian Root Words*, see the entry *Astuats*.

I have outlined above the known historical facts regarding the definition of the word Astuats. Remarkably, the same definition was repeated by the Armenian writers of the Middle Ages without being aware of these facts. Scholars of recent times are similarly unaware yet this has not prevented them from accepting the alien and enigmatic name of Sabazios, a secondary god of the Phrygians, and deriving from it the word Astuats ('Mighty Creator' = 'God'). I should add that no ancient Hay neighbouring Phrygia in Anatolia or Christian Hay of later periods had any knowledge of Sabazios for god, except the ingenious Marr and his followers. It should not be forgotten that during the time the Hays were the neighbours of the Phrygians and nearly a thousand years after that, they called their god by the name of Maha.

Reverting to the subject of Tork' Angeł and the hurling of hill-sized rocks after the enemy, many have thought that this story derives from Homer's *Odyssey*, where towards the end of Book IX the Cyclops Polyphemus hurls rocks after Odysseus' boat. This is a possibility which can neither be confirmed nor rejected, but in my opinion the Armenian story is not connected with that of the Cyclops. As indicated above, the story derives from the songs of the gusans, who were not educated people as we understand the term today but minstrels of a certain talent possessing the gift of the gab. The time when Tork' Angeł's story was composed could not have been prior to the seventh century BC (scholars of the opposite view consider Tork' Angeł was of second century BC), since after this period most of the details would have been forgotten. Futhermore Khorenats'i has not read Homer—his knowledge of the *Iliad* derives from the Mesopotamian Greek sources or Eusebius, which do not concur with Homer's original fables.

These facts can only present difficulties for scholars with opposite views. Indeed, I would also point out that between Homer of the eighth century BC, and the composition of the Armenian fable there was insufficient time for the transmission of the story from one nation to the other, and we may safely assume that there were not many copies of Homer's works available in the late eighth century BC. It would take a further five centuries for Homer's works to be rewritten and perhaps edited in Classical Greek from perhaps the third century BC. However, this is not all that significant and either way it does not affect the creativity of the gusans, nor the enjoyable fable Khorenats'i has saved for posterity.

The first Hays to set foot in the later Armenian highlands were those who were part of the Mushki movement. According to Tiglath-Pileser I of Assyria,[8] the Mushki had five kings, which means the movement comprised of five different ethnic units, each having its own leader. Of these five the Phrygians are certain because of the name Mushki; the Mysians too are certain in view of the name of the city of Mush.[9] The remaining three are conjectural since their presence is deduced from Homer's *Iliad* as the Balkan allies of Priam of Troy (Book ii, lines 840-44, 848-50 & 858-63).

According to Homer the enemies of Priam were the Mycenaeans from the mainland Greece, Crete, Rhodes and the Aegean and Ionian Islands. The allies of Priam that came from the Balkans were the Phrygians, Mysians, Paeonians, Pelasgians and the Thracians. These last five Balkan tribes constituted the Mushki movement after the end of the Trojan War, and as a part of the Population Movement arrived and initially settled around the confluence of the Euphrates and Murat Su (Arsanias/Aratsani).[10] From this conjectural description we can conclude that the remaining three tribes, besides the Phrygians and the Mysians, were the Paeonians, Thracians and the Pelasgians. I must add that the Paeonians of this conglomerate were those who arrived towards the end of the Trojan War under the leadership of Asteropaeus, and they were mainly from Pelagonia, neighbouring the Phrygians. The Pelagonian Paeonians and Phrygians were always allies and jointly undertook various operations.[11] We can conclude therefore that the Mushki comprised the Phrygians, Mysians, Paeonians, Thracians and the Pelasgians. It appears that the Paeonians of the Mushki and some of their allies eventually settled south of their original place, in and around Ingilene, where we find the settlement of the first Hays around Angeł Castle and Angeł Tun. This is the place Tork' Angeł comes from, where there was the temple of the god Tark or Tarku.

Tork' Angeł was the patriarch of Angeł Tun and appears to have been rather a wealthy leader, able to satisfy the Assyrian greed for gold and silver, which may have been the reason Sargon II of Assyria chose him

---

8.   A. K. Grayson, *Assyrian Royal Inscriptions*, vol. 2, §12 (p6).

9.   R. A. Crossland, 'Linguistic Problems of the Balkan Area in the Late Prehistoric and Early Classical Period', in *Cambridge Ancient History*, vol. iii, part 1, 1982, pp 834-49.

10.   Diakonoff, *Pre-History of the Armenian People*. He believes that the Mushki movement of the time of Tiglath-Pileser I were the Proto-Armenians; see p119, & note 87, p195.

11.   In the Balkans the Pelagonian Paeonians of the east of Lake Lychnides bordered on to the Phrygian or Brygian country to the west of the same lake. The two nations went to Troy together in support of Priam, they also migrated together at the end of the ninth century BC to Asia Minor, the Paeonians settling in the country of Tabal bordered Phrygia in the west. These are some of the joint undertakings. Besides, the Hays of Tabal had always had good relations with Midas of the Phrygians.

as the vassal king of Melid. The date of his accession to the Meliddin (Malatya) kingdom is unknown, since the Assyrians do not mention it. In my opinion, it is most likely that Sargon, at the time of his successful campaign against Kiaki (Głak) in 718 BC,[12] occupied himself also with the affairs of Melid and chose Tork' Angeł as a vassal king of the extensive country of Kammanu-Melid. The previous king, another vassal of Assyria, was acting contrary to Assyrian interests, because of which he had already fled the country before the arrival of the Assyrian army; he was Gunzinanu, the zƏndzak of Mosēs's History, Book 1, chapter 19.

It seems that after a few years of cordial relations with Assyria, Tork' Angeł felt secure enough to concentrate his efforts on the wellbeing of his own kingdom, which could not have suited Sargon, the Assyrian king. Sargon's inscriptions, the Annals, give the following information:[13]

> In the tenth year of my reign, Tarkhunazi the Meliddian, who did not fear the name of the great god—the wide Kammanu which I with the help of Ashshur, my lord, had taken, and Gunzinanu their king had driven out (of the country), and had set him (Tarkhunazi) upon his royal throne … and had caused him to pay homage, and the lordship over the wide countries had entrusted to his hand … perfidious messages against the land of Ashshur despatched. In the anger of my heart the land of Kammanu in its totality I conquered. The city of Meliddu, his royal city, like an earthen pot I destroyed, and all his subjects like a flock of sheep I treated. But he himself, to save his life, entered Til-Garimmu. That city like a cloud I covered. They feared the splendour of my weapons, and they opened their gates. Tarkhunazi, their prince, together with his warriors I put in iron fetters; his wife, sons and daughters together with 5,000 captives of his warriors into my city of Ashshur I brought.

Note that the kingdom of Melid encompassed a large country and comprised the two cities of Melid, the capital, and Kammanu. From the inscription it is obvious that at the time Til-Garimmu (house of T'orgom) was also a part of the kingdom.

It appears that the description of Tork' Angeł, being a great and powerful person, is correct. The name, both ancient and recomposed

12. A. G. Lie, 'The Inscriptions of Sargon II, King of Assyria', see *The Annals*, pp 68-71. Lukenbill, §7—The Fourth Year of Sargon.
13. Lie, §26—The Khorsabad Texts, see tenth year.

betray such a quality, particularly when we know that these are his demotic names as usually recorded by the Assyrians—what was he called prior to Tarkunazi, we do not know. As made clear in Sargon's inscription, this huge and powerful man, like a coward, left his city and the people to the mercy of the Assyrians and ran away to Til-Garimmu to save his skin instead of making a stand and fighting the enemy. So the people called him Tarkunazi, recomposed in Classical Armenian as Tork' Angeł. It is obvious that the truth is completely different to the parabolic description of his actions by gusans. But minstrels have to make a living and no one likes to hear stories about cowards, which is the reason why the entire scenario has been misrepresented in Khorenats'i's history. It is fortunate for Khorenats'i that he shows no conviction in the stories, for which reason I have called his stance a healthy attitude, unlike our modern scholars whose verbosity appear to be more gusan-like than logical scholarship.

It remains for me to explain the names of Tarkunazi and Tork' Angeł. Tarkunazi consists of three roots of *tark*, *un* and *az-i*. *Tark* means only 'thunder' and does not include the meaning of 'god', unless the hierglyphic sign for *Tark/Tork'* (no. 199) in the shape of a capital *W*, is preceded by the sign of GOD (no. 360) in the shape of a circle within a circle with double strokes from the north to south poles. In such cases the meaning becomes 'God *Tark*' ('God Thunder'), who was the head of the Hay pantheon when they lived in the lands of Tabal (later Cappadocia), Togarmah (house of T'orgom), Melid (Malatya), Cilicia (in its entirety), Gurgum (with its capital at Marash), Kummukh (the later Commagene) and Carchemish (the present ruins of Cherablus by the Euphrates, near the Syrian border). Panamuwatis, the queen of Kummukh, has used the sign of *Tark* (no. 199) in the sense of 'thunder' in her inscription of Boybeypinarı, Line 111B3,[14] saying *'par-na Tark wa nu wa tu tipa sa ti sa pawa tu-u tasa khara'*, which means 'if (the enemy) returns like Thunder *(par na Tark wa nu wa tu)*, mighty gods *(tipa sa ti)* condemn that king *(sa pawa tu-u)* to suffering and burning *(tasa khara)'*. The words God Thunder (signs 199 + 360) appear throughout the inscriptions. The conclusion is that Tark or Tarku has only one meaning, 'Thunder'.

The root *un* (> *unayn* 'empty, devoid, vain') and *an* (> *anazniv* 'ignoble, mean') are negative prefixes, which Modern Armenian has inherited from the Proto-Armenian language—these prefixes are similar

---

14. Soultanian, *Pre-History Volume II*, p131.

to the English *un-*. The root *az* in the ancient language had the meanings of 'fire, flame, blaze, spark'. Modern Armenian has inherited this root in its duplicated form as *azaz*, which we see in the words *azazun* ('dried-up, jaundiced, burnt-out'), *azazayel* ('to dry up'), *azazil* ('fiery person, fierce'), and so on. We can therefore conclude that the name Tarkunaz-i means 'Thunder Devoid of Fire', which describes the person and his action very well. There is no sense of god in the name; on the contrary, this is a name given by the people to a coward king.

As for the name Tork' Angeł, we notice the same *Tark* for 'thunder' has been used in a later phonetically changed manner of *Tork'*, which means, again, simply 'thunder' with no inherent sense of god. Angeł consists of the *an* negative prefix and the root *geł*, as explained above in the names of Vstamkar, Gełam, etc, means 'ignoble, not noble' only (in Armenian *anvest* [*anaznvakan*]). Thus the name means 'Tork' the Ignoble', which is the exact correlation of the ancient name Tarkunazi.

The person of Tarkunazi (Tork' Angeł) is completely opposite to the depiction created by Armenian and other historians and philologists. All the same, an enjoyable tall tale has never hurt anyone—and, in the end, are we not all storytellers?

*

Anushavan

Our only source for Anushavan is Khorenats'i's history, where at the end of Book 1, chapter 20, he mentions the name and provides a short explanation, saying:

> Arayan Ara died with Semiramis in a war, leaving a male child exceedingly accomplished in deeds and words, named Anushavan Sosanəver; for he was, according to religious practices, dedicated to the cult of plane trees of Aramaneak *at Armavir city*, since from the gentle or stronger rustle of the leaves and the direction of the wind, in our country they were used to practising divination for a long time.
>
> This Anushavan having endured Zameses's scorn for a long time, suffered at the royal court. But in time having help from friends succeeded to gain control of a part of our country as a vassal and later succeeded to the whole of the country.

Khorenats'i's source for this lovely story is without doubt the songs of the gusans, since it was impossible for Mar Abas to learn this from the Assyrian inscriptions. The Assyrians at the time of Ashurbanipal (668-c. 627 BC) had erased the name of Anushavan from their inscriptions, as we shall see below.

The story says that Anushavan was a son of Arayan Ara, which is certainly wrong. Arayan Ara's son was Baz/Bazuk. Anushavan was the son of Mugallu, the Hay's Mshak. There is also an interpolation in the story, which may be an addition by Mosēs, since he does not understand the word Aramaneak, or else the later editors of the history have made additions. The plane trees of Aramaneak means the trees in the circuit of Aram country, which cannot be transferred to Armavir city (in italics). The word Aramaneak comprises *Aram*, the country, plus the word *maneak*, which means a bracelet, a necklace and circle (in syllabic script two consonants cannot come together hence one of the *m*-s has been dropped). My claim is supported by the fact that Anushavan never set foot on the soil of the Armenian highlands since he was a king of the previous habitation places of the Hays, as we shall see below. But the claim that Anushavan endured the scorn of Zameses (Ashurbanipal) for a long time is amazing since it is true and historically attested.

Mugallu (Mshak) was king of Togarmah (house of T'orgom) and Kammanu Melid, while Ishkallu (Ska-Aɫu, father of Skayordi) was the king of Tabal. After the mysterious disappearance of Ishkallu, Mugallu extended his kingdom and became also the ruler of Tabal. At the time Assyria was ruled by Ashurbanipal, and Mugallu had submitted in *c.* 668 BC and sent him tribute together with one of his daughters.[1] Mugallu's actions were prompted by the imminent danger of a Cimmerian attack on his kingdom. Under the circumstances, an Assyrian alliance and military help might therefore have proved of utmost importance. When Mugallu died, his son Anushavan succeeded as ruler of the great country of Tabal, Kammanu-Melid and Togarmah. But Anushavan soon changed sides and started a cordial co-operation with Lygdamis (Dugdamme) the Cimmerian, a situation which,[2] besides being against Assyrian interest, was deemed by Ashurbanipal to be disloyal. This was the beginning of the animosity between Anushavan and Ashurbanipal, which prompted the Assyrians to erase the name of Anushavan from their inscriptions and leave just the last word of '...ussi'. This is the part Khorenats'i refers to as 'Anushavan endured the scorn of Zameses (Ashurbanipal) for a long time'.

We do not know much about Anushavan except that he died in a palace fire and that no trace of him was found.[3] Of course, Ashurbanipal considered his death as 'divine retribution' in view of the animosity between them. As for the period in which Anushavan ruled that extensive country of the Hays, I can only offer an estimate of *c.* 645 to *c.* 632 BC. In fact, there is very little written in Armenian sources about Anushavan—the *Armenian Encyclopaedia* does not even mention the name. Adjaryan in his *Dictionary of Personal Names* lists the name and derives it from the Zend-Avesta Anaoshō-urvān, meaning 'Deathless Spirit'[4] and cites Justi 17b (F. Justi, *Iranisches Namenbuch*, Marburg, 1895, reprint of Hildersheim, 1963), which derives the name from 'Sweet Village'. Akinian and Eɫishē say that the name Nushirvan derives from it. Adontz holds the same opinion as Adjaryan but conjures fantastic conclusions from the name,[5] such as the

1. Luckenbill, §781—The Cylinder Texts; see also II Cylinder B, §848.
2. Hawkins, 'The Neo-Hittite States in Syria and Anatolia,' *CAH*, vol. III, part I, pp 431-32.
3. Ibid.
4. Adjaryan, *Dictionary of Armenian Personal Names*, see the entry *Anushavan*.
5. N. Adontz, *Collected Articles*, vol. I, Yerevan University, 2006, p22.

idea that 'the name Anushavan is a reference to the immortality of Ara the Fair'.

I wonder whether these scholars have ever made the effort to analyse the name and find out what it means, bearing in mind the glaring fact that in the seventh century BC the impossibility of loanwords from the Zend-Avesta or Pahlavi, particularly when we know that the Avesta was not yet written. Khorenats'i mentions Zameses of Assyria—if our scholars are unaware of Zameses's identity, the least they could do is conclude that he was an Assyrian king, which means at the time of Anushavan there was an Assyria, which would give them a date prior to 612 BC (the fall of Nineveh) for the time of Anushavan. Furthermore, as Urartu was still a viable kingdom prior to the fall of Assyria, it means that the Hays were living in the places referred to by Khorenats'i when he describes Tigran Sakawakeats' as 'extending the borders of our country up to previous habitation places in antiquity' (Book 1.24).

The facts we have concerning Anushavan derive from the Assyrian records. If Anushavan was called Sosanəver by the Hays, the Assyrians would have had no reason to know this. However, I believe to be true the part of Khorenats'i's claim that 'in our country it was an accepted religious way of listening to the rustle of the foliage and make divinations'.[6]

As mentioned above, except for its final part, the Assyrians had erased the name of Anushavan from their inscriptions. If the Hay name Anushavan is successfully explained then it will also be possible to reconstruct the ancient name. Anushavan comprises three roots: *an* negative prefix, + *ush* 'memory, remembrance, to remember' (Modern Armenian preserves the word as *yush*) + *avan* 'habitation place, a house, a resting place'. Therefore, the name means 'No Memory (no) Resting Place', since he died in a palace fire and no remains of his were found (i.e. the resting place is a reference to his non-existent grave).

The Assyrians only mention '…ussi', which is the *ush/yush* mentioned above. The remaining initial part has to be *apanan (+ us-si)* = *apan-an-us-si*, where *apan > awan* is 'resting place' and the following *an* is the negative affix. Therefore, *an-ush-avan* → Anushavan = 'No Memory No Resting Place', *apan-an-us-si* → Apananus-si = 'No Resting Place No Memory'.

*

6. Hesiod, *Homeric Hymns, Epic Cycle and Homerica* (Loeb Classical Library, 1995): 'In Epirus there was Zeus's oracle first consulted by Deucalion and Pyrrha after the flood. Later writers say that the god responded in the rustling of leaves in the oaks for which the place was famous.' Epirus and Dodona were so named after the Trojan War. Epirus was to the southwest of Pelagonia, the first settlement place of the Hays, early in the second millenium BC. This excerpt does not need conclusion, which should be made by the reader.

Gurti of Til-garimmu

The Assyrian designation of Til-garimmu relates to an ancient town in the east of Tabal in Anatolia, in the west of the Armenian highlands. This town was known since the time of the Hittite Kingdom as Tegarama, a strategically important place to the east of the realm. During the course of history the name of this town was subject to minor phonetic changes, depending under whose hegemony it found itself at the time. However, the name maintained a recognisable phonetic pattern, e.g. Teg-arama under Hittite domination, Til-garimmu under the Assyrians, Togarmah as named by the Aramaeans and the Bible, house of T'orgom by the Armenians, Gaurēnē by the Romans (we note that the initial 'te' of Tegarama, the 'til' of Til-garimmu and the 'to' of Togarmah in time has dropped) and Gürün by the Turks.

The Armenian writers of the fifth century AD and onwards have supported the view that the Armenian nation derives from the house of T'orgom (Togarmah/Til-garimmu) and up to the present the use of 'T'orgomian azg' (Nation of Togarmah) is common, which, in my opinion, may be correct so far as the ethnic name of Armenian (not Hay) is concerned. However, we do not have supporting evidence for such a claim and the Bible,[1] freely quoted as support does not mention the Armenians,[2] even though Togarmah is mentioned a few times, such as Genesis 10.3, I Chronicles 1.6, Ezegiel 27.14 & 38.6. Additionally, the ethnic name Armenian (not Hay) has been known for the past 2,600 years, but we should remember that Armenian is not an appellation that the Armenians use, nor does such a word exist in their vocabulary, since they call themselves Hay and their country Hayastan. The ethnic name Armenian means 'people of Aram' and it was first used by their neighbours the Aramaeans in order to denote the new people who entered Urartu as their last settlement place. The original Semitic (Aramaean) version of the name Armenian was Armināiā, which the

---

1. Aram Kossyan, *The House of T'orgom*, Yerevan, 1998. He states on p6 that the Bible is the basis of the designation for the house of T'orgom.
2. It is possible that the first written reference connecting the Armenians to Togarmah is found in Eusebius, *Chronicle II*, p12. However, Fl. Josephus derives the Armenians from Aram, see book 1.6.4.

Persians of the time of Darius the Great (521-486 BC) adopted in the Behistun inscriptions as Armina and the Greek Hecataeus of Miletus (c. 500 BC) borrowed it from the Persians, writing it as Armenioi.

It is noteworthy that the Hittite name Tegarama for this town uses the root *aram*, a legacy from the times of Naram-Sin of Agade (2213-2176 BC), whereas the biblical name of Togarmah (based on the Aramaean usage) uses the root as *arm* which, in my opinion, explains the reason why the ethnic name Armenian omits the second 'a' of the ancient name Aram, where they dwelt for 600 years prior to entering Urartu. This matter of dropping the second 'a' in Aram also indicates when the ethnonym Armenian was composed, since we know that prior to Togarmah the town was known by the Assyrians as Til-garimmu, and the inhabitants as Hati ($t > y = Hayi$).

Scholarship, in general, considers the town of Til-garimmu/ Togarmah as a small unimportant place and we do not see many references to it in historical works until the time of Gurti's insurrection against the Assyria of Sennacherim in the very early seventh century BC. Til-garimmu has most of the time been overlooked by history prior to Gurti, which may be due to the fact that most of the time it was under the hegemony of Melid, which was strategically and size-wise a more important city on the border of Urartu. It is only in the course of the reigns of Sargon II and his son Sennacherim that we hear more about Togarmah. In the case of the first Assyrian king, Togarmah was the city to which Tarkunazi (Tork' Angeł) escaped in order to save himself, and in Sennacherim's case the rebellion of Gurti, i.e. of the Hay population, took place in Togarmah.

In this chapter I shall discuss the name of the rebellious Gurti and the response of Sennacherim, the Assyrian king. But let us see first what other writers had to say about the city of Togarmah and the person of Gurti. On the penultimate page of his study on Ara the Fair[3] Matikian tells us (p333) that: 'We do not know when the Hays migrated from the Balkans into Anatolia . . . We have more data about them starting with the eighth century BC . . . We find the Hays in Armenia Minor under the leadership of their king Gurti'; for this information he cites Friedrich Schmidtke in *Die Japhetiten in der Völkertafel* (Breslau, 1926), pp 51-52.

The times Matikian is alluding to coincides with L. W. King's 1909 translation of the Assyrian and Babylonian cuneiform texts[4] (Part xxvi).

---

3. A. Matikian, *Ara the Fair*, Mkhit'arian Press, Vienna, 1930.
4. L. W. King, *Cuneiform Texts from Babylonian Tablets, etc., in the British Museum*, part xxvi, London, 1909.

Seeing the place name Til-Garimmu, which he knew to be associated with the Armenians, he put two and two together and came to the conclusion that Gurti was a Hay (Proto-Armenian) king. It was not necessary for Schmidtke to know Armenian in order to connect Til-Garimmu with the Armenians, since the information would have been available to him in the works of Gutschmid, Jensen, Hübschmann and Markwart.[5]

In his *History of Armenia* (p128)[6] Adontz recalls Gurti as the founder of a new kingdom in Til-Garimmu (house of T'orgom). He also mentions Sennacherim's attack on this city on 695 BC, when Gurti disappeared and the Assyrians were content with plundering the whole land. Adontz equates Gurti with the Phrygian Gordius and speculates that he might have been a grandson, in other words a son of Midas of Phrygia. We see a similar confusion in Diakonoff,[7] who equates Kurti with Gurti and then derives both of these names from the Phrygian name of Gordias.

I find it remarkable that Schmidtke, Matikian, Adontz and other academics, familiar with the Assyrian inscriptions of Sennacherim, have shown no further interest in Gurti and Khorenats'i's history. One feels disappointment at Matikian and Adontz, since they both knew in addition to Khorenats'i's history the Assyrian inscriptions and Sebēos's history—in 1913 Matikian had even published his study on Sebēos.[8] In chapter 1 of Sebēos's history, paragraph 29, there is a reference to Gurti without mentioning his name: 'Assyrians ruled Armenia until the death of Sennacherim, when they rebelled against Assyrian subjugation.' The information from Sebēos combined with the contents of the cuneiform texts, particularly the lines quoted below from the translations by D. D. Luckenbill,[9] would have made it clear who Gurti was. It would have also pointed the way towards discovering who were the other kings mentioned by Khorenats'i since their names appear in the same Assyro-Babylonian inscriptions.

In 1998 A. Kossyan published a sub-standard study entitled *The House*

5. H. Hübschmann, *Armenische Studien*, Leipzig, 1883; H. Jensen, *Hithiter und Armenier*, Strasburg, 1898.
6. N. Adontz, *History of Armenia*, translated from the French by V. P. Selbosyan, Hayastan, Yerevan, 1972.
7. Diakonoff, *Pre-History of the Armenian People*; for more on Kurti, Gurdi and Gordias, see p184, note 12. Diakonoff also tries to equate Parwata and Paroyr. Parwata of Tabal of the eighth century has nothing to do with the Armenians, he is the Bar-ga'ya of KTK and the Payapis K'aałea of Book 1.14 of Khorenats'i's History. The transcription of Parwata yields Bargaya ($w \rightarrow g$, $t \rightarrow y$).
8. A. Matikian, *The Anonymous or Pseudo-Sebēos*, Mkhit'arian Press, Vienna, 1913.
9. Luckenbill, *Ancient Records of Assyria and Babylonia*.

of T'orgom wherein he addresses a wide range of topics not all connected with the house of T'orgom (Til-garimmu) or the rebellious Gurti.[10] When considering the Mar Abas Katina of Mosēs (p47) he claims that the person and his work are irrefutable, but produces no evidence whatsoever by way of support. He asserts, following Hawkins, that the hieroglyphic inscriptions of southeastern Anatolia frequently mention the word 'Mita(i)s' (p35, apparently the name of Midas, king of the Phrygians), but there is no such word in the whole of these inscriptions, since the word is *miti sa*, meaning 'counsellor, adviser'. Kossyan's 'Mita(i)s' is a corruption of the word *miti*, apparently with the meanings of 'servant, slave'—he is unaware that the word for slave and servant in the hieroglyphics was *zara*.[11] He equates the name Ėshpai with Kurti as the slayer of Sargon II, thinking that the first two are the same person.[12] Like Adontz, he finds a connection between Gordius and Gurti, which is light years away from the truth and is based on mere phonetic similarity. In fact Kossyan's study has so many flaws, and his thinking is spread over so many subjects which do not always comply with reality and ancient written records, that one is hard-pressed to find any realistic

10. Kossyan equates the name Kurti with that of Gurti. The Assyrian inscriptions explicitly ascribe Atuna of Sargon II's era to Kurtis, who is the Kornak of Khorenats'i's chapter 1.22, the Cilician branch of the Proto-Armenian kings. Gurti is a contemporary of Sennacherim and belongs to Togarmah of Tabal, and rightly is shown in the second name-list of Khorenats'i in chapter 1.19. The two names should not be equated, nor should they be connected with Phrygian names of royalty.

11. The *Miti sa* of the hieroglyphic inscriptions Kossyan writes as *Mita(i)s* . It is obvious that he has taken his transliteration/translation of Kurti's inscription (Bogça, no. 27 in Meriggi, part II) from Hawkins, which hardly has a correct sentence. *Miti* means an 'adviser' and never 'servant' or 'slave'. Yarairaisa, the prime minister of Astiruwa of Carchemish, in his A.6 (line 3) inscription says *'waza za na mi king ti miti ti izi'*, which means kings run to me in order to consult (the literal translation is 'great *(ti)* kings *(king)* run *(waza)* to me *(na mi)* to be tied (= *ti*, as in *sameti*), or Ruwas, the prime minister of Tuwatis, in his inscription Kululu I, line 1a writes: *'amu wa mi Ruwa sa Tuwati-i sa miti sa'* ('I am *[amu wa mi]* Ruwas *[Ruwa sa]* the adviser *[miti sa]* of Tuwatis *[Tuwati sa]*'). Finally, Kurti's inscription has the following sentence: *'WEST-i pama-i-ia EAST-mi ma ira ha PARA miti-ia'*, which means 'in the whole (= *pama-i-ia*) of the west *(WEST i)* and the east *(EAST)* my truthfulness *(mi ma ira ha)* and my wisdom *(miti-ia)* circulated *(para)*'.

12. Ėshpai and Kurti can never be equated. Ėshpai is called the 'Kulumean' because he was apprehended by Sargon II and exiled, prior to 705 BC, to southeastern Assyria where he lived for a number of years in the city of Kuluman. Khorenats'i tell's us that Hayk lived in Babylon, since he is trying to connect the story to the Bible. Ėshpai and Hayk are the same person and their abode in the lands occupied by the Proto-Armenians was Zapkaka (the later Kiakka); see R. Campbell Thompson & M. E. L. Mallowan, 'The Inscriptions of Ashurbanipal from the Temple of Ishtar', *Annals of Archaeology and Anthropology*, p96. It may also be of interest to the reader to look at the Bible, Isaiah 14, in connection with the death of Sargon II, even though the king's name is not divulged.

connection between Gurti, Til-garimmu, the Assyrian sources, Mosēs's History and the Armenians.[13]

Finally, we also have the opinions of G. Łap'ants'yan and S. Yeremyan, academics who both see a connection between Togarmah, Armenian ethnogenesis and Khayasha (which they write as Hayasa). Their far-fetched conjectures in the case of Khayasha have been discussed and discarded a long time ago, and I shall therefore pass over these without further comment.

If any one of these scholars who have come across the name of Gurti and the information concerning him had shown some faith in what Khorenats'i wrote in his Book 1, chapters 12, 19 and 22, they would have spotted that the name Gurti was recorded in chapter 19 as Goṛak. It would merely have been a matter of analysing the two names, and a little deliberation would have provided a resolution many years ago. However that was not done, deterred in most cases by the scholarly preconception that Khorenats'i was a historian of the seventh to ninth centuries. We know the views of Adontz (and Manandyan) in connection with Khorenats'i and his history, to which we can add Matikian's following statement: 'It is not possible to rely on the genealogy of the noble houses of Khorenats'i, since he had not seen the original Anonymous History (a nonsensical reference to chapter 1 of Sebēos' history or its alleged source) and in the course of the ninth century it was not possible to find the true traditions (of the Armenians).'[14]

Holding Matikian, Adontz and others to the few lines quoted above, one may conclude logically that Khorenats'i was not a historian of the seventh to ninth centuries but of the fifth, in view of the fact that he records in addition to the name of Gurti more than fifty names in his chapters 1.12, 19 & 22, each one of which is corroborated by Assyrian and Babylonian inscriptions starting from the tenth century BC. There are a few Proto-Armenian names that Mosēs does not record in his name-lists of chapters 1.12, 19 & 22. These omissions are mainly due to the fact that the Assyrian inscriptions do not recall these kings, or there was more

---

13.   Kossyan claims without any proof—and he is not on his own in this case—that archaeological evidence shows that in the second millenium and earlier there were Armenians living in the Highlands; in this connection see M. Israelyan, *The History of Erebuni Fortress-city*, 1971, pp 104-117. Obviously there were people living in the Highlands (where there is water there has always been habitation), but how does one know that they were Hays? How does one recognise the Hay language of those times (four to five thousand years ago), when the names and the language used in the inscriptions of Hay kings of the hieroglyphic era (1000-700 BC), and even the Classical Armenian names preserved for us by Khorenats'i have not been understood?

14.   A. Matikian, *Ananunə kam kełts-Sebēos*, 1913, p70.

than one person with the same name, e.g. the two names of Suhis (> Yoys, pronounced as Huys)[15] of which the Assyrians know only the second but Mosēs knows neither, the two Palalams (P'arokh) of whom the Assyrians know the second just as Mosēs, the three Khalparutiyas (Hrant) of whom the Assyrians know the second and third whereas Mosēs knows only the third.

Let us now examine the names Gurti and Gorak in order to establish what they mean and see if they correlate. Gurti consists of two root words, *gur* meaning 'rebellion, insurgency, to snarl' and *ti* meaning 'day, year, time, period', etc. Therefore Gurti means 'Time of Insurgency'. Gorak consists of two roots: *gor* is the same word and so has the same meanings as the Proto-Armenian *gur* (Proto-Armenian *'u'* of the hieroglyphic script transcribes as *u* and *o*), and *ak* meaning 'source, spring, eye'. Therefore the meaning of Gorak is 'Source of Insurgency'. The composer of the Classical Armenian version of the name managed to record a perfect correlation by keeping its meaning unchanged in the linguistic transfer.

We have little information about Gurti, except what the Assyrian king Sennacherim inscribed after 695 BC, describing the campaign against Til-Garimmu.[16] Khorenats'i too was unable to glean any additional information and only records the name. Sennacherim's short inscription says:

> In the eponymy of Assur-bel-usur, the governor of … against Til-garimmu, a city on the border of Tabalu, whose kingdom Gurti had consolidated, I levelled my weapons. bowmen, bearers of shield and lance, chariots, horses, my royal host, I sent against him. That city I besieged, and by the throwing up of earth(works) and the assault of siege engines, by the rush and attack of foot soldiers, they captured the city. The people, together with the gods dwelling there, I counted as spoil. That city (they destroyed), they devastated, to mounds and ruins they turned it.

Sennacherim's inscription does not mention what happened to Gurti. It has been conjectured that he escaped and was not heard of again. However the inscription says that Sennacherim himself did not

---

15. The original pronunciation was Yuyis, which, after the creation of the Armenian alphabet in the first decade of the fifth century, became Yoys (see Y. T'ireak'ian, *Studies in Armeno-Iranian*, pp 57-64). The transcription of Suhis as Yoyis is rather complicated, which I have explained in my *Pre-History Volume I*, pp 68-9.
16. Luckenbill, §§ 290-1—Sennacherim: The Historical Texts.

participate in the campaign, which was entrusted to one of his generals.

A Proto-Armenian hieroglyphic inscription known as the Karahöyük Elbistan Inscription has survived to our own times in connection with this 695 BC Assyrian campaign. Karahöyük was a place a few kilometres north of the present town of Elbistan and south of Gürün, the ancient Til-Garimmu (also known as the Biblical Togarmah, the Hittite Tegarama and the Armenian house of T'orgom). Scholars dealing with the Anatolian hieroglyphics ascribed this inscription to the fourteenth century on the basis of palaeography despite the fact that they did not understand a single sentence of the text. The inscription, belonging to the early seventh century BC, describes the disastrous consequences of the Assyrian campaign but makes no mention of Gurti.

The author of this inscription, as the case would have been with the Proto-Armenians in general, is unaware of the name Sennacherim, which is a biblical appellation. But he knows, and hence inscribes, the true Assyrian name of this king as 'Moon Made Wish Come True' ('*MOON sasa-sa*', where *sasa* → *hasa*)[17] which is the Proto-Armenian version of the Assyrian name Sin-ahhê-eriba. According to Assyriologists the story behind this name is that with the death of the first male son of Sargon II (722-705 BC), Sennacherim's birth was an act of compensation from the Moon god, giving the meaning of '(God) Moon Made [Sargon's] Wish Come True', as confirmed by both the Proto-Armenian and Assyrian versions. The inscription confirms that Sennacherim did not take part in the campaign against Til-Garimmu, since he was ill in Nineveh ('burning with fever' as the inscription has it). The author of the inscription does not divulge his own name and the whole exposition is in the manner of a dialogue with the god Tark. I quote below the whole of my translation of this important inscription:

Line 1: God Tark-the-Great-Charger 'Moon-Made-Wish-Come-True' sent his men to the country.

Line 2: because he (the king) was ill at the time, afflicted with fever. They advanced on my realm.

Line 3: The numerous soldiers that were in my country later caused great tumult in my city by attacking me.

Line 4: Afterwards, the punishment [= *sasa* > *sastel*] of all [the citizens] ceased. But later, the soldiers forced and penetrated

17. The ancient Armenian word *sasa* transcribes as *hasa*, which is the root *has* of the present verb *hasnil*, meaning 'to reach, to arrive, to have one's wish come true, to be promoted or advanced, comprehend, augment, ripen, grown up, share, tax', etc.

Line 5:   every corner of the storehouse, the palace and the citadel, which they had encircled [= *tsir ara*].

Line 6:   Later the cavalry attacked me, burning and pounding, and the soldiers in the plains of the country were doing the same

Line 7:   to them [to the people]. After that god Tark-the-Great-Charger they punished the kingdom and I had to surrender to them the greater part of my goods.

Line 8:   After that god Tark-the-Great-Charger they pounded and pounded and from my impoverished person they took a lot and went

Line 9:   into the country. God Tark-the-Great-Charger, they went all over the borders for provision and punished the [people of the] part of the plain [which] placed me in great difficulties, because at the time a mouse could not subsist [on what was left].

Line 10:   The soldiers had emptied the country. They came to my city where the storehouse of the kingdom was, the primary source of provisions for everyone of the city of the kingdom. They descended upon the city with a great assault and went to the storehouse, the house where I kept a great variety of foodstuff, which they carried away. They surrounded [= *tsir ara*] the lands of the priests and by force seized their cows. Marched on

Line 11:   to the palace and the stables. In a rage they arrived at the temple, they beat them [the priests]. They approached my residence and set it on fire. These men smashed the realm and the fire engulfed the stable and the temple. Thereafter, god Tark-the-Great-Charger their attacks for foodstuff ceased.

*

The Proto-Armenian Kingdoms

Beginning with the twelfth century BC the Hays (Proto-Armenians) started to migrate in waves from the central Balkans (Paeonia) to eastern Anatolia in the territories of Aram, Tabal and Cilicia. In waves, the migrations of the population of Paeonia continued for the next thousand years, finishing before 150 BC. Some of the population migrated also to the other parts of the then known world, such as the south of Greece.

Beginning with the tenth century BC we find that these migrants had settled and started to creat their own new city kingdoms in Anatolia, either for the first time or by taking over an existing system. In this chapter I shall list all the city names of the kingdoms and the names of the kings known to me so far. Considering that this more or less repeats my study in *Pre-History Volume I*, I shall only give a few details, some of which may have been overlooked at the time the previous volume was published. The names of the rulers whose inscriptions have reached us are in bold and those mentioned by Mosēs Khorenats'i are indicated with an asterick.

Carchemish

The exact date when the existing rulership was taken over by the Hays is not known, but it is thought Suhis I (Yoys, pronounced Huys) became the ruler in the first decade or so of the tenth century BC by marrying Watis, the daughter of Ura-Tark, the Hurrian king.

1. **Suhis I.** The meaning is 'Hope', which the ancients pronounced as Yuyis (Huyis).
2. **Asatuwatimaza.*** 'Togetherness Preacher' = Amasia.
3. **Suhis II.** The meaning is the same as no. 1 above.
4. **Katuwa.*** 'Solid Person' = Kaypak
5. Sangara.* 'Shepherd of His Lambs' = Garnik ('Little Lamb').
6. **Astiruwa.*** 'Mighty Thinker/Just' = Erast, also known as Ara and Ara the Fair.
7. Kamana.* 'No Will' = Havanak ('Consenter').

8. **Pisiri.*** 'Memory Left Behind by the Thinker/Just' = Husak ('Dear Little Last One').

The following two names were not rulers but important first ministers:

1. **Yarairaisa.*** 'Attached to Ira (Astiruwa)' = Arayan Ara ('Ara Belonging to Ira').
2. Sastura.* 'Grand Admonisher' = Baz/Bazuk ('Arm of the King/Executor of Law').

Körkün

We have two names from this place, that of father and son. They were cousins of Astiruwa of Carchemish. But it is not known whether their governing centre was in this place or it was just the inscribed stele that was found there. Körkün is a small settlement to the west of Carchemish and about 15 miles south of Marash.

1. **Azina.** 'The Fiery'.
2. **Ilapikasa.** 'Attacker and Smasher of States'.

Gurgum Markhazi (Marash)

Again, we do not know at what exact date this rule was established, but judging from the stele one may infer that it must have been at the latest in the first decade of the tenth century BC, if not earlier. Marash hitherto had no ruler and, according to the inscription, it was the people themselves who decided on a certain Larazamasa, the chief priest, to become their king. It is possible that this is the oldest kingdom of the Proto-Armenians.

1. **Larazamasa I.** 'Devoted/Attached to God's Fire. This is Parokh I.
2. Muwazisa.* 'Fiery Priest' = Manawaz ('Priest of Fiery Being').
3. Halparutiya I. 'The Battering Ram of God Rutiya'.
4. Muwazali.* 'Acerbic Fiery Priest' = Arbun ('Devoid of Intoxication').
5. **Halparutiya II.** Same as 3.
6. Larazamasa II.* Same as I, but the Assyrians called him Palalam ('Attached in Communion with God') = Parokh ('Unforgiving (to Abusers of God's) Glory').
7. **Halparutiya III.*** Same as 3. Hrant (the name of the god Rutiya with an initial emphatic *h* added).

8. Tarkulara. 'Thunder Took a Kid (for Wife)'.
9. Mutallu. 'Elegant and Affable'.

Melid (Malatya)

In the case of Malatya the Urartian sources confirm that at the start of the eighth century there was the kingdom of the Proto-Armenian Shakhu, which means, we can confidently say that by the end of the ninth century BC a kingdom was established. Unfortunately the inscriptions that have reached us are in fragments which do not divulge any information about the Hay kings. It is through the Urartian and Assyrian inscriptions that we have the following information.

1. Shakhu.* The first Hay king, whose name means 'Usury' = Shara (from *shariat*).
2. Khelaruata.* 'Noble Brave and Capable' = Vstamkar ('Noble and Capable').
3. Sulumal.* 'Radiance Wholly Affable' = Gełam ('Wholly Noble').
4. Gunzinanu.* 'Vainglorious Leopard' = zƏndzak ('Lovable Little Leopard').
5. Tarkunazi.* 'Thunder Devoid of Fire' = Tork' Angeł ('Ignoble Thunder').
6. Mugallu.* 'Augmented and Affable' = Mshak ('Cultivator').
7. ....ussi.* This is the end part of the original name with the meaning of 'Memory'. The whole name would have meant 'No Memory and Resting Place' (= Apananus-si) = Anushavan ('No Memory and Resting Place').

Note that the last two names, Mugallu and ...ussi, are also the rulers of Togarmah and Tabal. They will be mentioned again under these kingdoms.

Kummukh (Commagene)

This rulership of the Proto-Armenians starts in the early ninth century BC. We know the names through the Assyrian inscriptions since none of the rulers left their own inscription, except Queen Panamuwatis who is not remembered by Armenian traditions since she married a foreigner, a Hurrian prince named Suppiluliumas.

1. Qatazilu.* 'There is Overflowing Sparks/Fire' = Ampak

('Source of Lightning').

2. Kundashpi.* 'He Who Has Batallions of Cavalry' = Vashtak ('Source of Cavalry')

3. **Panamuwatis.** 'Great Lady Married to This Wind-like Person.

3. Suppiluliumas. The husband of Panamuwatis called Ishpilulume 'Where Did This Scar Swim in from'?

4. Kushtashpi.* 'Flanks Full with Cavalry' = Shavarsh ('One with Black Horse's).

5. Mutallu. 'Elegant and Affable'.

Tabal

The capital city of the extensive lands of Tabal is thought to have been the present village of Kululu, northeast of Kayseri. The rulership of Tabal starts around the middle of the ninth century BC. It is only in the seventh century BC that we find Tabal joined with Melid and Til-Garimmu under the rules of Mugallu and his son ...ussi.

1. Tuatte. 'Capable King'.

2. Kikki.* The meaning is not known but conjectured as 'Vigour' or 'Giant' = Sisak.

3. Tuwatis.* 'Wind Like King/Kingdom' = Aramayis ('Wind of Aram').

4. **Ruwas.** He was not a king but prime minister. It is through his inscription that we know of Tuwatis' death and the change of dynasty. The name seems to be Ancient Greek.

5. **Wasusaramimasa.*** 'Kingdom of God Sarami' = Harma (the god Sarami).

6. Khully.* 'Ram or Battering Ram' = Khoy ('Ram').

7. Ambaris.* 'Grossly Pompus' = P'arnak ('Source of Pomp').

9. Ishkallu. 'Affable Giant'.

10. Mugallu.

11. ... ussi.

Til-Garimmu (T'orgoma Tun)

For most of its history this city-state was under the hegemony of Melid. There are some inscriptions but these are all in fragments and the ones that would make sense contain mainly the names of the gods. The only indipendent ruler known is from the seventh century BC at the time of the Assyrian Sennacherim.

1. Gurti.* 'Time of the Insurgent' = Goṟak ('Source of Insurgency').

West of Tabal

The kingdoms in the following list are the minor city states spread to the northwest, west and southwest of Caesarea Mazaca (Mazhak = Kayseri). Most are not recorded in the *History of the Armenians* and are known either through their own or Assyrian inscriptions. With the exception of Pukhamme of the ninth century, they all belong to the second half of the eighth century BC.

1. Pukhamme of Khubishna. 'Carer of All'.
2. **Urballa* of Tukhana.** 'Good Satellite' = Arbak ('Good Satellite'). In his inscription he calls himself Warpalawa ('He Who Conducts Good Conversation').
3. Uirimme* of Khubishna. 'What a Loftiness' = Perj ('Elegant, Sumptuous').
4. Ushkhitti of Atuna. 'The Time of the Highly Intelligent'.
5. Tukhamme of Ishtunda. 'Resist All'.
6. Kiaki* or Kiyakiya of Shinukhtu. 'Life to the End' or 'Life! Life!' = Głak ('Extreme Desire [to Live Life to the Full]').
7. **Kurti* of Atuna.** 'The Time of the Shameful' = Koṟnak ('Head Bowed in Shame')
8. **Hurakhara of Porsuk.** 'Blaze of Fire'. He also gives in his inscription the names of his ancestors: his father was Atis ('Wind') and his ancestor Hurnasa ('The Fiery').
9. **Panuna of Kululu.** The meaning is not known.
10. **Tarkhuna of Bolkarmaden.** 'Thunder the Successful'.
11. **Sapi of Karaburna.** 'Valorous Feat, Victory'.

Cilicia

The extensive lands of Cilicia were divided into two parts, the eastern (Campestris) and the western (Aspera) sections. Most of the Proto-Armenian kingdoms were in the west. The exception was Azatiwata of Adana, who was the chief minister of the house of Mukasa, a Mycanean dynasty.

1. Pikhirim* of Khilakku. 'Rebellious for Which Admired' = P'aṟnavaz ('Famous for His Fiery Nature').
2. Kate of Que. 'The Durable' = Kay ($t \rightarrow y$, 'Exists').

3. Kirri of Que. 'The Lewd' or 'Effeminate' = Sir ('Womanish, Dissolute').
4. Tulli of Tanakun. 'The Forgiver'.
5. Kirua of Illubru. 'The Passionate'.
6. Sanduarri* of Sissu and Kundu. 'Fiery Brave Person' = Aṛnak ('Source of Bravery').
7. Sandasarme* of Khilakku. 'Fiery Look of the Moon' = Hrach'eay ('Fiery Eyes'). At the time of this king it was taboo to mention the word eye.
8. Syennesis* of Cilicia. 'Builder and Adorner' = Pachoych ('Embellisher').
9. Appuashu* of Pirindu. 'Person of Fearsome Talk' = Baos ('Idle Talker').
10. **Azatiwata* of Adana,** also known as Asizatiwara. 'Capable Flaming Dawn' = Norayr ('New Fire'). The second version of Asizatiwara means 'The Chosen Fire' = Norayr ('New Fire'), which has the sense of 'New Man of New Age'. He was chief minister of Adana.

Unqi (Patinu) on Orontes River in Hatay

We know of two rulers of this city state through the *History of the Armenians*, although there have been others such as Khalparutiyas, mentioned by the Assyrians. Since this place is away to the south of the concentration of the Proto-Armenians, I shall limit my explanation only to the two of which I am certain.

1. Surri.* 'Sharp' = Sur ('Sharp').
2. Kulani.* 'Radiance with No Say (in State Matters)' = Ts'olak ('Source of Radiance').

Kadmukhi

The Proto-Armenians had just one king in this large country with the capital city of Nisibis (Mtsbin) in the second half of the ninth century BC. The Kadmean house derives from it.

1. Dati* of Khubushkia. *Dat* means 'Law, Justice' = Kadmos does not correlate with the meaning of Dati and derives from the country name of Kadmukhi.

* * *

The Progeny of Hayk

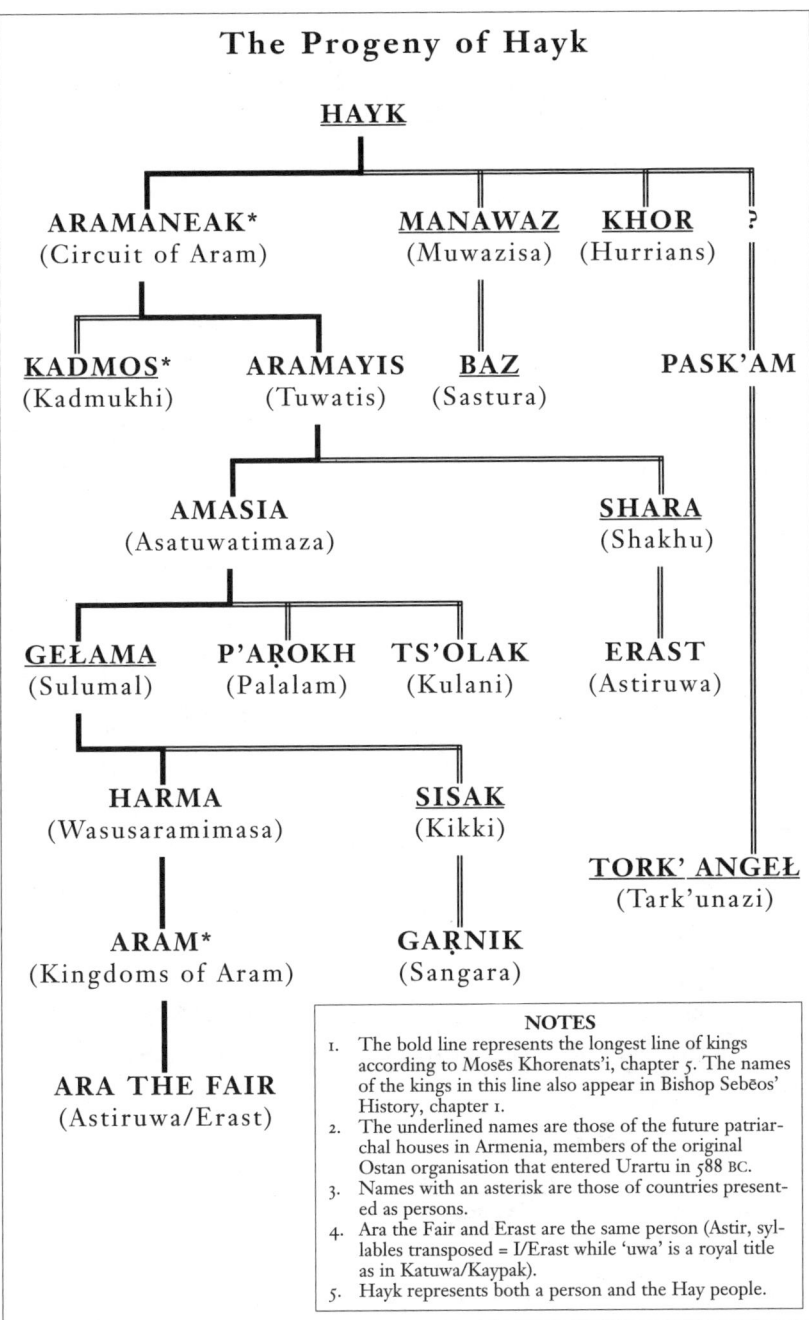

HAYK

ARAMANEAK* (Circuit of Aram)   **MANAWAZ** (Muwazisa)   **KHOR** (Hurrians)   ?

KADMOS* (Kadmukhi)   **ARAMAYIS** (Tuwatis)   **BAZ** (Sastura)   PASK'AM

AMASIA (Asatuwatimaza)   **SHARA** (Shakhu)

GEŁAMA (Sulumal)   **P'AŖOKH** (Palalam)   **TS'OLAK** (Kulani)   **ERAST** (Astiruwa)

HARMA (Wasusaramimasa)   **SISAK** (Kikki)

ARAM* (Kingdoms of Aram)   **GAŖNIK** (Sangara)

TORK' ANGEŁ (Tark'unazi)

ARA THE FAIR (Astiruwa/Erast)

NOTES

1. The bold line represents the longest line of kings according to Mosēs Khorenats'i, chapter 5. The names of the kings in this line also appear in Bishop Sebēos' History, chapter 1.
2. The underlined names are those of the future patriarchal houses in Armenia, members of the original Ostan organisation that entered Urartu in 588 BC.
3. Names with an asterisk are those of countries presented as persons.
4. Ara the Fair and Erast are the same person (Astir, syllables transposed = I/Erast while 'uwa' is a royal title as in Katuwa/Kaypak).
5. Hayk represents both a person and the Hay people.

The Central Balkans and the Paeonian settlements
(twelfth-eighth centuries BC)

Anatolia and the Balkans (circa twelfth century BC)

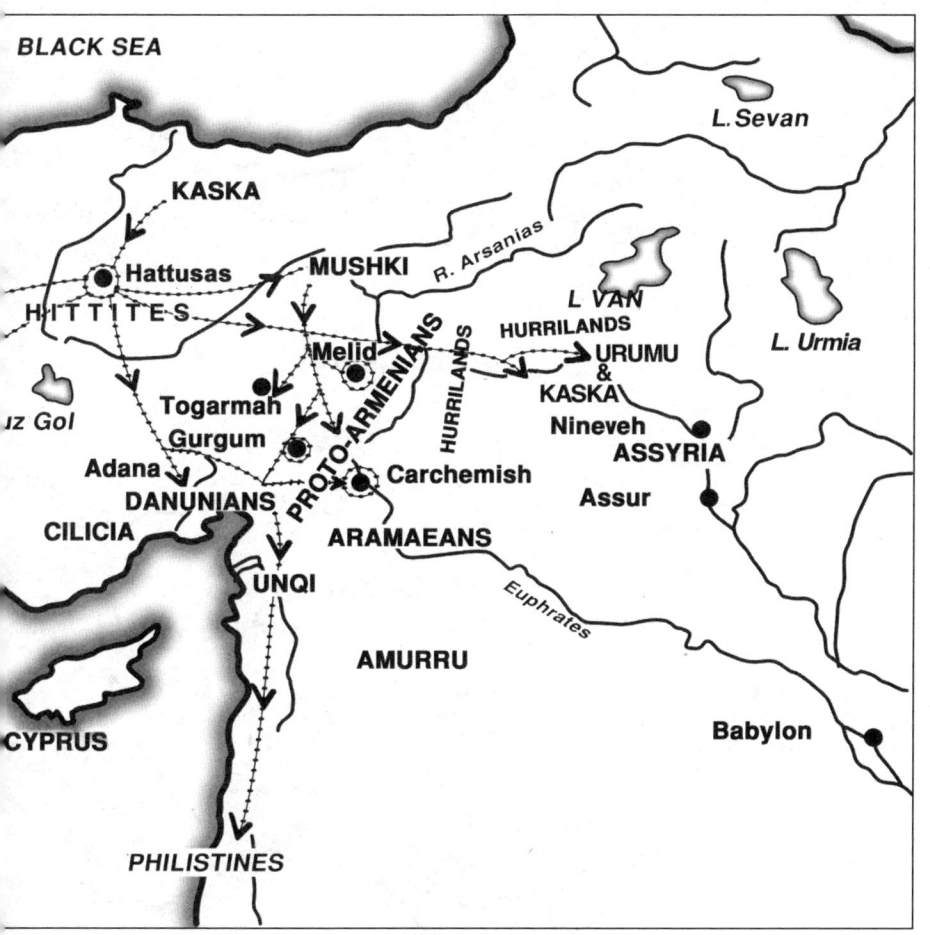

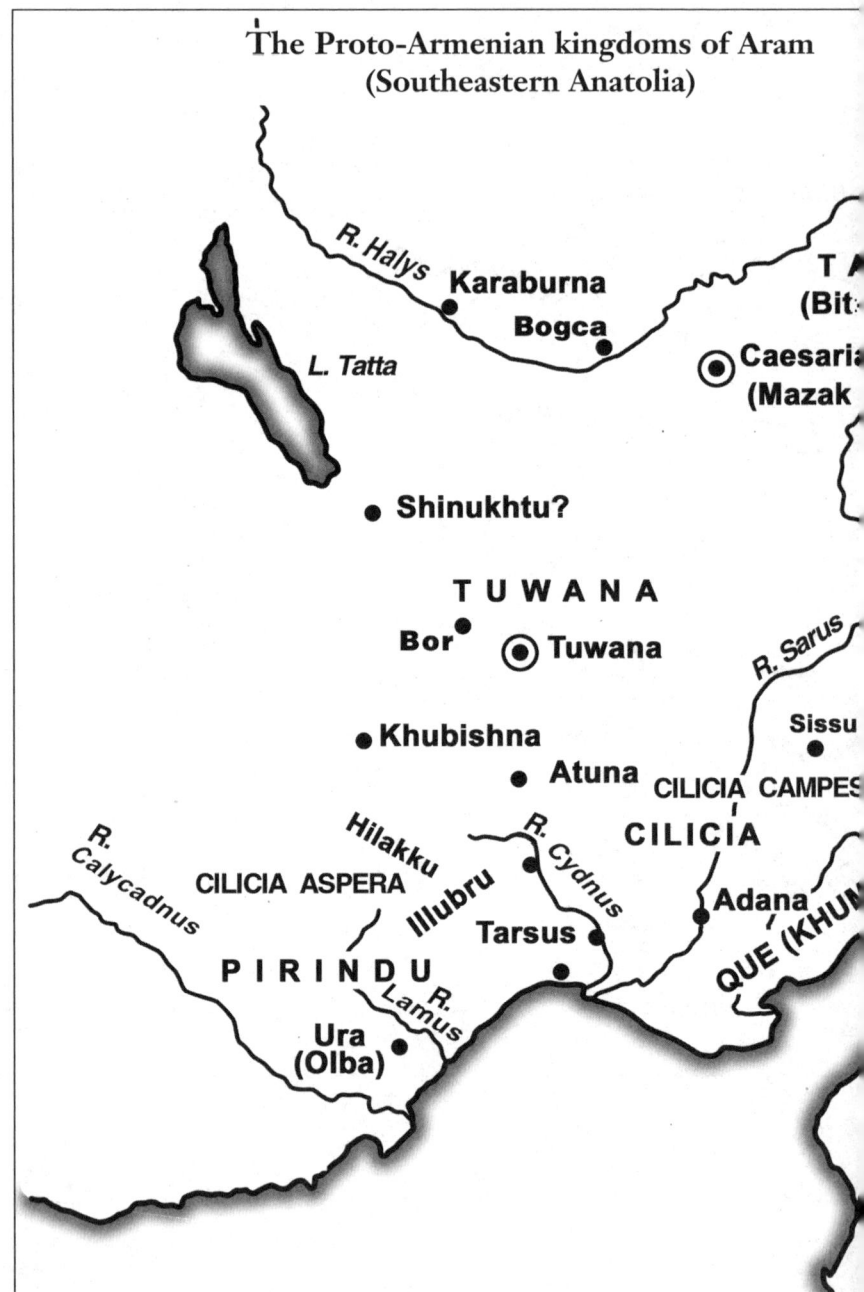

The Proto-Armenian kingdoms of Aram
(Southeastern Anatolia)

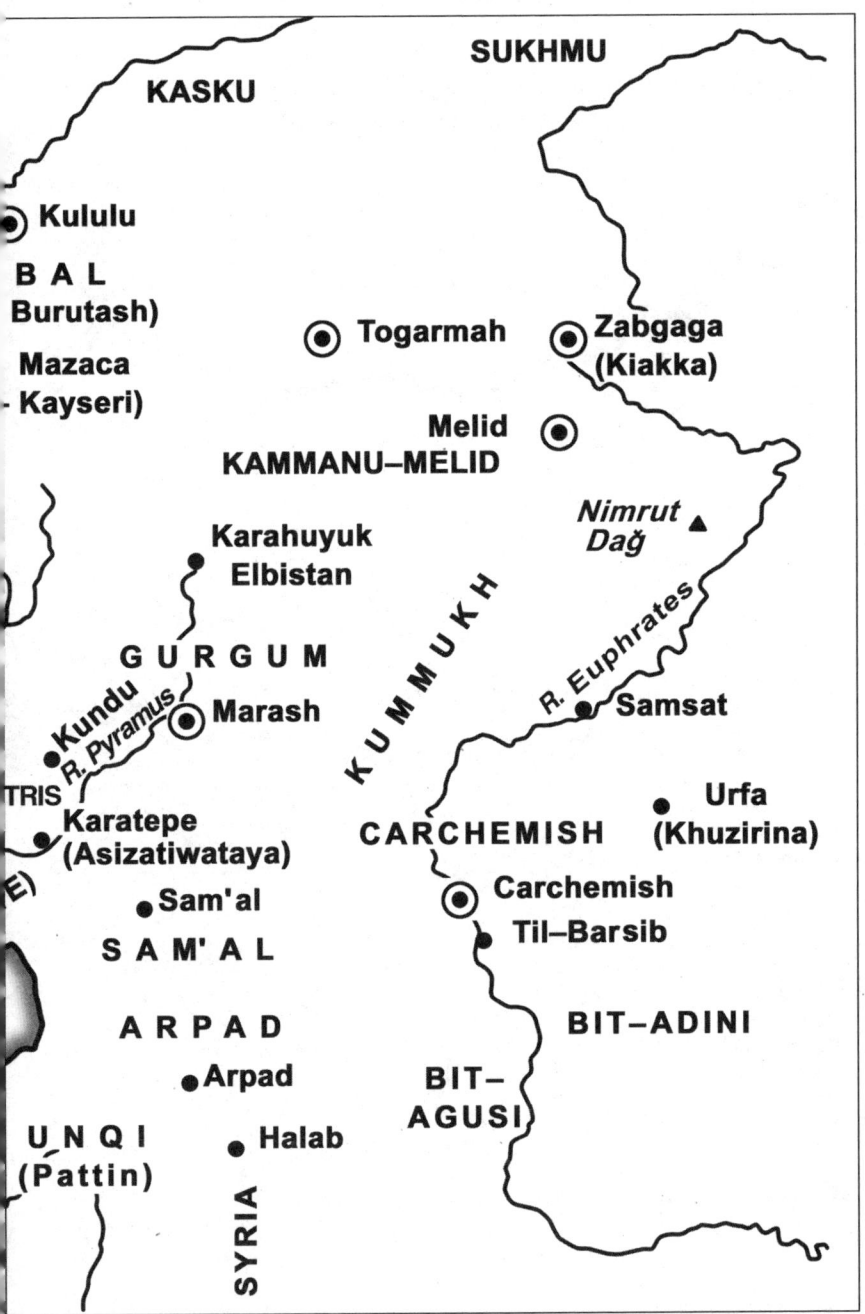

The original Ostan and politico-strategic settlement areas in the Armenian Highlands

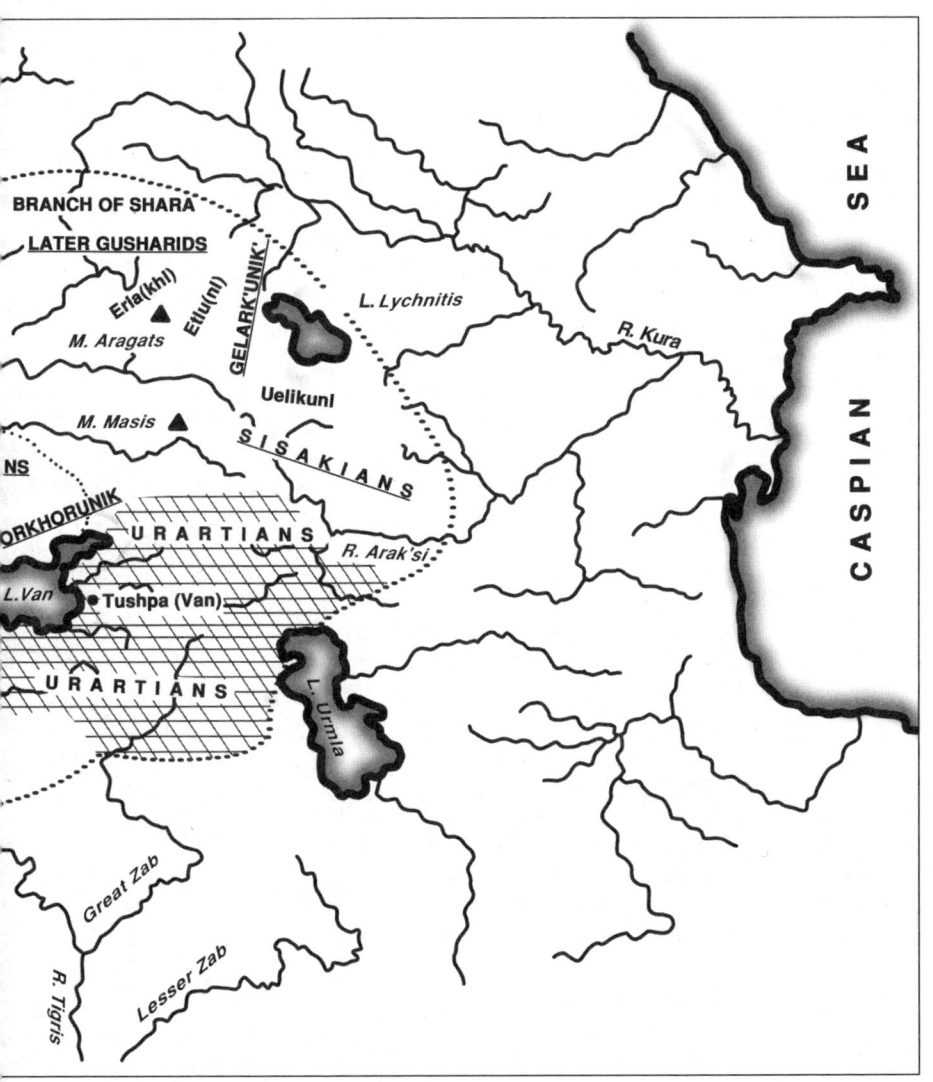

Bibliography

Armenian Texts

Abgaryan, G. V., *The History of Sebēos and the Problem of the Anonymous*, Academy of Armenia, Yerevan, 1965.

—— *History of Sebēos*, Academy of Armenia, Yerevan, 1979.

Adjaryan, H., *Dictionary of Armenian Root Words*, 4 vols, Yerevan University, 1971

——*Dictionary of Armenian Personal Names*, 5 vols, Sevan, Beirut, 1972.

——*Complete Grammar of the Armenian Language*, 8 vols, Armenian Academy, Yerevan, 1952-72

——*History of the Armenian Language*, 2 vols, State University, Yerevan, 1940 & 1951.

——*Armenian Letters*, University of Yerevan, 1984.

Adontz, N., *History of Armenia*, Hayastan, Yerevan, 1972.

——*Armenia in the Period of Justinian*, Hayastan, Yerevan, 1987.

——*Collected Articles*, 3 vols, University of Yerevan, 2006-2008.

Agat'angełos, *History of King Trdat and St Gregory*, Arapian, Constantinopole, 1824

——*Agat'angełos*, translated with commentary by A. Ter-Łevondyan, Soviet Writer, Yerevan, 1977.

Akinian, Fr. N. V, *Movsēs Daskhurants'i (Called Kałankatuats'i) and His History of the Albanians*, Mkhit'arian Press, Vienna, 1970.

——*Bibliographical Studies*, Mkhit'arian Press, Vienna, 1930.

Ananian, P., *On the Book of Sebēos*, Mkhit'arian Press, Venice, 1972.

Anonymous, *Chronology of the Seventh Century*, Mkhit'arian Press, Venice, 1904.

Artsruni, T'ovma, *History of the House of the Artsrunis*, University of Yerevan, 1985.

Bargirk' Haykazian Lezui, 2 vols, Mkhit'arian Press, Venice, 1836-37.

The Holy Bible, Old and New Testaments, Edition G. Pałtatlian, Constantinopole, 1895.

Biwzandats'i, N., & M. Minasian, *Collection*, edited by M. Minasian, Geneva, 1991.

Biwzandats'i, P'awstos, *History of the Armenians*, original edition of K'. Patkanyan, translation and commentary by S. Malkhazyants', Yerevan University, 1987
——*The History of P'awstos Biwzandats'i*, edited by A. A. Abrahamyan & V. D. Arak'elyan, Hayastan Press, Yerevan, 1968.

Carrière, A., *Nouvelle Sources de Moïse de Khoren*, Mkhit'arian Press, Vienna, 1893.
——*Nouvelle Sources de Moïse de Khoren 2*, études critiques, Mkhit'arian Press, Vienna, 1894.
——*Moïse de Khoren et le Généalogies Patriarcales*, Paris, 1897.
——*The Eight Temples of Heathen Armenia*, Mkhit'arian Press, Vienna, 1899.
——*The Story of Abgar in the History of Moïse de Khoren*, Mkhit'arian Press, Vienna, 1897.
Chamchian, M., *The History of the Armenians*, 3 vols, Mkhit'arian Press, Venice, 1784-86

Daghbashian, Y., *P'awstos Biwzand and the Falsifier of his History*, Mkhit'arian Press, Vienna, 1898 (in Armenian).
David Anhaɫt', *Collected Articles*, Academy of Armenia, Yerevan, 1983.

Eɫishē, *History of Vardanants'*, Haypethrat, Yerevan, 1958.
Eusebii Pamphili, *Chronicon Bipartitum*, in Armenian, Latin and Greek, Mkhit'arian Press, St Lazar, Venice, 1818.

Girk' T'ɫt'ots', Jerusalem Patriarchate edition, 1994.

Hats'uni, V. V., *Moses Khorenats'i Returns to Fifth Century*, Mkhit'arian Press, St Lazar, Venice, 1935.
Hesiod, *Homeric Hymns, Epic Cycle and Homerica*, Loeb Classical Library, 1995.

Israyelyan, M., *The Story of Erebuni Fortress*, Hayastan, Yerevan, 1971.

Kaɫankatuats'i, M., *The History of the Albanian World*, Hayastan Press, Yerevan, 1969.
Khalat'yants', G., *Movses Khorenats'i's Newly Found Sources*, Mkhit'arian Press, Vienna, 1898.
——*Ɫazar P'arpets'i and His Work: A Historical and Philological Study*, Moscow, 1883.
Khorenats'i, Moses, *The History of the Armenians*, critical edition by M. Abeɫian & S. Harutiwnian, reprinted Academy of Armenia, Yerevan, 1991.

Bibliography

——*The History of the Armenians*, translated with commentary by S. Malkhazyants', University of Yerevan, 1981.

Koryun, *The Life of Mashtots'*, Haypethrat, Yerevan, 1962.

Kossyan, A. *The House of T'orgom*, Institute of History, Yerevan, 1998.

Łap'antsyan, G., *The Worship of Ara the Fair*, Academy of Armenia, Yerevan, 1944.

Łevond Vardapet, *Armenian History*, Skorokhodov Press, St Petersburg, 1887.

Malkhazyants', S., *The History of Sebēos and Movsēs Khorenats'i*, M. D. Ṛotineants', Tbilisi, 1899.

Manandyan, H., *The Solution of the Enigma of Khorenats'i*, Pethrad, Yerevan, 1934.

——*Hunaban Dprots'ə ev nra Zargats'man Shrjannerə*, Mkhit'arian Press, Vienna, 1928.

——*A Critical Study of the History of the Hay People*, 2 vols, Haypethrat, Yerevan, 1945 & 1957.

——*The Greek Inscription of Garni and the Period the Temple was Built*, Pethamalsaran, 1946.

Mat'evosyan, A. S., *The Chronology of Movsēs Khorenats'i and At'anas Tarawnts'i*. Patma-Banasirakan Handes, University of Yerevan, 1989.

Matikian, A. V., *Ara the Fair*, Mkhit'arian Press, Vienna, 1930.

——*The Anonymous or Pseudo-Sebēos*, Mkhit'arian Press, Vienna, 1913.

Mgryan, M., *Movsēs Khorenats'i*, Hayastan, Yerevan, 1970.

Mushełyan, A. V., *The Century of Movsēs Khorenats'i*, Yerevan University, 2007.

Ormanian, M., *Azgapatum*: vol. i, Sevan, Beirut, 1959; vol. ii, Ter-Nersesian, Constantinople, 1914; vol. iii, Jerusalem Patriarchate, 1927.

P'arpets'i, Łazar, *History of the Armenians and Letter to Vahan Mamikonean*, critical edition by G. Ter-Mkrtchean & S. Malkhazyants', Mnats'akan Martirosean, Tbilisi, 1904.

——*History of Łazar P'arpets'i*, translated with notes by B. Ulubabyan, University of Yerevan, 1982.

Petrosyan, A. *Arami Aṛaspelə Hndevropakan Aṛaspelabanut'yan Hamatek'stum ev Hayots' azgatsagman khndirə*, Van Ardzan, Yerevan, 1997.

Sargisean, B. V., *Tesutiwn Sełbestrosi Patmut'ean ev Movsēs Khorenats'voy Ałberats'*, Mkhit'arian Press, St Lazar, Venice, 1893.

Sebēos, *Armenian History*, edited by S. Malkhazyants', Armfan, Yerevan, 1939.

——*The History of Bishop Sebēos*, edited by G. V. Abgaryan, Academy of Armenia,

Yerevan, 1979.
——*The History of Bishop Sebēos*, edited & translated by G. Khachaturyan & V. Eliazaryan, Zangak, Yerevan, 2005.
Shirakats'i Anania, *Collection of Works*, Soviet Writer, Yerevan, 1979.

T'op'chyan, A., *The Case of the Greek Sources of Movsēs Khorenats'i*, Sargis Khachents', Yerevan, 2001.

English Texts
Agathangelos, *History of the Armenians*, translation with commentary by R. W. Thomson, Albany State University, New York, 1976.
Ammianus Marcellinus, *History*, Loeb Classical Library, 2001/2005-6.
Apollodorus, *The Library*, vol. 1, Loeb Classical Library, 1995-6.
Appian, *Roman History*, Loeb Classical Library, 2002/2005.
Arrian, *Anabasis of Alexander*, Loeb Classical Library, 2000/2004.

Barnett, R. D., 'Karatepe: The Key to the Hittite Hieroglyphics', *Anatolian Studies*, 3, 1953.
—— 'Urartu', in *Cambridge Ancient History*, vol. III, part 1, 1982.
Burney, C. & Lang, D. M., *The Peoples of the Hills*, London, 1971.

Campbell Thomson, R., *A Selection of the Cuneiform Historical Texts from Nineveh*, 1927-32
Ceram, C. W. (K. W. Marek), *The Secret of the Hittites*, Phoenix Press, London, 1988.
Conybeare, F. C., 'The Date of Mosēs of Khoren', *Byzantiniche Zeitechrift*, 10, 1901.
—— 'An Old Armenian Version of Josephus', *Journal of Theological Studies*, 9, 1908.
Cook, J. M., *The Persian Empire*, London, 1983.
Cornelius Nepos, Loeb Classical Library, 2005.

Diakonoff, I. M., *The Pre-History of the Armenian People*, Caravan Books, Delmar, 1984.
Dio Cassius, *Roman History*, Loeb Classical Library, 2000/2006.
Diodorus Siculus, *Histories*, Loeb Classical Library, 1970/1986.
Dowsett, C. J. F., *The History of the Caucasian Albanians*, Oxford University Press, 1961.
Drews, R. 'The Babylonian Chronicles of Berossus', *Iraq*, 37, 1975.
Drijvers, H. J. W., *Bardaisan of Edessa*, Van Gorcum, Assen, 1966.
—— *The Book of the Laws of Countries*, Van Gorcum, Assen, 1965.

Bibliography

Eusebius, *Ecclesiastical History*, Loeb Classical Library, 1974/1992.

Florus, *Epitome of Roman History*, Loeb Classical Library, 1995/2005.

Gibbon, Edward, *The History of the Decline and Fall of the Roman Empire*, Everyman's Library, 1966.

Grayson, A. K., *Assyrian and Babylonian Chronicles*, Locust Valley, New York, 1975.

—— *Assyrian Royal Inscriptions*, Wiesbaden, 1972-76.

—— 'Assyria', in *Cambridge Ancient History*, vol. iii, part i, 1982.

Gurney, O. R., *The Hittites*, London, 1954.

Hawkins, J. D., 'Building Inscriptions of Carchemish', *Anatolian Studies*, 22, 1972.

—— 'Hieroglyphic Inscriptions of Commagene', *Anatolian Studies*, 20, 1970.

—— 'Assyrians and Hittites', *Iraq*, 30, 1974.

—— 'The Negatives in Hieroglyphic Luwian', *Anatolian Studies*, 25, 1975.

—— 'Some Historical Problems of the Hieroglyphic Luwian Corpus', *Anatolian Studies*, 19, 1979.

—— 'Kululu Lead Strips', *Anatolian Studies*, 37, 1987.

—— 'The Neo-Hittite States in Syria and Anatolia', in *Cambridge Ancient History*, vol. iii, part i, 1982

Hawkins J. D., & Morpurgo Davies, A., 'The End of Karatepe Bilingual', *Journal of the Royal Asiatic Society*, 1975.

—— 'On the Problem of Karatepe: The Hieroglyphic Text', *Anatolian Studies*, 28, 1978.

—— 'Hieroglyphic Hittite: Some New Readings and Their Consequences', *Journal of the Royal Asiatic Society*, 2. 1975.

Hammond, N. G. L., *The Miracle That Was Macedonia*, Sidgwick & Jackson, 1991.

Herodian, *History of the Empire*, Leob Classical Library, 1970/2002.

Herodotus, *The Histories*, Penguin Classics, 2003.

Hewson, Robert H., *Armenia: A Historical Atlas*, University of Chicago Press, 2001.

Homer, *The Iliad*, Loeb Classical Library, 2001.

Huxley, George L., 'On Fragments of Three Historians: I. The Son of Xenophanes; II. Kleidemos and the "Themistokles Decree"; III. Nikolaos of Damascus on Urartu', *Greek, Roman and Byzantine Studies*, 9, 1968, pp 309-320.

Josephus, *The Complete Works*, Translated by W. Whiston, Pickering & Inglis,

1960.

Koestler, Arthur, *The Thirteenth Tribe*, Pan Books, London, 1977.
Komoroczy, G., 'Berossus and the Mesopotamian Literature', *Acta Antiqua*, 21, 1913.

Lie, A. G., *The Inscriptions of Sargon II, King of Assyria*, Paul Geuthner, Paris, 1929.
Livy, *The Early History of Rome*, Penguin Classics, 1961.
Lloyd, Seton, *Ancient Turkey*, Guild Publishing, London, 1989.
—— *Early Highland Peoples of Anatolia,* Thames & Hudson, London, 1967.
Luckenbill, D. D., *Ancient Records of Assyria and Babylonia*, Chicago, 1926-27.

Mahé, Annie & Mahé, Jean-Pierre (translation & commentary), *The History of the Armenians by Moses Khorenats'i*, Gallimard, 1993.
Malory, J. P., *In Search of the Indo-Europeans*, Thames & Hudson, London, 1996.
Man, John, *Attila*, Bantam Press, London, 2005.
Merker, I. L. 'Kingdom of Paionia', *Balkan Studies*, 1965.

O'Callaghan, R. T., *Aram Naharaim*, Pontificium Institutum Biblicum, Rome, 1948.

Pausanias, *Description of Greece*, Loeb Classical Library, 1988/1995.
Piotrovskii, B. B., *Urartu: The Kingdom of Van and its Art*, Evelyn Adams & Mackay, 1967.
—— *Urartu*, Archaeologia Mundi Series, Geneva. 1969.
Plato, *The Republic*, Macmillan, London, 1950.
Plutarch, *Makers of Rome*, Penguin Classics, 1965.
Polybius, *The Histories*, Loeb Classical Library, 1927 (2003-6).
Postgate, J. N., 'Assyrian Texts and Fragments', *Iraq*, 35, 1973.
Procopius, *History of the Wars*, Loeb Classical Library, 2000/2006.
—— *Buildings*, Loeb Classical Library, 2002.
—— *The Secret History*, Penguin Classics, 1981.

Quintus Curtius Rufus, *The History of Alexander*, BCA, 2004.
Quintus Smyrnaeus, *The Fall of Troy*, Loeb Classical Library.

Saggs, H. W. F., *The Might That Was Assyria*, London, 1984.
Soultanian, Gabriel, *The Pre-History of the Armenians, Volume I*, Bennett & Bloom, London, 2003.

Bibliography

——— *The Pre-History of the Armenians, Volume II: The Proto-Armenian Hieroglyphic Inscriptions of Aram*, Bennett & Bloom, London, 2004.

——— *The History of Bishop Sebēos*, Bennett & Bloom, London, 2007.

——— *The Pre-History of the Armenians, Volume III: The Proto-Armenian Hieroglyphic Inscriptions of southeastern Anatolia*, Bennett & Bloom, London, 2009.

Steinherr, F., *Die Phonizisch-Hethitischen Bilinguen von Karatepe*, Gottingen, 1974.

Strabo, *Geography*, Loeb Classical Library, 1982-89.

Suetonius, *Lives of the Caesars*, Loeb Classical Library, 1998/2001.

Tacitus, *The Annals of Imperial Rome*, Penguin Classics, 1989.

——— *The Histories*, Penguin Classics, 1972.

Terry, Milton S. (trans.), *The Sibylline Oracles*, AMS Press, New York. 1973.

Thomson, R. W., *The History of the Armenians by M. Khorenats'i*, translation & commentary, Harvard University Press, Cambridge, Mass., 1978.

——— *Agat'angelos*, translation & commentary, Albany State University, New York, 1976.

——— *Lazar P'arpets'i*, translation & commentary, Scholar's Press, Atlanta, Georgia, 1991.

——— *The Armenian History Attributed to Sebēos*, translation with notes, historical commentary by James Howard-Johnston, Liverpool University Press, Liverpool, 1999.

Thucydides, *The Peloponnesian War*, Penguin Classics, 1979.

Toumanoff, Cyril, *Studies in Christian Caucasian History*, Georgetown University, 1963.

——— 'On the Date of Pseudo-Mosēs of Chorene', *Handes Amsorea*, 75, 1961.

Waterman, Leroy, *The Correspondence of the Assyrian Empire*, Ann Arbor, 1930-36.

Wilkes, John, *The Illyrians*, Blackwell, Oxford, 1992.

Wiseman, D. J., *The Vassal-Treaties of Essarhaddon*, British Schoool of Archaeology, 1958.

Xenophon, *Cyropaedia*, Loeb Classical Library, 1979/1983.

——— *The Persian Expedition*, Penguin Classics, 1949.

*

Index

The preparation of this Index has been problematic, since various scholars transcribe Classical Armenian names in different ways. My preference has been to transcribe in compliance with the critical edition of the History of Khorenats'i, yet such transcriptions can sometimes be alien to Modern Eastern Armenian as well as the various works quoted. For example, the Text says Ninos, which Diodorus gives as Ninus; Manawaz is Manavaz both in Malkhazyants' and Thomson; Yapet' is Hapet' in Malkhazyants' but Yapheth/Japheth in Thomson; Movsēs is Moses in Thomson and Moïse in Mahé; and so on. Therefore, in this index, wherever I have deemed it necessary, I have quoted my transcription followed by any other transcription that I have used in discussing such works.

Index

Index

Index

The Pre-History of the Armenians,
Volume 1

The Pre-History of the Armenians,
Volume 2: The Proto-Armenian
Hieroglyphic Inscriptions of Aram

The Pre-History of the Armenians,
Volume 3: The Anatolian
Hieroglyphic Inscriptions of the
Proto-Armenians

The History of Bishop Sebeos:
Redefining a Seventh-Century Voice
from Armenia

www.bennettandbloom.com